COMMODITIES DEMYSTIFIED

COMMODITIES DEMYSTIFIED

SCOTT FRUSH

New York   Chicago   San Francisco   Lisbon
London   Madrid   Mexico City   Milan   New Delhi
San Juan   Seoul   Singapore   Sydney   Toronto

1 2 3 4 5 6 7 8 9 0   FGR/FGR   0 9 8

ISBN: 978-0-07-154950-9
MHID: 0-07-154950-1

Printed and bound by Quebecor / World.

McGraw-Hill books are available at special quantity discounts to use as premiums and sales promotions, or for use in corporate training programs. To contact a representative please visit the Contact Us pages at www.mhprofessional.com.

To my clients

CONTENTS

Contents

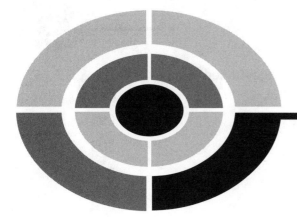

Acknowledgments

I once again am extremely grateful to the people at McGraw-Hill for giving me the opportunity to exercise my passion for writing. To all involved in the production of my fourth McGraw-Hill book, I say thank you. For their vision and commitment to publishing this book, I thank Dianne Wheeler, executive editor, and Herb Schaffner, publisher, at McGraw-Hill. I especially want to thank my good friends at DTE Energy in Ann Arbor for their insights and help with assembling information. Last but not least, I thank my wife for her patience, understanding, and assistance.

INTRODUCTION

Over the last several years investors have witnessed skyrocketing demand and rising prices for many commodities. Inspired by the moneymaking opportunities, individual and institutional investors are taking a closer look at commodities and making their first investments or increasing their commodity allocations. However, commodities are not a new asset class, nor are they a hot now, gone tomorrow investment. Unlike stocks, bonds, and mutual funds, commodities are a part of people's everyday lives and essential for their survival. Commodities are real and tangible assets that represent the food we eat, the fuel we use to power our automobiles, the metal we utilize to make jewelry, and the lumber we use to build our homes. Without commodities, our civilization would not exist today. The same cannot be said for stocks and bonds.

Commodities are not the final end products that consumers purchase. Rice, corn, wheat, and oats are used to produce cereal. However, cereal is the end product, not the rice and corn themselves. The same logic should be applied to your investments. Commodities should not be viewed as a final stand-alone investment. Rather, commodities should be purchased to optimize your portfolio. Oatmeal cannot be produced without oats, and an optimal portfolio cannot be built without commodities. By investing in commodities, you will gain a hedge against inflation and loss of purchasing power, stronger performance potential, and a lower risk of unfavorable correlations with traditional stock and bond investments. Commodities underscore many essential products, including your investment portfolio.

Commodities Demystified is written to arm you with the information and tools you need to invest successfully in commodities. Emphasis is placed on how to include commodities in your existing investment portfolio rather than investing exclusively in commodities. Perhaps you are not interested in investing in commodities but want to gain knowledge of commodities out of curiosity or for your job. This book will deliver exactly what you need to know in those cases as well. Finally, this book is aimed at readers who have little knowledge of commodities but have the intellect and appetite for a solid grounding in the fundamentals of commodities. Accordingly, my guiding principle was not to insult any reader's intelligence but instead to build on it.

Executive Summary: The 10 Defining Characteristics

This section presents a brief introduction to the 10 defining characteristics of commodities, an executive summary of sorts. Note that Chapter 18 provides detailed descriptions of each defining characteristic and that each one is mentioned and discussed in substantial detail throughout the book. The top 10 defining characteristics are the following:

- Commodities are *standardized* in each commodity class.
- Commodities are defined by their unique *tradability*.
- Commodities offer *deliverability* as a settlement option.
- Commodities exhibit a high level of *inelastic demand*.
- Commodities supplies are *finite and limited*.
- Commodities demonstrate a highly *global marketplace*.
- Commodities require *long production lead times*.
- Commodities offer investors an *investing safe haven* during uncertain times.
- Commodities provide a *hedge against inflation* and loss of purchasing power.
- Commodities yield *favorable correlations* for enhanced portfolio optimization.

Figure 1 shows the universe of investing opportunities, and Figure 2 displays the universe of commodities.

Before Getting Started

Time and time again I tell people, "Manage your portfolio before it manages you." Managing your portfolio always begins with you. Never rely on someone else to do what you should be doing. When it comes to your investments, you have two options:

Introduction

Figure I-1. Universe of Investing Opportunities

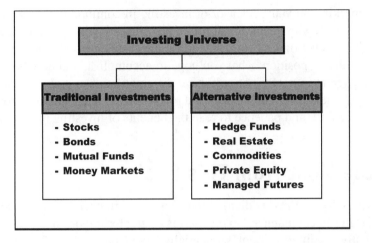

Figure I-2. Commodities Universe

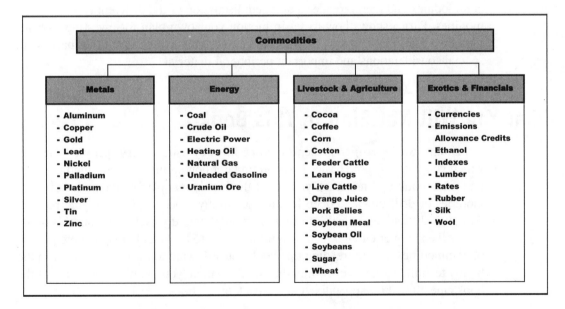

Accomplish the tasks that will help you manage your portfolio or forgo them and let your portfolio manage you. Since you are reading this book, you have demonstrated your ability and willingness to be proactive in managing your portfolio. Consider this book an invaluable tool to help you with this endeavor.

Self-Assessment

Before embarking on your endeavor of investing in commodities, I encourage you to complete a self-assessment. Since commodity investing is a personalized process and will change over time as your situation changes, understand as much as you can about your current position, what you hope to accomplish, and how best to bridge the gap. Different investors not only have different goals and obligations but also have varying financial circumstances and preferences. As a result, investors need to exercise care, skill, and patience to reap the benefits of investing in commodities.

How to Get the Most from This Book

Commodities Demystified is divided into four parts in each of which the chapters are similar in subject manner. No one part is of greater importance than the others. Consequently, reading this book sequentially from Chapter 1 to Chapter 20 is your best route. The book is structured to provide maximum benefit, ease of learning, and quick and simple referencing. It begins with a discussion of the essentials of commodities and then provides a detailed discussion of the different types of commodities. Part 3 shows how to set in motion your own plan for investing in commodities. The final chapters help reinforce and enhance the first three parts with special considerations and important peripheral material.

What You Will Not Find in This Book

Commodities Demystified presents commodities by using a very specific format in which you will learn the basics first and find out how to invest in commodities second. This book will not teach you about the highly complex mathematics of commodities or drill down so deep into a topic that you lose sight of the big picture. Although difficult technical information was deliberately excluded from this book, you will encounter enough technical information to learn and grasp the big picture of commodities. If after reading this book you still want to immerse yourself in the highly technical aspects of commodities, I encourage you to investigate some of the books mentioned in Appendix A at the back of the book.

A Review of the Chapters

Commodities Demystified is divided into four parts to help you find and learn what you want quickly and easily. Included in these four parts are 20 chapters covering all things commodities from the basics to the peripheral issues. The structure of this book is as follows.

PART 1: DEMYSTIFYING COMMODITY FUNDAMENTALS

The first chapter of *Commodities Demystified* presents an introduction to the commodities trade. This chapter examines the history of commodities and defines a commodity. The second chapter discusses the benefits of investing in commodities, and the third chapter looks at the risks inherent in commodity investing. Chapter 4 provides an inside look at the players and participants involved either directly or indirectly in the commodities trade. Chapter 5 examines general investing risks and rewards and considerations for investing in commodities. Chapters 6 and 7 discuss market indicators that drive commodity prices and commodity indexes, respectively.

PART 2: DEMYSTIFYING COMMODITY CLASSES

The second part of the book focuses on the different commodity classes: metals, energy fuels, livestock, agriculture, exotics, and financials. Chapter 8 begins the discussion with precious and industrial metals. Chapter 9 provides an in-depth look at energy fuels, specifically crude oil, natural gas, coal, heating oil, and uranium ore. Agriculture—both softs and grains and oilseeds—and livestock are discussed together in Chapter 10. The final chapter in this part focuses on exotic commodities and financial commodities such as foreign currencies, rates, and indexes.

PART 3: DEMYSTIFYING COMMODITY INVESTING AND TRADING

The third part shows how you can participate in the commodities markets. Commodity mutual funds are discussed in Chapter 12, and exchange-traded instruments such as ETFs and ETNs are presented in Chapter 13. Chapter 14 shows how investors can participate in commodities by taking an ownership stake in companies involved in the commodities market. Although not for many investors, hedge funds are discussed in Chapter 15 as an alternative for high-net-worth investors. The final chapter in this part provides a discussion of commodity futures and options on futures from the perspective of both managed futures funds and self-participation.

PART 4: DEMYSTIFYING SPECIAL CONSIDERATIONS

Part 4 is all about special considerations and important peripheral topics involving commodities. Peak performance investing is discussed in Chapter 17, providing investors with an understanding of how to build and manage optimal portfolios for the long term. The 10 defining characteristics of commodities are presented in Chapter 18.

These characteristics encapsulate the most important lessons about commodities and thus represent an executive summary of sorts. Chapter 19 offers a plan to help you search for, evaluate, and hire the right advisor to manage your portfolio. The final chapter in the book provides a basic introduction to online and electronic commodity trading with sources for online discount commodity brokers.

The appendixes offer some helpful resources to jump-start your endeavor of researching and investing in commodities.

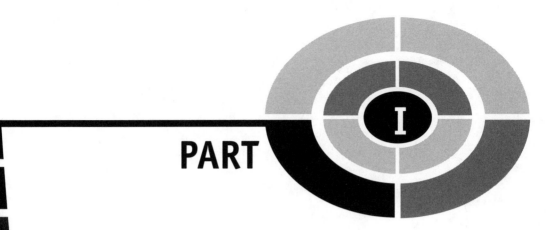

PART

I

Demystifying Commodity Fundamentals

1

CHAPTER 1

Getting Started in Commodities:

Understanding the Essentials

The production of commodities first occurred in world history 10,000 to 12,000 years ago with the domestication of wheat and barley in the Fertile Crescent, an area that encompasses present-day Iraq and Turkey. Commodity exchanges are more of a modern invention, however. The commodity futures markets were established to give farmers and merchants a way to manage the risks associated with harvesting and processing.

Although some historical evidence suggests that a crude form of commodity futures trading began over 6,000 years ago in China, that claim is very difficult to prove; the first recorded instance of commodity futures trading occurred over 300 years ago in seventeenth-century Japan. In 1730 the feudal government of Tokugawa established the Dojima Rice Market/Exchange in Osaka at the request of rice merchants who wanted to stabilize the price for rice. The cultivation of rice—a staple crop in Japan—was characterized by times during the year when rice was in tight supply and times when it was stored after harvest for future use. As a way to generate needed cash, farmers sold "rice tickets" that demonstrated the ownership of stored rice. Soon afterward standardized contracts were developed that represented specific quantities and qualities of rice for a predetermined price. As a result, both farmers and merchants knew how much rice they would purchase or sell and on what date regardless of what happened to the supply, demand, or price of rice. Tokyo followed Osaka's lead and established its own rice markets. Over time, rice tickets were accepted in the same way as any other currency, and thus began futures trading.

In 1848 the first commodity exchange in the United States was established in Chicago by 82 businesspeople seeking to make the marketplace for certain commodities more efficient. The Chicago Board of Trade (CBOT) was born and provided a formal and central meeting place for both farmers and merchants. Gone were the days of bringing one's product to Chicago and searching for a merchant to purchase it at a fair price. However, the earliest form of trading at the CBOT was called spot trading. This involved farmers selling their products to the highest-bidding merchants on the spot. Thus, the term *spot* was coined. Since many agricultural products are harvested in the fall, most of the products were brought to the CBOT in that season, and spot transactions were conducted. This meant that merchants had to store vast quantities of product during the peak harvesting months and thus incur higher costs and more volatile prices. Prices declined during the peak harvesting months, when supply was high, and advanced during off-peak months, when supply was very low. To resolve this problem, a new kind of transaction was created: The *to-arrive* contract was established in 1849. The first commodities underlying this new type of contract were flour, timothy seed, and hay; corn was added in 1851. This contract permitted farmers and merchants to transact a product at today's prices but not exchange the product until a certain date during the year. The farmer essentially provided "storage" for the product until a time when "delivery" was required. The result of the to-arrive contract was less product with the merchant and lower price volatility. Over time the to-arrive contract was standardized to meet the needs of the majority of farmers and merchants and was renamed the *futures contract.*

The Kansas City Board of Trade was established in 1856, and the New York Board of Trade in 1870 under the name the New York Cotton Exchange. Two years later, in 1872, the New York Mercantile Exchange was established as the Butter and Cheese Exchange of New York. In 1898 the Chicago Mercantile Exchange was established under the name the Chicago Butter and Egg Board to trade those products.

Futures trading in the United States experienced a significant increase in the 1970s when futures on currencies—the Swiss franc and Japanese yen—were introduced. During the 1980s futures on financial indexes were established, resulting in even greater trading. Today there are numerous commodity exchanges throughout the world, mainly in developed countries that trade many different commodities. In 2007 the Chicago Board of Trade and the Chicago Mercantile Exchange agreed to merge to become the world's largest commodities exchange.

The Commodity Futures Trading Commission (CFTC), part of the U.S. Department of Agriculture, regulates many aspects of futures trading, specifically, futures exchanges, broker-dealers, investment managers, and commodity trading advisors.

What Is a Commodity?

Commodities are the raw materials, hard assets, and tangible products that underpin civilization in nearly every way imaginable. Commodities are the building blocks for virtually everything people eat, use for energy, and use in construction and for many of the things people use on a daily basis. Commodities gave civilization life from the very beginning with the cultivation of wheat and barley. Moreover, commodities were instrumental in the development of civilization. Their importance shows in the fact that those early periods are named for them: Copper Age, Bronze Age, and Steel Age.

As a general rule, all commodities are defined by three characteristics. The first characteristic is standardization. This means that one can take one unit of a commodity and replace it with another unit of the same commodity. Thus, commodities are said to be *interchangeable*. The second characteristic is *tradability*, which refers to two distinct features: the existence of a robust marketplace consisting of many buyers and sellers and the unique futures market, a trading structure not found in traditional investments. The third characteristic is *deliverability*, which refers to the actual physical exchange of a commodity between the seller and the buyer.

The only exception to the rules that commodities must be raw materials and must have deliverability is the commodity class called financials. For the most part, financials are considered commodities even though they are intangible. Financials include currencies, indexes, rates, and emissions allowance credits.

Commodity Classes

The global marketplace is vast, with many different commodities. Commodities are classified in one of six major sectors: metals, energy fuels, agriculturals, livestock, exotics, and financials. Within certain commodity classes commodities are divided and classified in sector groups, such as precious metals and industrial metals. This book will mention a number of different commodities but will focus primarily on the core commodities listed below. The second part of the book provides a more detailed look at the different commodity classes.

PRECIOUS AND INDUSTRIAL METALS

Not all metals are the same, nor do they have the same or similar applications. Precious metals are defined primarily by their high resistance to corrosion and oxidation, in contrast to industrial metals with their low resistance. Furthermore, most industrial metals are found in much larger quantities than are precious metals. Thus, the demand and price for precious metals are much higher than those for industrial metals.

Precious Metals

- Gold
- Platinum
- Silver

Industrial (Base) Metals

- Aluminum
- Copper
- Lead
- Nickel
- Palladium
- Tin
- Zinc

ENERGY FUELS

Energy makes the world go round and is essential for modern civilization. Without energy, many parts of society would come to a halt, much as they did in the *Mad Max* movies. In those movies, the world was essentially without energy and people fought for the little that remained. The society was defined by chaos, violence, lawlessness, and uncertainty. Today most sources for energy are derived from fossil fuels. Tomorrow people hope to procure much energy from alternative renewable sources such as solar, wind, and hydro. Nevertheless, dependence on energy fuels is apparent in current society. That provides opportunities for investors in the following areas:

- Coal
- Crude oil
- Electric power
- Heating oil
- Natural gas
- Unleaded gasoline
- Uranium ore

AGRICULTURALS

Also known as ags, agricultural commodities are essential for human survival. This commodity sector is divided into two groups. The first is grains and oilseeds, the commodities most essential for human life. The second group is termed *softs* and contains the discretionary-use agricultural commodities. The commodities in this group are not essential for human life but improve it. Softs can be divided further into tropical and fiber.

Grains and Oilseeds

- Corn
- Soybeans
- Soybean oil
- Soybean meal
- Wheat

Softs

- Cocoa
- Coffee
- Cotton
- Orange juice
- Sugar

LIVESTOCK

Livestock, also referred to as meats, is composed of four major commodities, two related to cattle and two related to hogs. As with energy fuels, the demand for livestock commodities is highly correlated with economic prosperity. When countries prosper, the standard of living for their people increases, providing them with additional discretionary income. This typically means more demand for meat products, which are generally expensive. As China, India, Brazil, and other countries grow their economies, the long-term demand trend for livestock, including the following commodities, looks strong:

- Feeder cattle
- Lean hogs
- Live cattle
- Pork bellies

EXOTICS AND FINANCIALS

The exotic commodity sector is best defined as commodities that do not have the same demand as other commodities. Also, most of the exotic commodities do not trade on U.S. commodity exchanges or on many of the top global commodity exchanges. Financials are an intangible commodity and the only commodity that cannot be delivered physically to the purchaser. All financial commodities settle financially, that is, in some form of currency.

Exotics

- Ethanol
- Lumber
- Rubber
- Wool

Financials

- Emissions allowance credits
- Currencies
- Indexes
- Rates

Figure 1.1 lists the major traded commodities

Supply and Demand Fundamentals

Most people who know commodities agree that future prospects look very strong as a result of both favorable demand fundamentals and favorable supply fundamentals. Demand for nearly all commodities is expected to continue to rise, and the supply of many commodities is expected to fall over time. This creates an ideal long-term opportunity for those willing and able to invest in commodities. In 2007 the largest pension fund in the United States, the California Public Employees' Retirement System (CalPERS), announced its belief that commodities will experience continued strength in the future and therefore increased its allocation to commodities. The question is not whether commodities will continue to experience strong gains but rather by how much. The following section provides a framework that shows why commodities have favorable demand and supply fundamentals.

FAVORABLE DEMAND FUNDAMENTALS

The demand for commodities is projected to accelerate for three primary reasons: the continued general increase in global population, the development of economies around the world that are hungry for energy fuels and metals, and advances in consumers' standard of living, which means a greater desire to spend more on commodities.

Increasing Global Population

The population of the world has been increasing for some time, and a greater population means a greater demand for commodities. Agricultural commodities stand to

Figure 1-1. Major Traded Commodities

Commodity	Trading Unit (1 contract)	Trading Symbol	Exchange
Aluminum	44,000 pounds	AL	New York Mercantile Exchange (NYMEX)
Coal	1,550 tons	QL	New York Mercantile Exchange (NYMEX)
Cocoa	10 tons	CO or CC	New York Board of Trade (NYBOT)
Coffee	37,500 pounds	KC	New York Board of Trade (NYBOT)
Copper	25,000 pounds	HG	New York Mercantile Exchange (NYMEX)
Corn	5,000 bushels	C	Chicago Board of Trade (CBOT)
Cotton	50,000 pounds	CT	New York Board of Trade (NYBOT)
Electric Power	760 - 920 megawatt hours	JM	New York Mercantile Exchange (NYMEX)
Ethanol	29,000 US gallons	AC	Chicago Board of Trade (CBOT)
Feeder Cattle	50,000 pounds	FC	Chicago Mercantile Exchange (CME)
Frozen Concentrated Orange Juice	15,000 pounds	OJ or OB	New York Board of Trade (NYBOT)
Gold	100 troy ounces	GC	New York Mercantile Exchange (NYMEX)
Heating Oil	42,000 gallons	HO	New York Mercantile Exchange (NYMEX)
Lead	25 metric tons	LPB	London Metals Exchange (LME)
Lean Hogs	40,000 pounds	LH	Chicago Mercantile Exchange (CME)
Light Sweet Crude Oil	1,000 barrels	CL	New York Mercantile Exchange (NYMEX)
Live Cattle	40,000 pounds	LC	Chicago Mercantile Exchange (CME)
Lumber	110,000 board feet	LB	Chicago Mercantile Exchange (CME)
Natural Gas	10 mmBttu	NG	New York Mercantile Exchange (NYMEX)
Nickel	6 metric tons	LNI	London Metals Exchange (LME)
Oats	5,000 bushels	O	Chicago Board of Trade (CBOT)
Palladium	100 troy ounce	PA	New York Mercantile Exchange (NYMEX)
Platinum	50 troy ounce	PL	New York Mercantile Exchange (NYMEX)
Pork Bellies	40,000 pounds	PB	Chicago Mercantile Exchange (CME)
Propane	42,000 gallons	PN	New York Mercantile Exchange (NYMEX)
Rough Rice	2,000 hundredweight (cwt.)	RR	Chicago Board of Trade (CBOT)
Rubber	5,000 kilograms	JN	Tokyo Commodity Exchange (TOCOM)
Silver	5,000 troy ounce	SI	New York Mercantile Exchange (NYMEX)
Soybean Meal	100 tons	SM	Chicago Board of Trade (CBOT)
Soybean Oil	60,000 pounds	BO	Chicago Board of Trade (CBOT)
Soybeans	5,000 bushels	S	Chicago Board of Trade (CBOT)
Sugar	112,000 pounds	SB or SE	New York Board of Trade (NYBOT)
Tin	5 metric tons	LSN	London Metals Exchange (LME)
Unleaded Gasoline	42,000 gallons	HU	New York Mercantile Exchange (NYMEX)
Uranium Ore	250 pounds	UX	New York Mercantile Exchange (NYMEX)
Wheat	5,000 bushels	W	Chicago Board of Trade (CBOT)
Wool	2,500 kilograms	OL	Sydney Futures Exchange (SFE)
Zinc	25 metric tons	LZS	London Metals Exchange (LME)

do well as food will be needed to feed a larger populace. Metals will be in higher demand as more houses, schools, government buildings, and retail stores will be required to address the needs of a growing population. Energy fuels will be sought to power more automobiles and heat more homes as well. This trend can be offset by a greater supply of the needed commodities, but the supply of commodities stands a better chance of declining than rising over the long term. Figure 1.2 shows projections of the global population.

Development of Global Economies

Stagnant economies require a certain level of commodities, no more and no less. However, when economies are developing and expanding, an escalating amount of

Figure 1-2. Global Population Projections

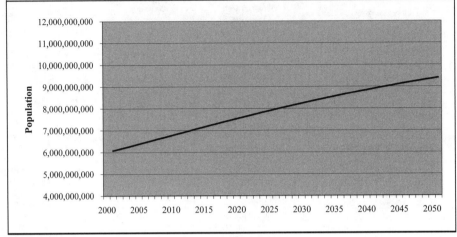

SOURCE: United Nations

commodities is needed to fuel that growth. China, for example, has been growing by leaps and bounds and gobbling up nearly every commodity it needs. Unfortunately, when China buys a certain commodity, everyone else throughout the world pays more because of the global reach of most commodities. As a country, China is nowhere close to full economic maturity, and that translates into continued strong demand for energy fuels, metals, and agricultural commodities. Only a few years ago China was a net exporter of crude oil. However, with its rapidly growing economy, China is now a net importer of crude oil, and that means more competition and price pressure on the crude oil currently on the market. China is not the only country with a rising economy. India and Brazil are two others of importance. As a whole, Africa, Central and South America, and Southeast Asia are developing their economies and demanding more commodities. This trend probably will continue into the future.

Increases in the Standard of Living

When the economy of a country accelerates, so does the standard of living for average consumers. A higher standard of living means more money available for discretionary spending. When times are tough, consumers spend less money on nonstaple items and more on staple items such as food. In contrast, when times are good, consumers have more money to spend on pork rather than wheat and on luxury items such as gold and silver jewelry and fancy automobiles that require palladium and aluminum. As the economies of China and other developing nations expand, consumers will reap the benefits with a higher standard of living. However, advances in the standard of living are not experienced only in developing countries. Even the most developed and mature countries experience economic growth, and that translates into higher standards of living for all. Commodities will benefit from this trend.

FAVORABLE SUPPLY FUNDAMENTALS

Although it may surprise most people, many of the commodities consumed around the world are not expanding but declining. Moreover, other commodities are experiencing growth but are forecast to experience a permanent decline that will lead to higher prices as demand exceeds supply. Energy fuels and metals are the best examples of commodities that exist in finite quantities. Once they are exploited, there are no substitutes. Agriculture has its own supply problems in which there is a lack of suitable farmland available to cultivate crops. Once this farmland is in use, nothing more can be done to increase production. Finally, a lack of sufficient infrastructure to produce commodities and meet current demand is obvious.

Limited Quantity of Raw Materials

Coal, crude oil, natural gas, gold, silver, and many other energy fuels and metals exist in finite quantities. Once these quantities are used up, they are done. When crude oil runs out in the next 100 or so years, society will be unable to produce any more and will have to find alternatives. The thought of a world without crude oil and its component products is mind-numbing. Furthermore, even though the world may have ample supplies of certain commodities for 50 or 100 years, the production of those commodities is declining. All the low-hanging fruit has been picked. For example, crude oil production in the United States and Norway has been in decline for many years and will continue to decline until all economically feasible crude oil has been exploited. The same pattern is being experienced everywhere. Many experts claim that Saudi Arabia is also at historical peak levels and will not produce more oil in the years to come. Production of many commodities throughout the world has only one way to go—down. When supplies fall or stay constant while demand rises, that can lead to only one result: higher prices. As an investor, that means opportunity.

Lack of Agricultural Acreage

Much like energy fuels and metals, agricultural commodities have a significant drawback, in this case a limitation on the amount of land available to grow crops. The world is a big place with many open areas untouched by civilization and, more important, farming. However, not all land is ideal or even suitable for cultivating certain crops. There is a reason why oranges are not grown in the state of Michigan and cocoa is not cultivated in Alaska. Furthermore, as the population of the world grows over the next few decades, people will need to live and work somewhere new. They will not be able to cohabit with existing families and work for the same companies. An increasing population means more intrusion on some of the more fertile growing areas. Cities and towns sprang up around ideal farming areas, and when a city or town expands, those croplands are replaced with homes and businesses.

Cropland—both suitable and unsuitable—can be fertilized to increase production, but that solution can only go so far. The lack of agricultural acreage will result in supplies of many needed commodities not meeting demand.

Insufficient Infrastructure

Mining for gold, drilling for crude oil, and harvesting wheat require substantial investments in equipment and facilities throughout the food chain. When infrastructure is inadequate, increasing production to meet higher demand is not feasible. For example, a few years ago the price for crude oil was much lower than it is today. That meant that crude oil exploration and production companies made less money per barrel of crude oil brought to the market. When profits are lower, there is less incentive to spend capital to improve and upgrade equipment and facilities with the hope of increasing production. However, when prices rise, there is more incentive to increase production. This is much easier said than done since the infrastructure was not built in anticipation of higher demand. As a result, companies that produce certain commodities may have difficulty increasing production as demand for many commodities continues to accelerate. Infrastructure is very important in mining and drilling because the commodities that are easiest to exploit already have been found and extracted. To increase production, companies must drill in difficult to reach areas where the risks are higher. Without increased spending on higher-technology equipment, this cannot be accomplished. A fair amount of time must pass before many of the companies involved in mining and drilling develop their infrastructure to produce the quantities demanded. Until that is accomplished, demand will outpace supply, and that is good news for investors.

Major Commodity Exchanges/Designated Contract Markets

Officially known as designated contract markets (DCMs), commodity exchanges facilitate the trading of commodities and the underlying derivative products, trading over $1.5 trillion worth of contracts daily. This is accomplished through the listing and execution of specific and standardized commodity contracts, including spot prices, forwards, futures, and options on futures. The majority of commodities exchanges throughout the world trade in the core commodities: energy fuels, agricultural products, and metals. However, a few commodities exchanges also trade exotics and financials.

Commodities exchanges bring together many participants involved in the commodities trade, such as producers, merchants, and speculators. Individuals are permitted to trade on commodities exchanges, but most of the trading is conducted by large institutions or governmental entities that make very large trades.

As the central figure in the futures markets, commodities exchanges serve many roles and provide many benefits. First, commodities exchanges provide an environment that makes it possible to establish global prices for commodities. Without commodities exchanges, commodity participants would not know where to transact business or how to obtain the best prices. Transparency is an essential element of commodity exchanges. Second, commodity exchanges through futures markets allow participants not involved in producer or merchant activities to speculate on the prices of commodities. Speculators participate in the commodity futures market to make gains by correctly forecasting the direction of prices. Speculators assume some degree of price risk and inject significant liquidity into the markets. This allows producers and merchants to hedge their price exposure and protect their positions. Third, commodity exchanges establish what are called *clearing firms*: legal corporations charged with protecting the financial integrity of the commodities markets, facilitating the settlement of trades, and ensuring delivery.

Most commodities exchanges emphasize certain commodities over others. For instance, the Chicago Board of Trade is recognized for the trading of agricultural commodities, the New York Mercantile Exchange is known for trading energy and metals commodities, and the Chicago Mercantile Exchange is known for trading livestock. In addition, most commodity exchanges trade in multiple commodities, whereas some target a small number. The Kansas City Board of Trade lists for trading wheat and natural gas, and the Chicago Mercantile Exchange lists for trading butter, milk, feeder cattle, pork bellies, lean hogs, live cattle, lumber, and more.

No single commodity exchange has exclusive trading rights to a specific commodity. For example, one can trade gold on both the Chicago Board of Trade and the New York Mercantile Exchange. West Texas Intermediate (WTI) crude oil is traded on both the New York Mercantile Exchange and the Intercontinental Exchange. However, there is little overlap of the commodities traded on exchanges. For example, pork bellies are traded only on the Chicago Mercantile Exchange.

All commodity exchanges in the United States have physical trading locations with the exception of the Intercontinental Exchange, which trades electronically.

Market Indicators

There are many indicators that affect commodities markets. Some of the indicators are called *fundamental indicators*, and others are called *technical indicators*. Fundamental indicators relate to the supply and demand dynamics of a particular commodity. The hope is to gain more insight into a commodity's value, which then is evaluated against current market prices. With technical analysis, no emphasis is placed on supply and demand for a particular commodity. Rather, many aspects relating to price, volume, and open interest are looked at with a keen eye. Below is a list of the key commodity market indicators divided into fundamental indicators and technical indicators. Chapter 6 discusses each market indicator in detail.

Technical Indicators

- Price
- Volume
- Support and resistance
- Trend lines
- Momentum
- Moving averages
- Relative strength

Fundamental Indicators

- Crude oil
- Gross domestic product (GDP)
- U.S. dollar exchange rate
- Consumer price index
- Discount and federal funds rates
- London InterBank Offered Rate
- EIA inventory reports
- Nonfarm payrolls
- London Gold Fix
- Purchasing Managers Index
- Commodities indexes

Investment Approaches

Once you know what commodities are all about, you can invest in and trade commodities. Remember that for the typical investor, investing and trading commodities should be considered within the context of one's total portfolio, not as a stand-alone investment.

There are five general approaches to participating in the commodities markets: purchasing exchange-traded instruments, buying into commodity mutual funds, taking an ownership stake in companies involved in commodities, investing through hedge funds, and the most basic approach: investing through futures and options on futures. The last approach can be accomplished either through a managed futures fund or by means of self-directed participation. No single approach is ideal for all participants, but some approaches carry more risk than others. For the typical investor who is looking to maximize portfolio returns and manage volatility risk, purchasing commodity indexes is a good fit. These instruments offer broad exposure to multiple commodities at a low cost because of their passive management style. Commodity mutual funds are better suited for investors who want to assume greater risk for the chance to earn higher returns than the market earns. Commodity hedge funds have limitations and are generally higher-risk but can deliver superb returns. Buying shares of stock in a corporation or master limited partnership is another approach that can generate attractive returns if the right companies are purchased.

Below is a short description of each approach. However, note that Part 3 of this book provides an in-depth discussion of the different investment approaches available to market participants.

EXCHANGE-TRADED INSTRUMENTS

Exchange-traded funds, exchange-traded notes, and closed-end funds all are exchange-traded instruments. These investments are characterized by their passive management style, in which each instrument tracks a certain commodities market. Since there is no active management for the purchase and sale of component investments, costs are much lower than those of comparable actively managed funds. Exchange-traded instruments provide instant exposure and diversification across a broad spectrum of commodities. For the typical investor, greater diversification is ideal since risk is kept to a minimum.

COMMODITY MUTUAL FUNDS

A commodity mutual fund is just like any other mutual fund except that it targets and holds companies involved in the commodities trade. These companies mine for metals, drill for energy fuels, harvest agricultural crops, generate electric power, or operate regulated utilities. Most commodity mutual funds exhibit a bias toward companies involved in energy fuels, though some take a more balanced approach and incorporate metals and other commodities. The primary reason for purchasing a commodity mutual fund is to earn above-market rates of return through active management. Active management attempts to generate attractive returns through security selection with a little assistance from market timing of purchases and sales. Annual expense ratios are generally high with commodity mutual funds, but that is expected in light of the expertise money managers must have to run such a fund.

STOCKS AND PARTNERSHIPS

Many different types of companies are involved directly or indirectly in the commodities trade. Companies that explore and drill for oil or mine for gold are considered to be directly involved, whereas transportation companies such as railroads and barges are considered to be indirectly involved. Companies that are directly involved tend to offer higher risk and higher return potential, whereas companies that are indirectly involved prosper when an entire industry, such as coal mining or crude oil drilling, is performing well. Companies that are indirectly involved present less risk to investors but have less return potential. Companies can be defined as either corporations or master limited partnerships. Corporations are by far the most popular legal form of entity, whereas master limited partnerships offer unique tax advantages. Taking an ownership stake in either type of company is a good method for many investors new to commodities investing.

COMMODITY HEDGE FUNDS

Commodity hedge funds are managed by professionals who many believe are the top minds on Wall Street. A hedge fund is not really an asset class but an account type that allows money managers to use various alternative tools and strategies. Hedge funds are not for everyone, nor can everyone invest in a hedge fund. The U.S. Securities and Exchange Commission has established very strict requirements for who qualifies to invest. Only those with substantial wealth and high annual incomes can satisfy the "qualified investor" criterion. Hedge funds can invest in nearly anything, including commodities. Some hedge funds invest in a broad basket of commodities, whereas others invest in only one or two commodities. Hedge funds present greater risk to investors but offer high return potential.

FUTURES AND OPTIONS

Commodities are defined by the trading of futures and options on futures with specific commodities as the underlying asset position. Futures and options are the most basic and most elementary of all the instruments that are used to provide commodity exposure. Significant expertise and a higher risk profile are needed before one embarks on trading futures and options. The reason for this is that futures and options exhibit much higher volatility than do other types of investments and can be employed with the use of leverage, in which only a portion of the traded amount is required to be posted.

Many professional commodities money managers also use futures and options. The most common type of account is called a futures managed fund. With this account, a sponsor, such as a brokerage firm, hires a professional commodities trading advisor to make investing decisions.

Each of the commodities profiled in Part 2 of this book is listed with contract specifications for futures contracts that trade in that particular commodity.

Quiz for Chapter 1

1. About how long ago did the production of commodities begin?
   a. 2,000 years
   b. 5,000 years
   c. 10,000 years
   d. 100,000 years

2. The first commodity exchange was established in Florence in 1153.
   a. True
   b. False

3. Which two commodities are considered the first to be produced?
   a. Copper and bronze
   b. Lumber and silk
   c. Tin and lead
   d. Wheat and barley

4. Which of the following was the first commodity exchange in the United States?
   a. Chicago Mercantile Exchange
   b. Chicago Board of Trade
   c. New York Board of Trade
   d. Kansas City Board of Trade

5. All but which of the following characteristics define a commodity?
   a. Elastic
   b. Standardization
   c. Tradability
   d. Deliverability

6. Which of the following is not classified as a precious metal?
   a. Gold
   b. Silver
   c. Nickel
   d. Platinum

7. Foreign currencies generally are considered commodities.
   a. True
   b. False

8. Which of the following commodity exchanges was acquired by the Chicago Mercantile Exchange in 2007?
   a. New York Mercantile Exchange
   b. Intercontinental Exchange
   c. Chicago Board of Trade
   d. Minneapolis Grain Exchange

9. Which of the following commodities is not considered an exotic commodity?
   a. Electric power
   b. Rubber
   c. Wool
   d. Lumber

10. All but which of the following is a reason why the demand for commodities is expected to increase in the coming decades?

    a. Advances in consumers' standard of living

    b. Increasing global population

    c. Development of global economies

    d. Adequate infrastructure

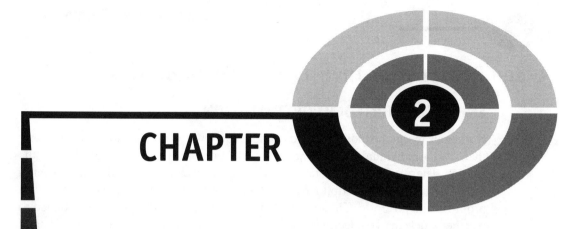

CHAPTER 2

Attractions and Merits:

Making the Case for Commodities

For investors who want to gain an edge, investing in commodities can produce the golden results they are looking to achieve. Investing in commodities provides many advantages and benefits that are not available with traditional stock and bond investing. Smart investors know the benefits of allocating to fundamentally different asset classes such as commodities. If an investor does not invest in commodities, he or she will build a suboptimal portfolio in which there is lower return potential and higher risk levels, leading to underperformance.

Thus far you have learned about the fundamentals and history of commodities and the broad reasons for investing in commodities. Many specific aspects of commodities support the idea that even a small portfolio allocation can generate solid results over time. But what are those specific aspects? The following sections explain the important reasons—presented as golden, silver, and bronze, depending on their importance—why commodities can make a solid addition to an investment portfolio.

Golden Reasons for Investing in Commodities

ENHANCED PORTFOLIO OPTIMIZATION

Numerous research studies have concluded that *how* you allocate investments rather than *which* individual investments you select or *when* you buy or sell them is the leading determinant of investment performance over time. By allocating even a small portion of your portfolio to commodities, you will enhance the risk and return profile of the portfolio. This means that your portfolio will be better positioned to weather stock market declines, will be safeguarded against large swings in total portfolio value, and will have greater opportunities for higher performance over time. But what is enhanced portfolio optimization, and how does investing in commodities make this happen? Investing in commodities leads to greater portfolio efficiency and diversification, reduced volatility risk and the corresponding smoother returns, and higher risk-adjusted returns—the elements that define enhanced portfolio optimization. Following are discussions of each of these three elements of commodities investing.

Greater Portfolio Efficiency and Diversification

Every investor has a tolerance for risk as well as specific goals and needs. Those goals sometimes are related to wealth accumulation, wealth preservation, or both. Once you identify your risk profile and specific goals and obligations, you can design an optimal portfolio that will achieve them. More specifically, you want suitable portfolio performance over the long term. This is important because many portfolios are designed with little regard for an investor's risk profile or goals and needs.

Commodities provide investors with an opportunity to incorporate assets that best align their risk profile with their asset allocation. By adding a commodities element to your portfolio, you effectively create a more optimal and diversified portfolio.

Reduced Volatility Risk and Smoother Returns

Nothing can devastate a portfolio like market crashes and prolonged market weakness. Over the history of the stock market, investors have experienced some crashes and numerous periods of prolonged weakness. At times one investment will perform well, and at other times another investment will perform well. Commodities provide another investment option. If you allocate to multiple asset classes, including commodities, which do not move in perfect lockstep with one another, your portfolio will be shielded to a degree from excessive portfolio volatility. Holding a portfolio of only stocks and bonds generally has greater portfolio risk than does holding a balanced portfolio of stocks, bonds, and commodities. This means that your portfolio will experience lower price volatility than it would if you did not invest in commodities; this equates to lower portfolio risk and smoother returns over time. Most investors would agree that smoother returns from month to month are more desirable than returns that fluctuate greatly during the same time period. Adding commodities to a portfolio can help you accomplish this aim.

Higher Risk-Adjusted Returns

Modern portfolio theory says that when an investor is faced with two investments with identical expected returns but different levels of risk, he or she should select the investment that has the lower risk. Put a different way, a rational investor will select the investment with the higher return when faced with two investments that have different expected returns but identical levels of risk. By combining fundamentally different investments with various forecast returns and risk levels, you build a portfolio that provides a higher risk-adjusted return. Commodities can do this.

INFLATION PROTECTION

Inflation rates and commodity prices are strongly linked and highly correlated because commodities are an essential component of any economy. When inflation rates rise, commodity prices typically rise as well. This means that your portfolio is protected against the negative impact of inflation and the subsequent loss of purchasing power. Few investments offer that benefit.

Keep in mind, however, that inflation is caused by rising commodities prices rather than the other way around. When energy prices are increasing because of higher crude oil prices, prices in any economy typically advance across the board. For instance, the cat food you purchase requires factories to produce the food, trucks to transport the finished product to stores, and stores to inventory it until final purchase. Each part of this cycle requires energy to power the factory, gasoline to power the trucks, and electric power to operate the lights and natural gas to heat the store. A small increase in crude oil, natural gas, or coal has ripple effects in the economy, and the end-use consumer incurs the cost increase. People who have invested in commodities have a way to hedge some or all of the extra costs that result from rising commodities prices.

INELASTIC PRICING

Many people have heard the terms *elastic* and *inelastic*. Basically, elasticity is the measurement of demand for a product at different price levels. The more elastic a product is, the less of the product customers demand when prices are rising. Likewise, when prices are falling, products with substantial elasticity have proportionately greater demand. So what does this mean? There are some products in the marketplace that must be purchased regardless of price levels. These products are considered inelastic. For instance, gasoline for your automobile, natural gas to heat your home, and grains for the food you eat are relatively inelastic. When prices increase, you may be able to purchase substitute products such as corn instead of wheat or cut back on how much you use by driving less or carpooling, but for the most part you still have to purchase those commodities. Elasticity of demand, as it is known in economics, is not black and white; there are many shades of gray. Commodities are some of the most inelastic products in the world. You simply cannot get away with not purchasing and consuming them. All else being equal, this means that demand for commodities is relatively stable. As an investor, this means greater comfort because you know that rising crude oil prices will not be offset by lower demand that negates any gains made.

POTENTIAL FOR AGGRESSIVE RETURNS

For investors looking to assume greater risk in the hopes of earning higher returns, commodities can provide the means to accomplish this goal. Although the aim of investing in commodities is to construct an optimal portfolio and hedge against inflation, it also can be done with the hope of earning high returns. Because prices for many commodities are highly volatile, there is an opportunity for investors to trade commodities and earn high returns. People who participate in commodities in this manner are better described as speculators or traders rather than traditional investors. To become a speculator, people need strong knowledge, good trading skills, and, most of all, the time to monitor the markets and execute trades.

For investors interested in assuming greater risk without becoming a trader or speculator, investing with a money manager such as a commodities pool or hedge fund can be a good move. With this approach, investors assign the time and effort to professionals who have the requisite knowledge of commodities markets and experience with futures and options. This comes with a cost in the form of investment management fees. Chapter 19 discusses investing with a professional money manager in greater detail.

NO RISK OF PRODUCT OBSOLESCENCE

Investing in stocks demands a watchful eye and defense against obsolescence risk: the risk that a product will become worthless because of product innovations, changing consumer tastes, or product degradation. Think of the products sold by technology and pharmaceutical companies. At one time, the Intel 386 was the best microprocessor one could purchase. Not long thereafter Intel released the upgraded 486 model. During the same period AMD, a competing firm, released its own microprocessors. For investors, keeping up on the latest and greatest products is not practical. Fortunately, this scenario does not occur with commodities. Gold, silver, oil, and wheat may decline in price, but they will not become worthless or be discarded as a result of changing consumer tastes. This means greater certainty and extra safeguards for your investments.

MINIMAL EXTERNAL AND MANAGEMENT ISSUES

Scandals beset both public and private corporations every day. Investors in Enron and Tyco experienced firsthand what happens to investments when things go drastically wrong because management does not work for the shareholders but places its own interests first. In addition to unethical or questionable management actions, changes in analysts' recommendations, management's earnings announcements, and legal proceedings are examples of how stock prices can be influenced to go either up or down. By investing in commodities, you can avoid these potentially risky issues and ensure greater protection for your portfolio. In contrast to most other investments, commodities prices are driven by simple supply and demand economics. The exception to this rule occurs when you invest in companies that participate in the commodities market, such as gold mining companies and railroad companies. Extra discretion is warranted in these cases.

Silver Reasons for Investing in Commodities

GREATER PRICE PREDICTABILITY

Research has shown that commodity prices are slightly more predictable over time than are the prices of publicly traded companies. This is the direct result of the long-term supply and demand trends that many commodities experience over long periods. Why is greater price predictability important? Uncertainty creates risk. The more uncertain an investment's returns are, the greater risk that investment exhibits. More certain investments offer less risk. Of course, less risk comes with lower return as risk and return are inherently linked. You cannot earn high returns without accepting higher levels of risk. However, do not confuse price predictability with price volatility. Commodities are typically more price-volatile than are stocks and bonds, but with somewhat greater certainty in regard to price direction. Higher volatility does translate into greater risk, but the incremental risk is offset by greater price predictability with regard to long-term price direction.

FAVORABLE TAX TREATMENT

Commodities offer more favorable tax treatment (Section 1256 of the Internal Revenue Code) to investors than do many other investments, particularly stocks and bonds. Instead of paying 100 percent short-term capital gains taxes on profitable trades purchased and sold within one year, with commodities 60 percent of the profits are taxed as long-term capital gains—which means a lower taxable rate—and the other 40 percent is taxed at the short-term capital gains tax rate, which is the investor's federal tax rate. Capital gains tax rates are typically lower than an investor's marginal federal tax rate. As a result of this more favorable tax treatment, investors in commodities walk away with more money in their pockets than do other investors even when their gains are the same.

OPPORTUNITY TO HEDGE BUSINESS OPERATIONAL RISK

Many investors in commodities are companies that hedge their business operations with commodities futures and options. For instance, consider the cereal companies Kellogg's and Post. Those companies buy enormous quantities of grains and other agricultural products to make their cereals. As a result, they are very much exposed to the risk of prices escalating and thus forcing them to increase the prices of their cereals. If Post or Kellogg's believes that grain prices will rise in the next 6 to 12 months, it can hedge its forecast price increase through the use of futures or options. In this example, Post or Kellogg's will execute a contract to buy now at today's prices and accept delivery of the grains in six months. It typically will pay more for a future delivery than it would pay if it purchased now in what is called the spot market and took delivery immediately. The price it will purchase the grain for is dependent on the forward price curve. This curve will show market prices—again based on supply and demand—for each month for the next two years or more. Thus, if you want to receive grain six months from today, you look at the forward price curve, locate the price for the particular month you are targeting, and execute the contract at that price. Chapter 16 gives a fuller description of how futures and options work when one is investing in commodities.

Bronze Reasons for Investing in Commodities

BETTER INVESTMENT DECISION MAKING

Information on commodities is significantly more objective and concrete than information on stocks. Numerous factors drive stock prices, but there is only one factor that drives commodities prices: supply and demand economics. Research reports on supply and demand are typically very objective and leave little room for subjectivity. Because of the numerous factors that drive stock prices, analysts often stumble in their attempts to deliver quality research that is of material help to investors. This typically does not happen with commodities.

FOLLOWS THE INVEST IN WHAT YOU UNDERSTAND PRINCIPLE

The legendary investor Warren Buffett is known for his belief that people should invest in what they know and understand. If you do not understand how a product works, you should avoid making an investment in a company that produces that product. Commodities and real estate are the most basic and fundamental investable products and therefore lend themselves to being easily understood. Being comfortable with your investments goes a long way and can be worth more than its weight in gold—no pun intended.

LESS TIME AND RESEARCH

When people invest in stocks and bonds, they often need to review numerous research reports and, for more involved investors, research financial statements and perhaps conduct proprietary research. In contrast, investing in commodities does not require much time and research since it typically is done to take advantage of long-term price trends without the goal of zeroing in on specific individual investments. Investors in commodities still need to do research on supply and demand dynamics, but this work pales in comparison to what investors in stock or bonds should be doing. Figure 2.1 lists the major reasons for investing in commodities.

Figure 2-1. Reasons for Investing in Commodities

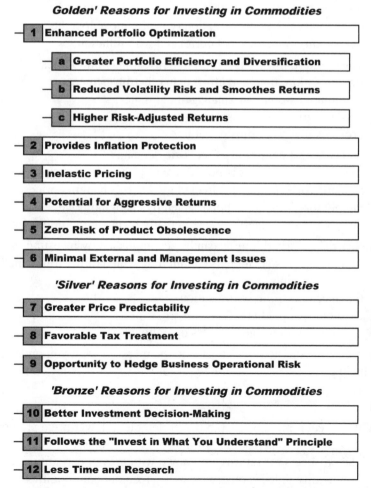

Quiz for Chapter 2

1. All but which of the following are reasons to invest in commodities?
   a. Elastic pricing
   b. Enhanced portfolio optimization
   c. Higher price predictability
   d. Hedge against inflation

2. Investing in commodities typically results in portfolios with higher volatility and more variable returns.
   a. True
   b. False

3. Why do commodities provide a hedge against inflation?
   a. Inflation causes consumer demand for raw materials to skyrocket.
   b. Inflation is controlled with robust commodity demand.
   c. Commodity prices and inflation typically move together.
   d. Commodity prices are not correlated with inflation.

4. Which of the following is a reason to invest in commodities?
   a. Requires more time and effort than other investments
   b. Maximum external and management issues
   c. Zero risk of product obsolescence
   d. Provides low risk-adjusted returns

5. What is the best definition of inelastic demand?
   a. Demand for a product is not affected by changing prices.
   b. Demand for a product is affected greatly by changing prices.
   c. Supply for a product is not affected by changing prices.
   d. Supply for a product is affected greatly by changing prices.

6. Higher risk-adjusted returns can be accomplished by investing in commodities. This attribute is captured by which of the following?
   a. Inelastic pricing
   b. Enhanced portfolio optimization
   c. Greater price predictability
   d. Opportunity to hedge business operational risk

7. Investing in commodities adheres to the invest in what you understand principle.
   a. True
   b. False

8. Why is greater price predictability preferable to lower price predictability?
   a. You are able to invest in multiple commodity classes.
   b. The prospects for returns are known with greater certainty.
   c. Commodity indexes otherwise will screen out commodities.
   d. Commodity mutual funds invest only in relatively guaranteed securities.

9. Less time and research typically is required with commodities than with traditional investments for which of the following reasons?
   a. Commodities have little in the way of published reports and forecasts.
   b. Commodities exhibit little volatility and pay higher average dividends.
   c. For the most part, commodity futures are easy to master and trade.
   d. Generally only macro-level supply and demand factors have to be evaluated.

10. Investing in commodities is underscored by which investing strategy?
    a. Asset allocation
    b. Market timing
    c. Security selection
    d. Tactical occurrence

CHAPTER

All about the Risks:

Commodities Challenges and Concerns

As many investors know and the media never miss an opportunity to point out, there are many pitfalls in the commodities trade. Some of the banner news stories you probably watched over the last couple of years include cold spells in Florida that impacted orange crops, hurricanes in the Gulf of Mexico that impacted natural gas prices, OPEC cutting oil production thus driving up prices, and new laws restricting the use of coal to power electric generating plants. This chapter touches on the most common macro commodity investing risks (see Figure 3.1).

Macro Commodity Investing Risks

As with mutual funds and more traditional investing, there are risks associated with investing in commodities. Moreover, commodities offer very unique risks not inherent in other asset classes. Exercising extreme caution when investing in commodities is strongly encouraged to ensure you do not fall prey to them. Always remember that investment risk and return go hand-in-hand.

Figure 3-1. Commodity Risks

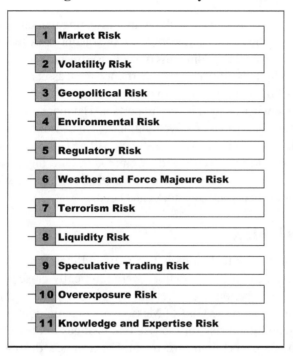

Said another way, since commodities offer above average return potential, that also means above average risk.

MARKET RISK

Market risk refers to external factors that can cause declining values in commodities investments. Some of these external factors, which are discussed in detail in Chapter Six include the following:

- Gross Domestic Product
- U.S. Dollar Exchange Rate
- Consumer Price Index
- Discount Rate
- EIA Inventory Report
- Nonfarm Payrolls
- London Gold Fix
- Purchasing Managers' Index
- Crude oil prices

VOLATILITY RISK

Volatility risk is the risk associated with highly fluctuating market prices. Unlike blue chip stocks, commodities have significant levels of volatility risk that can make many investors uncomfortable with holding this type of investment. Why is volatility considered a risk factor? High volatility creates uncertainty about asset availability. For example, if you need $500,000 in five years to purchase a vacation home, knowing that the money will be there when needed is very important. The more certain you are that the money will be available, the less risk you will have, whereas more uncertainty means more risk. If your portfolio is highly volatile, you will be less certain of the amount of money you will have to meet your needs. Commodities are highly volatile, and that means investors need to exercise more caution with their commodities investments than with their other investments, such as stocks and bonds.

GEOPOLITICAL RISK

Commodities investing is truly a global activity and therefore is fraught with pitfalls. It would be nice if all commodities were physically close by, but that is not the case. Crude oil can be found all over the world from Saudi Arabia to Venezuela and from the North Sea to the Gulf of Mexico. As a result, commodities investors are exposed to geopolitical risk, or the risk that changes in the political landscape will have negative impacts on an investment. For instance, during 2006 and 2007 many governments forcefully took control of private energy projects in their countries and essentially created state-owned companies. Two of the biggest countries in that group were Venezuela and Russia. Energy companies spent billions of dollars exploring, drilling, and bringing to market oil from those countries and were forced to sell those assets at a significant discount to the government even though fairly negotiated agreements were in effect. Bolivia is another case in which the government nationalized natural gas projects owned by companies, leaving investors feeling victimized. Among all the investment alternatives available to investors, commodities are at the top for having geopolitical risk.

ENVIRONMENTAL RISK

Environmental risk is the risk that producing or sourcing commodities can have long-lasting negative effects on the surrounding environment that permanently damage the landscape, require substantial capital for cleanup, or both. Damaging a company's image and reputation is another typical result of environmental damage. This means that investors can lose big when companies do not take environmental concerns seriously and cause the unthinkable, such as the *Exxon Valdez* oil spill in Alaska.

REGULATORY RISK

Regulatory risk, which sometimes is called corporate governance risk, refers to the current and future restraints imposed on investing in commodities that create extra financial costs or impede investment strategy and potentially reduce performance. As recently as 2007, the Securities and Exchange Commission toughened requirements for individuals to qualify for "accredited investor" status and thus be eligible to invest with hedge funds, which often invest in commodities. Another way regulators can affect commodities investing is through changes in margin requirements by the Federal Reserve. If the Fed requires investors to post additional margin, thus reducing leverage, some investors will have to alter their strategies, with potential implications for generating gains. Changing the tax rate on capital gains is another way regulators can affect investors in commodities. Two other entities that regulate the commodities trade are the Commodity Futures Trading Commission (CFTC) and the National Futures Association (NFA).

WEATHER AND FORCE MAJEURE RISK

This risk factor is best described as acts of God. *Force majeure* is the term the commodities industry employs to describe events that are out of the control of people. There are many events that constitute force majeure, with weather being the most prevalent. Hurricanes, droughts, floods, and extreme heat or cold are a few examples of weather-related events that can cause commodities prices to rise and fall quickly. For instance, too much rain or too little rain can cause many agricultural commodities to fail, and extreme heat and extreme cold can cause demand for energy fuels to increase or decrease quickly. For a real-world example, think of the 2005 hurricanes Katrina and Rita. Those storms brought destruction to most of the oil platforms and underwater oil transportation pipelines that were in their path in the Gulf of Mexico. This region is a vital source of energy for the United States, and the result was substantial price increases for energy fuels, especially natural gas. Nearly overnight the price for natural gas doubled, crushing those with short natural gas positions and handsomely rewarding those with long positions, especially Amaranth Advisors, which made a killing.

TERRORISM RISK

Although commodities prices are driven by long-term supply and demand dynamics, those prices are affected greatly by worldwide events, in particular terrorist attacks. Nigeria has been the target of many terrorist attacks on its vast oil infrastructure. Those attacks, although sometimes not significant, can have huge repercussions on the global crude oil market. It sometimes takes only a small act of terrorism to send energy prices soaring. Once the event is resolved, prices slowly but surely move back into balance. This is one reason for the high volatility in commodities prices. Investors need to be aware of the possibility of prices fluctuating widely and avoid making emotional decisions that can impede their long-term plans.

LIQUIDITY RISK

Liquidity is defined as the degree of ease investors have in selling an investment at or near the current market price. The closer the executed price is to the current market price, the more liquid an investment is said to be. In contrast, investments that are sold at prices that materially deviate from the current market price are considered illiquid. Publicly traded stocks are the most liquid investments. This means that if you buy or sell shares of a stock, you most likely will execute at the current market value. This cannot be said about less liquid investments such as real estate and some commodities. Depending on the commodity, an investment may be quite liquid or somewhat illiquid. It is the less mature commodities, such as emissions credits and coal that are less liquid. Thus, investors in this market need to realize that the market price they see may not be the price at which they will buy or sell. Investments with less liquidity also make valuing a fund or portfolio more challenging since determining the best price to use is not an easy thing to do. The bid-ask spread for a commodity is the best way to measure its liquidity. Wider spreads mean less liquidity, and narrower spreads mean greater liquidity.

SPECULATIVE TRADING RISK

The commodities market is made up of both hedgers and speculators, and each group has its own agenda. Like most other investment types, commodities involve participants whose single purpose is to profit from trading in specific commodities. Speculators are vital, as they provide liquidity and risk transfer, but they also can move the market in adverse directions and move it quite quickly. One of the main reasons speculators can be a thorn in your side is that they often do not pay attention to fundamentals and instead trade on the basis of technicals or other trends. That can make the job of identifying profitable opportunities much more difficult for investors who simply want to take advantage of long-term trends in which demand outstrips supply. For the most part, speculators account for approximately 20 to 25 percent of the total futures market, with hedgers accounting for the remaining 75 to 80 percent. For an inside look at the current market participants, investigate the *Commitment of Traders* report from the Commodities Futures Trading Commission at www.CFTC.gov.

OVEREXPOSURE RISK

Investing in commodities does not mean that investors always must seek out commodities mutual funds or exchange-traded funds or notes or play the futures market. Purchasing an S&P 500 index fund will provide commodities exposure since many of those companies participate directly in commodities, such as ExxonMobil. However, nearly all the rest participate indirectly, such as American Airlines through its exposure to jet fuel and Kellogg's through its exposure to the price of grains. If jet fuel declines, American Airlines will spend less on that commodity and report somewhat higher earnings, causing its stock price to increase.

For investors looking for only a modest exposure to commodities, investing in the S&P 500 may be the right approach. In contrast, for investors looking to gain additional exposure to commodities, investing in a commodities-related investment is the right approach. However, investors need to be aware of the commodities exposure they already have in their portfolios through investments such as the S&P 500 and not invest in more commodities than is appropriate for their risk and return profile. Doing so can create more risk than is suitable in a portfolio, and that can make for sleepless nights, uncertainty over future performance, and greater swings in a portfolio's market value. Make sure to consider the impact of commodity exposure from your present investments before deciding to add more commodities to your portfolio.

KNOWLEDGE AND EXPERTISE RISK

As with other investments, having solid knowledge of and expertise in the product you are looking to purchase is very important. Although most people know what commodities are about, they may be unfamiliar with how to invest in commodities, particularly the futures and options market. Once they learn where to go to invest, such as an online commodities broker, they must learn how commodities trade and what type of order to place. This means that investing in commodities requires more knowledge and expertise than does investing in most other investments. If you possess this knowledge and expertise, you are positioned well to invest in commodities. If you do not, seeking the help of a professional advisor with the requisite knowledge and expertise may be a smart move.

Quiz for Chapter 3

1. What is the risk associated with highly fluctuating market positions?
    a. Price determinacy risk
    b. CAF measurement risk
    c. VaR metrics
    d. Volatility risk

2. Geopolitical risk is more prominent with commodity investing than with traditional stock and bond investing.
   a. True
   b. False

3. Regulatory risk also is referred to as which of the following?
   a. Geopolitical risk
   b. Corporate governance risk
   c. Commodity registration risk
   d. Political resistance risk

4. Which type of risk often is described as an act of God?
   a. Regulatory risk
   b. Force majeure
   c. Volatility risk
   d. Geopolitical risk

5. Which type of risk is best defined as selling an investment at or near the current market price?
   a. Terrorism risk
   b. Weather risk
   c. Geopolitical risk
   d. Liquidity risk

6. With commodity trading, which of the following spreads is considered to represent a liquid market?
   a. Narrow spreads
   b. Wide spreads
   c. Contango spreads
   d. Correlation spreads

7. Environmental risk is a type of macro commodity investing risk.
   a. True
   b. False

8. Which of the following is not a macro commodity investing risk?
   a. Environmental risk
   b. Market risk
   c. Transparency risk
   d. Over exposure risk

9. Gaining additional exposure to commodities is ideal for nearly all types of investors, both conservative and aggressive alike.
   a. True
   b. False

10. Who issues the *Commitment of Traders* report detailing current participants in the futures market?
    a. National Futures Association
    b. New York Mercantile Exchange
    c. Securities and Exchange Commission
    d. Commodities Futures Trading Commission

CHAPTER

Players and Participants:

The Who's Who of All Things Commodities

Many people and entities participate in the commodities trade in one way or another. Each plays a very important role, and any broken link in the commodities food chain can have drastic effects on the other participants. When all participants are fulfilling their roles properly, the commodities market is an efficient marketplace that offers substantial investing opportunities for investors who recognize its potential. This chapter covers most of the key players in commodities, with an emphasis on where they fit in the commodities food chain. For instance, producers are discussed at the beginning of the chapter and end-use consumers conclude the list of participants. There are other participants, but the most important ones directly related to the commodities trade are included here (see Figure 4.1).

Figure 4-1. The Who's Who of Commodities

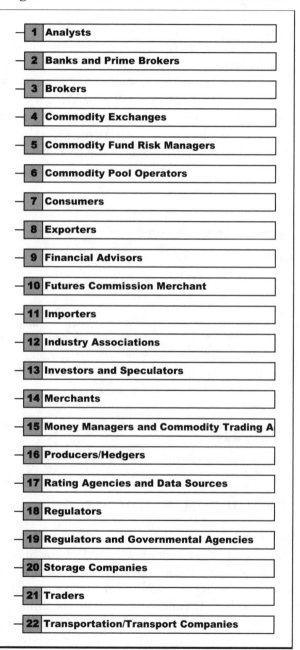

1. Analysts
2. Banks and Prime Brokers
3. Brokers
4. Commodity Exchanges
5. Commodity Fund Risk Managers
6. Commodity Pool Operators
7. Consumers
8. Exporters
9. Financial Advisors
10. Futures Commission Merchant
11. Importers
12. Industry Associations
13. Investors and Speculators
14. Merchants
15. Money Managers and Commodity Trading A|
16. Producers/Hedgers
17. Rating Agencies and Data Sources
18. Regulators
19. Regulators and Governmental Agencies
20. Storage Companies
21. Traders
22. Transportation/Transport Companies

Industry Associations

Industry associations enhance the industry for all the participants, from producers and exporters to importers and investors. Industry associations promote increased trade, improve product quality, sustain efficient markets, regulate members, and combat overly assertive government intrusion. Each commodity type has one or more associations; some are limited to a small geographic region, whereas others encompass the global marketplace. Some industry associations are open to new members, and others act as oligopolies, such as the Organization of Petroleum Exporting Countries (OPEC). Figure 4.2 lists some of the major commodities-related industry associations.

Figure 4-2. Commodity Industry Associations

Association	Location	Website
Aluminum Association	Arlington, VA USA	www.aluminum.org
American Forest and Paper Association	Washington, D.C. USA	www.afandpa.org
Copper Development Association	New York, NY USA	www.copper,org
Cotton Incorporated	Cary, NC USA	www.cottoninc.com
Futures Industry Association (FIA)	Washington, D.C. USA	www.futuresindustry.org
International Cocoa Organization	London, UK	www.icco.org
International Coffee Organization	London, UK	www.ico.org
National Association of Wheat Growers	Washington, D.C. USA	www.wheatworld.org
National Cattlemen's Beef Association	Centennial, Colorado, USA	www.beef.org
National Corn Growers Association	Chesterfield, MO USA	www.ncga.com
National Mining Association	Washington, D.C. USA	www.nma.org
National Pork Producers Council	Washington, D.C. USA	www.nppc.org
Organization of the Petroleum Exporting Countries (OPEC)	Vienna, Austria	www.opec.org
United Soybean Board	Chesterfield, MO USA	www.unitedsoybean.org

Regulators and Government Agencies

Regulators are the watchdogs of the commodities industry. There are many regulating agencies, such as the Securities and Exchange Commission (SEC), the Commodity Futures Trading Commission (CFTC), the Financial Industry National Regulatory Association (FINRA), the National Futures Association (NFA), the Federal Reserve, and the U.S. Treasury Department. The primary aims of regulators are to ensure that the laws of the land are upheld to prevent fraudulent activities, ensure open and efficient commodities and related futures markets, provide for full disclosure of the risks of investing in commodities (including conflicts of interest), and avoid financially catastrophic events such as hedge fund or managed futures fund failures and their subsequent negative impacts on the domestic and global financial marketplaces. Figure 4.3 lists U.S. regulators and government agencies.

Figure 4-3. U.S. Regulators and Government Agencies

Entity	Location	Website
Commodity Futures Trading Commission (CFTC)	Washington, DC USA	www.cftc.gov
Financial Industry National Regulatory Association	Washington, DC USA	www.finra.org
National Futures Association (NFA)	Chicago, IL USA	www.nfa.futures.org
Securities and Exchange Commission (SEC)	Washington, DC USA	www.sec.gov
U.S. Department of Agriculture	Washington, DC USA	www.usda.gov
U.S. Department of Energy (Energy Info. Admin.)	Washington, DC USA	www.eia.doe.gov
U.S. Department of Interior	Reston, VA USA	http://minerals.er.usgs.gov/minerals

Producers/Hedgers

This category of participants includes companies that produce commodities by mining them, such as gold mining companies in South Africa; drilling for them, such as oil and gas exploration companies in the Gulf of Mexico; or growing and harvesting them, such as wheat farmers in Nebraska and corn farmers in Iowa. These companies are the backbone of the commodities trade, and their efforts are the most important part of the commodities food chain. Producers often want to protect against price risk, or the risk that the commodities they want to sell in the future will decline in price. To accomplish this goal, many producers hedge their risk exposure by selling futures contracts, which involves selling a commodity now for delivery at some point in the future. Producers therefore are considered hedgers as they want to lock in prices for their goods without taking on the risk of prices falling, which will cause them to earn less for their efforts.

Exporters

Exporters are the entities, typically companies, involved in the distribution of commodities from one nation to other nations. These exporters can be the producers of a commodity, but that is not always the case. Many small producers do not have the size and scale to produce a commodity and then sell that commodity on the open market for export to another country. As a result, exporters serve the vital role of taking a commodity from the producer and facilitating its transfer to another nation. This should not be confused with transportation, which is another entity in the commodities food chain. Exporters can be thought of in terms of nations as a whole, such as Saudi Arabia, which is the largest exporter of crude oil to the world and in the world.

Importers

In contrast to exporters, importers are entities that transfer commodities from exporters into nations. Importers often are national governments that import rice or grain to their countries for subsequent distribution to companies that will distribute the rice or grain to the markets for consumers to purchase. In many other cases importers are companies that purchase from exporters and import a commodity to a nation for subsequent distribution. For instance, a wine importer from the United States may import wine from Italy or France and distribute that wine to retail markets for final purchase by end consumers. As with exporters, nations can be classified as importers; for example, the United States is the largest importer of crude oil in the world.

Commodity Exchanges

When people envision commodities investing, one of their first thoughts is commodities exchanges. Commodities exchanges are active hubs where most of the buying and selling of commodities is accomplished. In the past, exchanges were dominated by pits where traders physically gathered to execute purchase and sale orders through an open-outcry system. This system is still in use, but much commodities trading is handled by electronic systems that enhance the efficiency of the exchange and provide for greater trading volumes. The first global exchange in the world was established in Amsterdam by Italian immigrants to the Netherlands. Today global exchanges can be found all over the world in both developed and developing nations. The recent trend, however, is all about consolidation, in which the bigger and more established exchanges either purchase existing exchanges or establish new ones.

Depending on the type of transaction, some commodities are purchased and sold over the counter as forward contracts, whereas commodities traded on exchanges are sold as futures contracts. Exchanges serve many important roles for commodities producers and investors, including standardized contracts (and thus standardized terms), more reliable prices, mitigation of credit risk, and new product innovation.

Each exchange does not trade every commodity available. Rather, many exchanges target only a select few commodities. Figure 4.4 provides a list of the major global commodities exchanges and the commodities they trade.

Transportation/Transport Companies

Transportation refers to the physical distribution of commodities from one point to another, typically from the source to the final delivery point. This can refer to companies or to systems, such as the natural gas distribution system in the United States for transporting the commodity from Louisiana—the primary point of entry for foreign imports—to natural gas markets throughout the country. Other transportation entities include shipping vessels that deliver coal, grains, liquidized natural gas, or crude oil and railroads that play a critical role in the transportation of coal from mines to power plants. Transportation is typically a significant component of the

Figure 4-4. Major Global Exchanges

Exchange	Principal Commodities Traded
Australian Securities Exchange (ASX)	Agricultural
Brazilian Mercantile and Futures Exchange (BMF)	Agriculture, Biofuels, Precious Metals
Chicago Board of Trade (CBOT)	Corn, Ethanol, Gold, Oats, Rice, Silver, Soybeans, Wheat
Chicago Climate Exchange (CCX)	Emissions Allowance Credits
Chicago Mercantile Exchange (CME)	Butter, Milk, Feeder Cattle, Frozen Pork Bellies, Lean Hogs, Live Cattle, Lumber
Dubai Mercantile Exchange (DME)	Energy
Intercontinental Exchange (ICE)	Coal, Crude Oil, Electric Power, Natural Gas
Kansas City Board of Trade (KCBOT)	Wheat, Natural Gas
London Metals Exchange (LME)	Aluminum, Copper, Lead, Nickel, Plastics, Tin, Zinc
Minneapolis Grain Exchange (MGE)	Corn, Soybeans, Wheat
New York Board of Trade (NYBOT)	Cocoa, Coffee, Cotton, Ethanol, Frozen Concentrated Orange Juice, Sugar
New York Mercantile Exchange (NYMEX)	Aluminum, Coal, Copper, Crude oil, Electric Power, Gasoline, Gold, Heating Oil, Natural Gas, Palladium, Platinum, Propane, Silver
Shanghai Futures Exchange (SFE)	Aluminum, Copper, Energy, Rubber
Tokyo Commodity Exchange (TOCOM)	Agriculture, Energy, Precious Metals, Industrial Metals
Tokyo Grain Exchange (TGE)	Agricultural
Winnipeg Commodity Exchange (WCE)	Wheat, Barley, Canola

overall price structure for a commodity. In light of the vast world markets for some commodities, transporting them from the source to the final destination can be quite expensive. Shipyards are classified under this title since they facilitate the transportation of commodities from one source to another.

Storage Companies

Except for standardized financial instruments, commodities are tangible physical products, sometimes referred to as hard assets. As a result, commodities require storage when they are not in the process of being transported. Some commodities cannot be stored, such as electric power, which always must be moving from the power plant to the end consumer. However, the vast majority of commodities must be stored before final use. For natural gas, this means storage in gigantic tanks or underground storage facilities in remote areas to minimize the cost. Storage is used to address the cyclicality of commodity usage. For instance, natural gas usage is far greater in the colder months than in the warmer months, when running furnaces is at a minimum. However, utilities cannot simply purchase natural gas during peak months and cease making purchases in down months because they would never have the supply they need to keep up with demand. As a result, the summer months are called the injection months because natural gas is purchased and stored for future usage, and the winter months are called extraction months because natural gas is withdrawn to supplement the supplies needed to heat homes and businesses. Other commodities that require storage include grains, gasoline, coal, and agricultural softs.

Brokers

Brokers are companies that facilitate commodities purchases and sales between two other participants. Brokers are needed to help producers/hedgers locate suitable speculators and investors for their products. Brokers also help manufacturers with the purchase of large-scale commodities for their own inventory and eventual utilization. One well-known broker for futures trading is Lind-Waldock in Chicago. This broker allows individual and institutional investors to purchase and sell futures and options for various commodities. Without brokers, investors and speculators would have to search for producers/hedgers, which would be quite expensive. Brokers help facilitate efficient markets and help open up markets to the general investing public.

Traders

Traders are the people who make financial transactions happen. These people typically are glued to a computer monitor or multiple monitors. Traders execute transactions as instructed by various market participants. Transactions are executed with traders who can be anywhere around the globe. Traders need to react quickly to execute orders and generally fight hard for pennies on the dollar. Traders do not always sit in front of computer monitors or at desks. Rather, some trade in large "pits" at exchanges such as the New York Board of Trade and the Chicago Mercantile Exchange. These traders facilitate the purchase and sale of commodities for their own accounts or the accounts of their clients. They use various hand signals to express their desire to buy or sell specific commodities. Trading pits can be calm or busy, and traders need to be on their toes to avoid falling prey to other traders. Traders often wear different colored jackets to represent their different roles in the trading system. In addition, trading companies have their traders wear the same color jackets to represent their companies. Some of those jackets can be quite exotic so that a trader is easily recognized and not mistaken for a trader from a competing company.

Commodity Pool Operators

Commodity pool operators (CPOs) are people who establish futures managed funds. Commodity pool operators serve as the administrators of the fund and hire external managers—commodity trading advisors—to manage all or part of the capital in the fund. Many CPOs employ multiple commodity trading advisors and thus pursue a multimanager approach. The primary benefits of this approach are greater diversification, more specialized knowledge in each commodity trading advisor, enhanced risk management, and broader product offerings.

Futures Commission Merchants

A futures commission merchant (FCM) is an individual or organization that is responsible for soliciting and accepting futures and commodity option contract orders. In addition, futures commission merchants accept capital or provide credit to investors who want to enter into commodity transactions but do not have the required capital. Many global broker-dealers provide these services to their client base and often are affiliated with CPOs.

Money Managers and Commodity Trading Advisors

Commodities money managers and trading advisors are the lifeblood of a commodities fund: commodities mutual fund, hedge fund, managed futures fund, or private money manager separate account. Managers are typically the people who took the initiative to establish the fund and often have a vested interest in how well it does because of the wealth they have tied up in the funds they manage. Commodities managers are first and foremost responsible for the investment decisions of a fund. They make the buy and sell decisions and may execute the trades in smaller firms. The vast majority of managers are actively involved in researching investing opportunities and deciding which strategies or tools of the trade to employ. Obviously, this is the most important and most celebrated participant in the commodities trade.

Note that money managers who run managed futures funds are referred to as commodities trading advisors, whereas hedge funds and mutual funds are run by managers. Although they are different titles, both managers are responsible for

managing the capital invested in their funds. Unlike money managers, commodity trading advisors (CTAs) never take or receive invested funds. CTAs only make decisions on how the funds are to be invested.

Financial Advisors

Financial advisors play an important role in commodities because they are typically the first persons to expose many investors to all things related to commodities. Financial advisors emphasize a company's sponsored commodities, but this is not always the case. Financial advisors often have the trust and confidence of their clients and are the natural connection and source of education on commodities for many clients. They typically provide excellent ways for clients to discuss commodities and the best ways to incorporate commodities into their portfolios.

Analysts

The typical role of an analyst is to research investment alternatives and provide recommendations to a commodity manager. Analysts can recommend buying a certain investment or even recommend selling an existing investment. Of course this process is reversed for selling short rather as opposed to going long. Analysts typically target one or more commodities sectors and drill down into the details that can affect valuation. Some analysts use a top-down methodology, whereas others use a bottom-up methodology. They pore over financial statements and ask numerous questions to company executives in the hope of gaining better insight and making smarter investing decisions.

Commodity Fund Risk Managers

Risk managers are responsible for performing compliance-related tasks. Their first task is to identify the positions, performance, and level of risk of commodities. Once this is done, they report that information to commodities executives for their due diligence activities. Another vital role risk managers play is to implement control and restrictions on commodity fund managers once certain risk parameters have been breached. For example, if a certain commodity fund breaches its VaR (value-at-risk) risk metric, a risk manager may force a commodity manager to flatten out some of his or her positions that are considered too risky for the fund. Risk managers are responsible for helping to draft risk and performance reports for interested clients.

Banks and Prime Brokers

Banks provide the necessary financing for commodity importers to purchase products and bring them to market or to begin highly expensive projects such as natural gas exploration. Without banks and their extension of credit, many profitable but high-cost projects would never get off the ground. Banks also help many companies bridge the time gap between project initiation, when many of the expenses are due, to project completion, when the revenues are earned.

Prime brokers are the investment banks and financial institutions that serve as custodians for invested capital in commodity funds, such as hedge funds and mutual funds. In addition, prime brokers provide loan sourcing and securities for hedge funds that sell short. This service is not free, however; prime brokers charge fund managers for their services. Most global investment banks compete in this space because of the explosive growth in both the number of commodity funds and the assets they manage.

Investors and Speculators

This group participates in the commodities trade to provide efficiency, enhance liquidity, and assume price risk from producers and hedgers. Investors and speculators execute purchase and sale orders in the hope of profiting from the price appreciation or depreciation of a commodity. They typically do not hold a commodity until the expiration and take physical delivery. Instead, they typically close or flatten out their positions with an offsetting deal sometime before expiration so that they will not need to assume physical delivery. Investors typically do not participate directly through the use of commodities futures but instead target commodity funds and individual stocks of companies involved in the commodity space or work through exchange-traded commodities. Speculators are comfortable with assuming price risk, whereas investors generally try to avoid it and instead target the long-term trends in commodities demand.

Depending on the commodity investing approach, investors and speculators may have to meet certain requirements for income and assets owned. One such product is hedge funds. With hedge funds, a person needs to meet the following requirements before investing with a hedge fund manager:

- Earned at least $200,000 annually in income in the last two years and has a reasonable expectation of doing so into the future
- Earned, with the spouse, at least $300,000 annually in income
- Has a net worth of at least $2,500,000 after excluding the personal residence and automobiles

A qualified eligible participant (QEP) is a person who satisfies the requirements to trade in different investment funds, such as managed futures funds. According to the Commodity and Exchange Act, a person must meet the following requirements to be classified as a QEP:

- Must own securities and other investments with a market value of at least $2,000,000
- Has or has had an account open with a futures commission merchant at any time during the preceding six-month period (along with $200,000 or more initial margin and option premiums for commodity interest transactions)
- Has a combined portfolio of the investments specified in the two requirements above

Merchants

Merchants are companies that utilize commodities in their products for sale but are not considered the end consumer. Auto companies, for example, use tremendous amounts of industrial metals and energy fuels to manufacture cars, trucks, buses, and sport utility vehicles. Those products then are sold to a participant called the end consumer. In addition to auto companies, merchants include cereal companies, fast-food restaurants, gas stations, and home and business construction companies.

Rating Agencies and Data Sources

Rating agencies such as Standard & Poor's provide needed credit information and ratings on the various public companies involved in the commodities trade. These companies include coal mining companies, railroad companies, oil and gas exploration companies, and grain distribution companies. Companies rely on rating agencies for their credit ratings to ensure that they are entering into deals with a low risk of default. For instance, utility companies use credit ratings to help them identify which coal mining companies to deal with and the maximum credit exposure they should assume for each company. This allows the users of the credit ratings to control and manage their risk.

Data sources are actively involved in collecting performance data on commodity money managers such as mutual fund managers and hedge fund managers. Data sources attempt to provide objective information on money managers so that investors can make sound investing decisions. One key data source is Morningstar in Chicago. This company collects performance data on a wide range of mutual funds, hedge funds, and exchange-traded funds and provides ratings—from one to five stars—that are based on that information.

Consumers

Consumers are people who purchase commodities such as food, energy sources, collectible precious metals, and products that contain commodities, such as someone who builds a new home and installs new copper pipes. The end-use consumer is the final piece of the commodity food chain and is responsible for the demand side of the supply-demand equation for any commodity. All the other players and participants are involved in the supply side of the supply-demand equation. The end-use consumer is king with commodities and commodities market prices.

Quiz for Chapter 4

1. Which of the following helps regulate commodities markets?
   a. Securities and Exchange Commission
   b. Commodity Futures Trading Commission
   c. National Futures Association
   d. All of the above

2. The United States is a member of OPEC.
   a. True
   b. False

3. Which of the following was established in 1982 as a nonprofit independent self-regulating organization?
   a. Securities and Exchange Commission
   b. National Futures Association
   c. U.S. Department of Energy
   d. Organization of Petroleum Exporting Countries

4. Which of the following are best described as active hubs where buying and selling of commodities is accomplished?
   a. Commodity houses
   b. Storage facilities
   c. Export/import centers
   d. Commodity exchanges

5. All but which of the following commodity exchanges have physical locations?
   a. Intercontinental Exchange
   b. Chicago Mercantile Exchange
   c. New York Mercantile Exchange
   d. Chicago Board of Trade

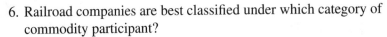

6. Railroad companies are best classified under which category of commodity participant?
   a. Importers
   b. Transportation/transport
   c. Exporters
   d. Storage

7. Brokers are people and firms that help facilitate commodities purchases and sales between two other market participants.
   a. True
   b. False

8. Which of the following is best described as an administrator of managed futures funds?
   a. Commodity pool operator
   b. Trading manager
   c. Commodity prime broker
   d. Futures risk manager

9. How much net worth must an individual have to qualify for accredited investor status?
   a. $200,000
   b. $500,000
   c. $2,500,000
   d. $5,000,000

10. What does QEP stand for?
    a. Quantity elasticity price
    b. Quality energy platform
    c. Quantitative extrapolation program
    d. Qualified eligible participant

CHAPTER 5

Investing Fundamentals:

Risk, Return, and Commodity Considerations

No one particularly likes risk, especially when risk turns into reality and brings misfortune. Avoiding risk is therefore ideal. However, this is not feasible in the world of investing since there is a clear and profound relationship between risk and return. Risk is an inherent part of any investment undertaking, and so it is critical to understand this inescapable trade-off. The possibility of being blindsided by the realization of risk needs to be evaluated in making investment decisions, as does the potential for strong returns.

Unfortunately, one hears the very opposite practically every day in nearly all places. People say that reward can be earned with little or no risk, but reward without risk does not exist in the investment marketplace. Don't let anyone tell you otherwise. Abnormally high returns are not uncommon, but they are neither predictable nor consistent over time. Consequently, if you want a return that outpaces both inflation and taxes, you must be prepared to assume some level of risk. You get what you pay for and earn what you invest in; you do not get something for nothing.

Two of the most important concepts an investor should learn and understand are investment return and investment risk. These two concepts and the way they work together are the foundations of asset allocation and its application to building an optimal portfolio. Depending on your objectives and constraints, you may invest in assets that have low risk and therefore have the potential for low but stable returns or invest in assets that have high risk and therefore have the potential for high but often volatile returns. In basic asset allocation theory, the higher the potential risk you take, the higher the potential return you can earn. Moreover, rational investors will not assume a higher level of risk in the hopes of earning a return that another investment may earn with a lower level of risk.

The million-dollar question is how to enhance your returns and still avoid risk. Although risk cannot be eliminated from a portfolio, it can be controlled and managed with a proper asset allocation policy. A portfolio that is optimally designed, built, and managed will exhibit a higher risk-adjusted return than will a portfolio not informed by proper asset allocation even if there are high-return investments in that portfolio.

Investment Return

Investment return is of primary importance. Why would a person invest otherwise? Without appropriate compensation in the form of returns, people would not invest their hard-earned money. Earning the highest return for the least amount of risk assumed is at the core of asset allocation. Return can come in many different ways. Although we will be discussing quantitative measures of return, do not forget that return often has qualitative aspects. Qualitative rewards include comfort, peace of mind, security, simplicity, and a feeling of control over one's life.

It is vitally important to consider the return you wish to receive and what risk you must assume to obtain that return. Moreover, investing more money in a higher-return asset class does not mean your return will be any higher than that of someone who invested less in that asset class. It is not the individual investments that constitute your portfolio that are important; it is the portfolio as a whole. For this reason, it is wise to build a portfolio with multiple asset classes rather than allocating to only the current high-return-potential asset class. Generally speaking, a higher probability of return also means a higher probability of losing some or all of an investment. Some people are willing to assume that risk, and others are not. This is what makes asset allocation and portfolio construction different from person to person.

The profit or loss from an investment consists of both appreciation and depreciation in market value over the holding period and dividends or interest received during the same holding period. Summing the two profit or loss components and dividing by the market value of the investment at the beginning of the period will give what is referred to as total return. This measure takes into account both the change in price of the security and any cash flow received during the holding period. It is commonplace in the investment field to measure return by using the total return calculation. An example of calculating total return follows.

EXAMPLE   The Smith Foundation purchased 1,000 shares of Deere & Co. at $40 a share. One year later the foundation sold the investment for $44 a share. During the one-year period, Deere & Co. paid a dividend of $1 per share. The total return on the investment, not including transaction costs, is 12.5 percent: $4 appreciation plus $1 dividend divided by $40 cost. Thus, to calculate total return, add the appreciation (ending value minus the beginning value) and all interest and dividends received during the period and divide by the beginning value.

The concept of return can be divided into two parts: actual return and expected return. Actual return is the return you have realized or the return that has occurred in a past holding period. Conversely, expected return is an estimate of what you will earn, both appreciation and income (dividends and interest), in a future holding period. Both actual return and expected return commonly are expressed as annualized percentages. The process of forecasting expected returns is especially difficult. However, the following steps will give you a basic understanding:

1. Forecast all possible material outcomes that may occur.
2. Assign probabilities of occurrence to each outcome.
3. Forecast the return for each specific material outcome.
4. Multiply the probabilities by their related forecast returns.
5. Add the results for each possible outcome.

EXAMPLE   An analyst estimates that the Smith Company has a 50 percent probability of returning 12 percent, a 25 percent probability of returning 5 percent, a 15 percent probability of returning 0 percent, and a 10 percent probability of returning –5 percent. Thus, the estimated return is as follows:

$$(.50 \times .12) + (.25 \times .05) + (.15 \times 0) + (.10 \times -.05) = 6.75 \text{ percent}$$

Potential outcomes usually are based on estimates of how well the economy will perform in the future holding period. The resulting return is simply an estimate that is based on each economic scenario.

Investment Risk

Investment risk can be defined in many ways, and different investors view risk differently. Some investors define risk as losing money, whereas others define it as unfamiliar investments. Still others define risk as contrarian risk, or the risk investors feel when they are not following the crowd. If you toss out all the subjective definitions, risk is defined more objectively as the uncertainty that actual investment returns will equal expected returns. Pension funds and insurance companies view risk as the uncertainty that they can meet future benefit obligations, whereas mutual funds view risk as the possibility of underperforming peer mutual funds and/or an industry benchmark such as the S&P 500. Individual investors tend to view risk as losing money in their portfolios, whether that loss is temporary or permanent. This may not be the best method for viewing risk, but it is the one that is understood and applied by most individual investors.

In the aggregate, most investment experts define risk quite rigidly as the volatility of returns over a specific time period. Most risk measurements are accomplished by using monthly price movements for individual securities, whether those movements are up or down. The greater the monthly movement, regardless of direction, the larger the volatility measure and therefore the greater the risk. Volatility also affects total performance. Portfolios with more volatility exhibit lower long-term compounded growth rates of return. Thus, it is essential to minimize volatility in a portfolio to achieve maximum appreciation over time.

Risk management and proper asset allocation reduce both the frequency and the amount of portfolio losses. Since you rely on estimates of future returns to design your optimal portfolio, it is critically important that actual returns come close to matching expected returns. Investments with more predictable returns are considered lower-risk. Conversely, investments with less predictable returns are considered higher-risk. Risk thus can be called uncertainty, more specifically, the uncertainty that actual returns will match expected returns.

SOURCES OF INVESTMENT RISK

There are two primary sources of risk. The first is called systematic risk, or risk attributed to relatively uncontrollable external factors. The second is called unsystematic risk, or risk attributed directly to the underlying investment.

Systematic Risk

Systematic risk results from conditions, events, and trends that are outside the scope of the investment. At any point, there are different degrees of each risk occurring. These risks will cause the demand for a particular investment to rise or fall, thus affecting actual returns. The four principal types of systematic risk are the following:

- *Exchange rate risk*: the risk that an investment's value will be affected by changes in the foreign currency market
- *Interest rate risk*: the risk attributed to the loss in market value caused by an increase in the general level of interest rates
- *Market risk*: the risk attributed to the loss in market value caused by the declining movement of the entire market portfolio
- *Purchasing power risk*: the risk attributed to inflation and the way it erodes the real value of an investment over time

Unsystematic Risk

Unlike systematic risk, unsystematic risk is not attributed to external factors. This source of risk is unique to an investment, such as how much debt a company has, what actions a company's management takes, and what industry it operates in. The principal types of unsystematic risk are the following:

- *Business risk*: the risk attributed to a company's operations, particularly those involving sales and income.
- *Financial risk*: the risk attributed to a company's financial stability and structure, namely, the company's use of debt to leverage earnings.
- *Industry risk*: the risk attributed to a group of companies in a particular industry. Investments tend to rise and fall on the basis of what their peers are doing.
- *Liquidity risk*: the risk that an investment cannot be purchased or sold at a price at or near market prices.
- *Call risk*: the risk attributed to an event in which an investment may be called before maturity.
- *Regulation risk*: the risk that new laws and regulations will affect the market value of an investment negatively.

Systematic risk plus unsystematic risk equals total risk. Since the goal of asset allocation is to create a well-diversified portfolio, unsystematic risk is considered unimportant because it should be eliminated with proper diversification. Therefore, an optimal portfolio should have only systematic risk, or risk resulting from market and other uncontrollable external factors.

Measuring Investment Risk

Since different investments have different types of risk and different degrees of risk, it is essential to quantify risk to make comparisons across the broad range of asset classes. As was mentioned above, risk can be defined as the uncertainty that actual returns will match expected returns. Intuitively, one can see that the greater the difference is between actual and expected returns, the less predictable and uncertain that investment is considered. This translates into greater risk.

By using historical return data, one can define risk more accurately. Historical volatility data can be obtained by using numerous intervals of time: days, weeks, months, and years. Monthly volatility generally is used in practice. In a simple analysis, averaging the degrees of difference between actual returns and expected returns for a specific investment provides the statistical measure called the standard deviation. A higher standard deviation means higher risk.

It is important to remember that standard deviations for investments or asset classes are not static but change over time. Some asset classes change more frequently and to a greater degree than others. Historically, small-cap stocks have exhibited the greatest amount of variability with regard to the standard deviation. Large-cap stocks follow right behind them.

Volatility has been shown to rise during periods of falling prices and to moderate during periods of advancing prices. Even with changes in asset class volatility in the short term, the range of asset class volatility has remained relatively stable over the long term. That is good for investment planning. The standard deviation is a statistical measure of the degree to which actual returns are spread around the mean actual return. Expressed as a percentage, the standard deviation is considered the best measure of risk.

Since actual returns are affected by both systematic and unsystematic risk, the standard deviation is a measure of total risk. As a result, the standard deviation gives an investor a way to evaluate both the risk and return elements of an individual investment. Although the standard deviation is one of the best measures of risk, it is not without issues. Depending on the holding periods selected for comparison, the standard deviation may vary from analysis to analysis.

Trade-Off between Risk and Return

The relationship between risk and return is central to the investing decision framework. This relationship essentially says that to earn higher level of returns, investors need to assume higher levels of risk. There is no other way to accomplish this aim. In addition, investors looking to assume low levels of risk will earn lower returns. Asset allocation is closely related to risk and return and the role they play in portfolio construction. Commodities should not be approached as a stand-alone single investment. Rather, they should be approached as part of the overall picture, a component of asset allocation. It is for this reason that this chapter is dedicated to asset allocation, including risk and return. For a more detailed discussion of asset allocation, pick up a copy of *Understanding Asset Allocation*, published by McGraw-Hill.

Asset allocation is founded on two celebrated and highly influential investment theories: modern portfolio theory (MPT) and the efficient market hypothesis (EMH), which is essentially a refinement of MPT. These two theories are the most widely discussed and widely used theories in investment management. You cannot pick up a book on commodities without reading discussions of the risk-reward profile of individual commodities strategies. Those books provide charts and graphs and typically incorporate Sharpe ratios. All this is directly related to both of these theories.

Modern portfolio theory says that investors and portfolio managers should not evaluate each investment on a stand-alone basis. Rather, each investment should be evaluated on the basis of its ability to enhance the overall risk and return profile of a portfolio. When faced with two investments with identical expected returns but different levels of risk, investors should select the investment that has the lower risk, according to MPT. From another approach, a rational investor will select the investment with the higher return when faced with two investments that have different expected returns but identical levels of risk. Figure 5.1 shows the relationship between investment alternatives and rational decisions.

When faced with investments A and B, a rational investor will select investment B over investment A because the total return of B is higher, with both having the same level of risk. Moreover, when faced with investments B and C, a rational investor will select investment C over investment B because the total risk of C is lower, with both having the same total return. Pretty simple stuff, but it was revolutionary when first put forth.

Modern portfolio theory introduces the concept of correlation and stresses how it enhances the risk and return profile of a portfolio. The Employee Retirement Income Security Act of 1974, which governs the management of pension funds, emphasizes this point, essentially endorsing MPT. Harry M. Markowitz, who was awarded the Nobel Prize in Economics in 1990, is considered the father of modern portfolio theory for his work in this area.

Figure 5-1. Investment Alternatives and Rational Decisions

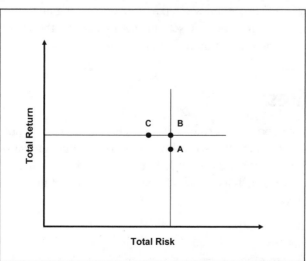

Source: Frush Financial Group

Understanding Asset Classes

An asset class is a group of securities that have similar underlying characteristics as well as very similar risk and return trade-off profiles. As a result of their similarities, the market prices of securities within each asset class tend to move together. The market price for each security within an asset class is influenced strongly by events that involve other securities within the asset class or the asset class as a whole. Whether this is justified or not, even one security can have a great influence on the prices of the other securities within the asset class. Asset classes sometimes are referred to as investment classes. The four primary asset classes are

- Equity investments
- Fixed-income investments
- Cash and equivalents investments
- Alternative investments

Each asset class can be divided into asset subclasses, such as large- and small-capitalization equity securities or taxable and tax-exempt fixed-income securities. Market capitalization is defined as the total market value of a publicly traded company; it is obtained by multiplying the number of shares outstanding by the market price per share.

As with the primary asset classes, each asset subclass is distinguished by its own unique risk and return characteristics. The benefit of asset subclasses lies in their less than perfect correlations to other asset classes, specifically to other asset subclasses. Thus, you can add different asset subclasses to your portfolio to enhance the portfolio's risk and return trade-off profile. For instance, a portfolio with both international and U.S. large-capitalization equity securities will have a better risk and return trade-off profile than will a portfolio containing only international large-capitalization equity securities. Asset subclasses can be thought of as providing enhanced asset allocation within the primary asset classes.

Asset Class Profiles

As was mentioned above, securities within each asset class have similar underlying characteristics. Each characteristic allows for portfolio customization. This is beneficial since different investors have different needs. But what are the underlying characteristics within each asset class? The most important underlying characteristics are the following:

- Total return potential
- Price volatility
- Correlation to other asset classes and asset subclasses

- Growth versus income trade-off
- Liquidity
- Market efficiency
- Factors that influence market value
- Type of underlying entity (corporation, government)

EQUITY INVESTMENTS

Equity investments represent an ownership interest in a corporation and signify a claim to a corporation's assets. To fund business operations, corporations raise capital by issuing equity securities. Each share of stock owned gives an investor a proportional share of the corporation's profits, which usually are distributed in the form of dividends. In addition, the owners of most equity securities are given voting rights. Voting rights allow a shareholder, for instance, to vote for a corporation's board of directors, approve or disapprove of employee stock option programs, and vote for or against acquisitions. In the author's experience, individual investors do not exercise their right to vote. As a result, more power shifts to corporate management and large institutions. Each has its own agenda, which isn't always the same as that of individual investors. Remember to exercise your right to vote.

There are essentially two types of equity securities: preferred stock and common stock.

Preferred Stock

Preferred stock represents ownership of a corporation but is slightly different from common stock. Preferred stock shareholders do not have voting rights. In exchange, they have a higher priority in terms of the assets of the corporation in the event of liquidation caused by bankruptcy. Furthermore, it is common for holders of preferred stock to receive not only a higher dividend but also priority in receiving dividends compared with common stock shareholders. For example, if a corporation is having difficulty making its dividend payments to both preferred and common stock shareholders, the corporation must make dividend payments to the preferred stock shareholders first. Afterward, if enough cash remains, common stock shareholders receive their dividend payments.

Many corporations issue what is called convertible preferred stock. This type of preferred stock is very similar to nonconvertible preferred stock, with one significant difference. Convertible preferred stock gives the owner the option to convert, or exchange, his or her preferred shares into a fixed number of common stock shares after a predetermined date. The market value of this type of preferred is more volatile since it is influenced by the market value of the related common stock.

Common Stock

Common stock is the most widely used form of equity ownership. Common stock shareholders have voting rights and often receive profits in the form of dividends. However, not all corporations distribute profits in that form. Some reinvest the dividends back into the company to fund existing and planned operations.

Two of the most common asset subclasses are growth stocks and value stocks. A growth stock is a common stock that produces higher rates of return than do the stocks of its industry peers, and a value stock is a common stock that is considered undervalued in light of its expected rate of return and current stock price. Again, each possesses its own unique risk and return trade-off profile. Both of these asset subclasses have similar characteristics since both are equity securities; however, they also have very important differences. As a result, growth stocks and value stocks tend to have a low correlation with each other, a risk-reducing and return-enhancing benefit.

FIXED-INCOME INVESTMENTS

Fixed-income investments represent a loan to a corporation or governmental entity to raise capital. Fixed-income investments commonly are referred to as debt in the investment community. In most cases, assets of the issuer back each fixed-income security, providing the purchaser with some protection in case of default. These assets, or debt instruments, hold the issuer to a contractual obligation to make periodic interest payments to the purchaser on predetermined dates in predetermined amounts until the security reaches maturity or is called by the issuer. Maturity is defined as the date on which an issuer is obligated to pay the principal of a fixed-income security to the purchaser. The call date thus is an event in which a fixed-income security is redeemed by the issuer before maturity. Typically, the longer the time to maturity for a fixed-income security is, the higher its yield tends to be. Thus, short-term securities typically have lower yields than do long-term securities. Yield is best described as an annual rate of return determined by dividing the annual interest payments by the purchase price or market value (depending on when and how one is evaluating the security).

For a real-world example, look at cash and equivalents. Cash and equivalents have many similarities with fixed-income securities, but the one characteristic that defines them as cash and equivalents rather than fixed-income investments is their short-term maturity. Why do securities with longer maturities have higher yields? The principal and most accepted theory (there are other theories) says that investors demand higher rates of return for each progressively longer period because they must forgo current consumption of the money they invest and assume risk for a longer time than they would if the holding period were shorter.

CASH AND EQUIVALENTS INVESTMENTS

Cash and equivalents investments are a very broad category that defines assets that are highly liquid and very safe and can be converted easily into cash, such as money market funds, or are already in that form, such as coins and bills. Cash and equivalents usually have a maturity date of less than one year. The returns of this asset class generally correlate with the rate of inflation. Thus, as inflation rates fall, so do the rates on money market funds and certificates of deposit. Cash and equivalents are differentiated by the issuer, maturity date, interest rate (referred to as the coupon rate), credit quality, and tax status (taxable or nontaxable).

Alternative Investments

Alternative investments are a very broad category of assets, mostly encompassing what are referred to as hard assets. In contrast to the other primary asset classes, alternative investments are more dissimilar in their inherent characteristics than they are similar. Furthermore, most alternative investments are tangible rather than intangible.

The principal reason for the purchase of alternative investments is to hedge inflation. In practice, this is referred to as protecting purchasing power. Another strong reason to invest in alternative investments is that they tend to have very low, sometimes negative, correlations with equities. Alternative investments do well in times of high inflation and often capture more investment inflows during times of market weakness regardless of their valuation.

Primary alternative investments include the following:

- Commodities
- Hedge funds
- Real estate
- Private equity
- Collectibles

Understanding each asset class, its expected risk and return trade-off profile, and the correlations among the classes is essential to asset allocation theory and its application to an investment portfolio. Asset classes represent building blocks for the selection of appropriate investments and their weightings within a portfolio.

Because of the different asset classes available, you can customize your portfolio in the way most appropriate to your objectives and constraints. Utilizing each asset class is central to enhancing a portfolio's return while reducing its risk. Consider a football team. A team composed only of linemen most likely will not reach the playoffs. Odds are that it won't even win a game! It takes a well-balanced team with players at all positions to reach the championship game. Building an optimal portfolio requires the same approach.

Understanding Correlation

An optimal portfolio is not just the sum of its parts. Rather, it is the sum of its synergies. Synergies are created by the interaction of the investments held in a portfolio. This interaction is referred to commonly as correlation and is a critical input to the asset allocation process. *Correlation* is the technical term used to measure and describe how closely the prices of two investments move together over time.

Positively correlated assets move in the same direction, both up and down. Conversely, negatively correlated assets move in opposite directions. Correlations between two assets are expressed on a scale that runs from −1.0 to +1.0. The more two assets are correlated, or move together, the closer they are to +1.0. Similarly, the more two assets move in opposite directions, the closer they are to −1.0. Two assets that move exactly together have a +1.0 correlation, whereas two assets that move exactly opposite have a −1.0 correlation.

EXAMPLE: The correlation between stock A and stock B is 0.8. As a result, for every $1 price movement in either stock, the other will move 80 percent in the same direction over the same period.

Correlations between −0.3 and +0.3 are thought to be noncorrelated. This means that the two asset classes move independently of each other. With noncorrelated assets, when one is rising in price, the other may be rising, falling, or maintaining its current price.

A properly allocated portfolio has a mix of investments that do not behave the same way. Correlation is therefore the measure about which you need to be concerned. To maximize the portfolio benefits derived from correlations, you need to incorporate assets with negative correlations, assets with low positive correlations, and even assets that have noncorrelations. Noncorrelated investments move independently of each other. By investing in assets with low correlations, you can reduce total portfolio risk without affecting the return of the portfolio. Doing this will minimize the overall investment-specific risk attributed to each investment.

The greatest portfolio risk reduction benefits occur during periods when correlations across the board are low, noncorrelated, or negative. When correlations increase, risk reduction benefits are partially lost. Over time, some correlations will increase and some will decline.

Since you cannot predict which correlations will change or to what degree they will change over time, successful investors allocate to a number of fundamentally different investments to reap the benefits of asset allocation.

Time Horizon Explained

The time horizon is another important input variable. Most investors pay too little attention to the time horizon and the important role it plays. The time horizon affects expected rates of return, expected volatility, and expected investment correlations.

As a result of the important role it plays, the time horizon is the first constraint that should be identified. Overestimating or underestimating your time horizon can affect the way you allocate your assets and thus affect your risk and return profile.

The primary role the time horizon plays is to help you select and evaluate the appropriateness of each asset class and asset subclass as an investment alternative. Specifically, the time horizon helps determine the balance between equity investments and fixed-income investments. The shorter your time horizon is, the more emphasis you should place on fixed-income investments. Conversely, the longer your time horizon is, the more emphasis you should place on equity investments. In the short term, equities are volatile and possess high levels of uncertainty. Put another way, equities exhibit unacceptable levels of risk in relation to their expected returns. In contrast, fixed-income investments are significantly less volatile in the short term and have much lower levels of uncertainty. As a consequence, fixed-income risks are more favorable in the short term in regard to expected returns.

As your investment time horizon increases, so does the probability of your equity assets experiencing positive returns. Over longer periods equity returns become more stable because there is more time for positive equity returns to offset negative equity returns. The returns of equities become significantly more clear and predictable as the investment time horizon lengthens.

Quiz for Chapter 5

1. Who is considered the father of modern portfolio theory and received a Nobel Prize for that work?
   a. Merton C. Miller
   b. Harry Markowitz
   c. Myron Scholes
   d. Warren Buffett

2. What theory says that each investment should be evaluated on the basis of its ability to enhance the total portfolio's risk-adjusted return?
   a. Security premium theory
   b. Market premium theory
   c. Modern portfolio theory
   d. Allocation efficiency theory

3. The Employment Retirement Income Security Act of 1974 officially recognized and required the use of modern portfolio theory.
   a. True
   b. False

4. What are the two types of equity stock?
   a. Limited stock and preferred stock
   b. Preferred stock and yield stock
   c. Yield stock and common stock
   d. Common stock and preferred stock

5. All but which of the following are underlying characteristics of asset classes?
   a. Price volatility
   b. Type of underlying entity
   c. Factors that influence market prices
   d. Type of products sold

6. Preferred stock does or does not provide voting rights to the shareholder.
   a. Does
   b. Does not

7. Fixed-income assets represent a loan to a corporation, institution, or governmental entity.
   a. True
   b. False

8. For the most part, alternative assets are financial in nature rather than physical in nature or what is called hard assets.
   a. True
   b. False

9. All but which of the following are considered alternative assets?
   a. Preferred stock
   b. Collectibles
   c. Private equity
   d. Hedge funds

10. The longer an investor's time horizon is, the more he or she should allocate to which of the following?
    a. Equities
    b. Fixed-income investments
    c. Alternative assets

CHAPTER 6

Market Indicators:

Understanding What Moves Commodities Prices

This chapter discusses market indicators that are considered the most important drivers of commodities prices. Some of these indicators are best described as economic indicators, whereas others are considered technical indicators. As we have learned, the price for any commodity is driven primarily by supply and demand; greater demand means increasing prices, and lower demand means decreasing prices. At the same time, greater supply of any commodity will tend to place downward pressure on prices, whereas reduced supply caused, for example, by production problems typically translates into higher prices. Identifying which indicators influence commodity prices and to what degree is therefore of the utmost importance to investors, traders, and all others who participate in the commodities market. This chapter presents the key fundamental and technical indicators that drive commodity prices higher and lower. This list is not exclusive as there are many factors that can influence prices. Nevertheless, it will give you a solid understanding of the key factors affecting prices.

Technical analysis and fundamental analysis are very different approaches to valuing a security. Technical analysis involves evaluating past price movements to forecast future price movements. This approach looks at the supply and demand for a particular security and the relevant price. This price is driven by the interactions between and the relationship of buyers and sellers. By using this information, technical analysis attempts to estimate purchase and sale entry and exit points for a particular security and provide a forecast value that is based on known price movements. In contrast, fundamental analysis does not place much emphasis on technical supply and demand factors but instead evaluates the financial well-being of a security's underlying company. Fundamental analysis focuses on balance sheets, income statements, cash flow statements, disclosure documents, and even discussions with management. The goal of fundamental analysis is to derive a fair value for a company and then compare that value with the current value to facilitate purchase and sale decisions. For instance, fundamental analysis will reward a company's strong free cash flow by forecasting a higher fair value. Technical analysis will not do this directly but may make estimates of fair value that are caused by changes in supply and demand for the company's security as a result of the news about strong free cash flow. Each approach has its proponents, and many investment professionals believe that each approach can be used to make a good investment decision. Figure 6.1 lists indicators for commodity markets.

Technical Indicators

PRICE

The price of a particular commodity is the chief technical indicator since forecasts of future price movements are based on past price movements as well as the other technical indicators you will read about in this chapter. Price is the point at which buyers and sellers are in equilibrium or, better said, where supply and demand are in balance at that specific point in time. Many factors can affect supply and demand, and so the equilibrium balance will change over time as new information is learned. Price is what clears the market for any commodity and drives both demand and supply. When prices are rising, demand can fall; when prices are falling, demand can rise. On the other side of the equation, when prices are rising, producers will have an incentive to supply more of that commodity, and when prices are falling, producers will want to supply less. The actions of producers and consumers thus are intertwined and dependent on one another. For investors, price is what determines gains and losses. For investors who are long a commodity position, gains are made when prices are rising. For investors who are short, the commodity will experience losses. Forecasting which direction price will move and how quickly underlies technical analysis.

Figure 6-1. Important Commodity Market Indicators

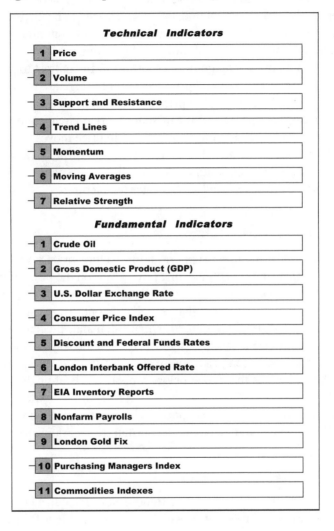

VOLUME

Price and volume are the two most important technical indicators for any commodity and provide an excellent way to ascertain the psychology of the market. Volume serves two important roles: a measure of interest and confirmation of price trends. Volume illustrates the interest that investors have in any particular commodity, whether that interest is for purchasing the commodity or selling it. The greater the volume, the greater the interest and trading activity in that commodity. When the price for a commodity is rising and so is the trading volume, investors are said to be accumulating that commodity. Likewise, when the price for a commodity is falling, accompanied by an increase in volume, investors are said to be dispensing with that commodity. Therefore, volume serves as confirmation of commodity price trends. That is good for investors as it signals how strong the interest is in a commodity and in which direction its price may go in the short term. In contrast to strong volume, weak volume can represent artificial price trends since there are many fewer buyers and sellers to ensure highly reliable prices. This means that a rising price trend together with weak volume can result in sudden price changes to the downside. There is greater uncertainty and lower confidence in price moves that are accompanied by lower levels of volume. The same can be said of price movements to the downside when there is weak volume. Any declines here can reverse course and move higher once more buyers and sellers enter the picture.

SUPPORT AND RESISTANCE

Most commodities have multiple support and resistance price levels. Support is a line or price level that supports preexisting price levels on the basis of past demand. As long as demand remains robust, prices will remain at or above a particular level: the point where demand is stronger than supply. In contrast, resistance is the point or price level at which supply begins to outpace demand, precluding prices from moving higher. Resistance levels are established the same way as support levels: by preexisting price levels. When prices move above resistance levels, they are called *breakouts*, whereas prices that move below support levels are called *breakdowns*. Once a breakdown or breakout is achieved, the price for the commodity can move quickly until the next resistance or support level is reached. Knowing resistance and support levels will help you understand the normal trading range for a commodity.

TREND LINES

Have you ever heard the expression "the trend is your friend"? This expression is relevant to commodities investing in which participants identify trends and then ride those trends until they stop or reverse. This is of the utmost importance since technical analysis is founded on the notion that prices move in established patterns that can be identified, forecast, and acted on. The two primary trend lines you have to be aware of are an uptrend line and a downtrend line. An uptrend line is a positively sloping line that mirrors the direction of prices over the period in question. An uptrend occurs when there are more buyers than sellers for the commodity as a result of greater demand. A downtrend line is the opposite of an uptrend line; in this case the trend line is downward-sloping. This scenario illustrates the fact that there are more sellers than buyers because of lower demand for the commodity over the period in question. Paying attention to trend lines will help you identify the direction in which prices are moving and how quickly they are rising or falling. Steeper-sloping trend lines, whether positive or negative, signal faster-moving prices, and more flat trend lines signal slower-moving prices.

MOMENTUM

The goal of this indicator is to measure the changes in consensus mass optimism or pessimism by comparing the price for a commodity today with the price for the same commodity from an earlier trading day. When momentum is weak and prices are rising, a top is probably near. However, when momentum is strong and prices are rising, the top could be some time away. Many traders follow this indicator and use it to make purchase and sell decisions.

MOVING AVERAGES

A moving average is an indicator that measures the average price for a commodity over a certain period as a stand-alone illustration or against other moving averages for the same commodity in different periods. Many technicians use two moving averages—typically the 50-day and 200-day averages—and compare them with each other to signal entry and exit points. The two important signals when one is using these moving averages are the point where the 50-day crosses above the 200-day and the point where the 50-day crosses below the 200-day. Bullish signals are represented by the 50-day moving average crossing above the 200-day moving average, whereas bearish signals are represented by the 50-day moving average crossing below the 200-day moving average. This indicator is best used when the commodity is following a confirmed trend and should be used with caution when the commodity is not following a confirmed trend.

RELATIVE STRENGTH

Relative strength is a statistical measurement of the price momentum or velocity of the price of a commodity. This indicator is calculated by comparing the average upside price change with the average downside price change for a particular commodity. The goal of this indicator is to illustrate how quickly the price for the commodity in question is changing over the period selected, which is typically 14 trading days, and is represented by a numerical value between 0 and 100. Results with values of 70 or higher (some say 80 and higher) are thought to signal overvalued commodities, whereas values below 30 (some say 20 or below) are thought to signal undervalued. As with most other indicators, the results should not be thought of as black and white. Rather, they should be evaluated within the context of many shades of gray. Thus, even a value of 50 is considered to represent a slightly more overvalued condition than a value of 35. For best results, this indicator should be used in conjunction with other technical—and perhaps fundamental—indicators to gain a solid perspective on the bullishness or bearishness of sentiment about a commodity.

Fundamental Indicators

CRUDE OIL

Crude oil is perhaps the most widely monitored and quoted price relating to energy fuels in the world because so many of the energy fuels that are purchased and used are derivations of crude oil. Gasoline, jet fuel, kerosene, and propane are only four of the energy fuels extracted from crude oil and sold as final products. As a result, when the price of crude oil is rising, the prices of each of the energy fuels created from crude oil also will rise. Two of the most recognizable crude oil brands are West Texas Intermediate crude (WTI crude) and Brent North Sea crude. Each is traded separately as they are considered entirely different from each other. For a real-life example, think of crude oil prices and how they affect what you pay at the pump for a gallon of gasoline. When prices of crude oil rise, you surely will see the signs change at the gas station to reflect an increase in gasoline prices. The change is not $1 for $1 as there are other factors that contribute to the price of gasoline, including refinery utilization and supply and demand.

GROSS DOMESTIC PRODUCT

Interested in knowing what the granddaddy of all economic performance indicators is? Look no further than the gross domestic product (GDP). This indicator is a broad measurement of all the goods and services produced in a country over a specific period by businesses, consumers, government entities, and international trade, which is defined as exports minus imports. Another helpful measurement is GDP per capita, a measure of the economic purchasing power per person in a country. When purchasing power is high or advancing, that can mean greater demand and spending on commodities and the related products. GDP is a big picture indicator that helps investors determine the economic activity of a country and the potential demand for commodities such as crude oil, copper, steel, and natural gas to fuel its economic growth. Strong GDP growth is bullish for commodities, and weak GDP growth or declining GDP is bearish.

U.S. DOLLAR EXCHANGE RATE

Many of the most important commodities traded globally are priced in U.S. dollars, commonly referred to as USD. Some of these commodities are gold, crude oil, and coffee. When the U.S. dollar appreciates or depreciates in value, the cost for these commodities will change. For instance, during the second half of 2007 the U.S. dollar was in a free fall against most of the currencies around the world. This meant that coal mined in the United States became more favorably priced to buyers whose currencies appreciated against the U.S. dollar. The result was increased demand for and purchases of U.S. coal by European energy companies. Even with the extremely high cost of transporting the coal from the United States to Europe, it was profitable to make the purchase. In contrast, when the U.S. dollar is appreciating in value, the cost of commodities produced in other countries becomes more favorable. A good example is steel. U.S.-based manufacturers enjoyed a prolonged period of favorably priced steel from abroad because of the strength of the U.S. dollar. That hurt domestically produced steel and drove many steel-producing companies in the United States to near bankruptcy. The important lesson here is that foreign currency exchange rates have a significant influence on the price of commodities, and that means profits and losses for commodities investors.

CONSUMER PRICE INDEX

Compiled by the U.S. Bureau of Labor Statistics, the consumer price index (CPI) is a measure of price inflation for a basket or set of goods and services typically purchased by consumers throughout the country. The consumer price index is the most widely quoted and used measurement for gauging inflation and the average cost of living. The CPI also can be quoted as the core CPI, which is the CPI minus food and energy products with their inherent high volatility from month to month. Consequently, investors can compare the traditional CPI with the core CPI to ascertain how prices for food and energy commodities are faring. The greater the difference between CPI and core CPI, the greater the inflation of food and energy prices during the period of measurement; the narrower the difference between the two, the lower the inflation of food and energy commodities.

Commodity prices and inflation rates are highly correlated: Increasing crude oil prices typically result in higher prices for gasoline and other energy fuels. One of the golden reasons for investing in commodities is to hedge inflation since investing in commodities provides a hedge against the loss of purchasing power caused by advancing inflation. For an investor, monitoring inflation is important as it provides an indication of the price trend for commodities prices. When inflation rates are forecast to rise, investors are given a signal to purchase the specific commodity to take advantage of the price rise. If inflation is forecast to decline over a certain period, commodities prices could come under pressure and fall. This is a signal to investors that purchasing commodities may not be a smart move and that going short commodities could generate nice gains.

DISCOUNT AND FEDERAL FUNDS RATES

The discount rate and the federal funds rate are two of the most important and most closely monitored interest rates in the investing marketplace. Both rates are established by the Federal Open Market Committee (FOMC), a branch of the Federal Reserve. The discount rate is the short-term rate banks are charged for borrowing from the Federal Reserve to satisfy their overnight reserve requirements. The federal funds rate is the rate banks charge one another to meet the same overnight reserve requirements. Banks typically borrow money from other banks first and borrow from the Federal Reserve second. In the past, borrowing from the Federal Reserve was considered a signal of a bank's potential problems since it could not borrow from other banks. Today, the Federal Reserve and many money center banks are trying to break this long-held belief by going to the Federal Reserve first and bypassing other banks altogether.

The discount rate and the federal funds rate provide an indication of how well or poorly the economy is doing and also help provide a forecast of future inflation. When the economy is weakening, the FOMC generally will reduce rates to lower the cost of borrowing for banks. In turn, banks will reduce the cost of borrowing for corporations and consumers. This equates to more robust economic activity, and it is hoped that this will invigorate the macro economy. Similarly, when the economy is strong and in danger of overheating and spurring inflation, the FOMC generally will increase both the discount rate and the federal funds rate, and that will have a ripple effect on the entire economy by raising the borrowing rates for all borrowers. The hope is to curb economic activity to prevent escalating inflation.

LONDON INTERBANK OFFERED RATE

LIBOR, the London InterBank Offered Rate, is one of the most frequently used benchmark rates for futures and options trading. Nearly all futures and options contracts incorporate an interest rate to determine a price and discount future cash flows. LIBOR is the rate most widely used for this purpose. When LIBOR is higher than normal, futures and options contracts tend to be lower in price; they tend to be higher in price when LIBOR is lower than normal. Monitoring LIBOR is therefore important when an investor is trying to get a handle on how the pricing of contracts will be affected.

EIA INVENTORY REPORTS

Released by the Energy Information Administration (EIA), a branch of the U.S. Department of Energy, EIA inventory reports go behind the scenes to provide information on the supply and demand for energy products in the United States. These reports detail information such as crude oil supply, consumer consumption, crude oil production, and refinery utilization. These statistics rarely are quoted in the mainstream media but are vitally important as they are the backbone for energy prices in this country. Many traders, speculators, investors, and companies involved in some aspect of the energy trade rely on this information. If you are looking to trade energy fuels, monitoring these reports is a must. The website for the U.S. Department of Energy is www.eia.doe.gov.

NONFARM PAYROLLS

In basic economics, when people are employed and are earning good wages, purchasing power is strong, and that translates into a bullish environment for commodities. In contrast, when people are out of work and wages are weak, purchasing power comes under pressure, and that means a bearish environment for commodities. One of the indicators that measure payroll activity is nonfarm payrolls, released by the U.S. Bureau of Labor Statistics. Nonfarm payrolls are a measurement of the number of individuals with paid wages employed by businesses throughout the country. This measurement does not include people employed at government entities, people at not-for-profit organizations, people employed by agricultural companies, and those who work at home as homemakers. The total number of people captured by this measurement accounts for about 80 percent of the country's total workforce and thus is used to gauge unemployment levels. The information released in a nonfarm payroll report indicates the total number of new jobs created from the last monthly period to the current monthly period. When higher levels of new jobs are created, that is a bullish signal for economic growth and rising purchasing power and demand for commodities. Monitoring this indicator thus will present investors with information on the direction in which demand for commodities will move.

LONDON GOLD FIX

The London Gold Fix is the benchmark for spot gold prices worldwide and serves as a measure of inflationary pressure in the global financial marketplace. Many economists consider the price of gold to be a measure of inflation expectations. When inflation is anticipated to be rising, gold prices typically increase; when inflation is expected to decline, the price for gold typically falls. The London Gold Fix is set by five prominent members of the commodities trading community on a daily basis. The New York Mercantile Exchange (NYMEX) is another solid source for gold pricing via COMEX (Commodities Exchange) gold futures prices.

PURCHASING MANAGERS INDEX

Complied and released on the first business day of every month by the Institute of Supply Management (ISM), the Purchasing Managers Index (PMI) is a measurement of broad economic activity in manufacturing. When the PMI indicates strong economic activity, the demand for commodities is considered to be strong since manufacturing companies are some of the biggest purchasers and consumers of commodities. For instance, if an automobile manufacturing company was experiencing strong sales for its automobiles, it probably would increase production to meet the new demand.

This means the automobile manufacturer would have to make greater purchases of steel, aluminum, copper, palladium, and other industrial metals. Those interested in viewing PMI reports can visit www.ism.ws/ISMReport.

COMMODITIES INDEXES

Another solid indicator of commodity prices are commodities indexes such as the Dow Jones-AIG Commodity Index. These indexes rise and fall with the performance of the underlying commodity or commodities. Although monitoring commodities indexes will not provide a forward-looking view of commodities, it will help paint a picture of how well commodities are performing at the present time and how they performed historically. In addition, capital inflows into or outflows from investable commodity indexes will provide insight into the degree of interest among investors for investing in commodities. When inflows are strong and greater than normal, demand for commodities is high; when capital inflows are weak and lower than normal, demand for commodities is low. Commodities indexes also provide investors with ways to invest in commodities and gain exposure to select commodities or multiple commodities.

Quiz for Chapter 6

1. Market indicators can be called technical or what other term?
   a. Asset allocation
   b. Fundamental
   c. Focused
   d. Dynamic

2. Price is the leading fundamental market indicator.
   a. True
   b. False

3. Support and resistance is classified as which type of market indicator?
   a. Fundamental
   b. Technical

4. Which indicator is best described as a measure of the changes in consensus optimism or pessimism by comparing the price for a commodity today with the price for the same commodity on an earlier trading day?
   a. Trend line
   b. Moving average
   c. Volume differential
   d. Momentum

5. Which technical indicator defines the point at which buyers and sellers are in equilibrium and supply and demand are balanced?
   a. Support and resistance
   b. Trend line
   c. Price
   d. Moving average

6. All but which of the following are considered fundamental indicators?
   a. Crude oil
   b. Gross domestic product
   c. Relative strength
   d. Consumer price index

7. The consumer price index is a measure of supply for commodities.
   a. True
   b. False

8. The discount rate and the federal funds rate are set by which organization?
   a. Federal Deposit Insurance Corporation
   b. Federal Open Market Committee
   c. Bureau of Economic Affairs
   d. Department of Labor

9. Which of the following best describes the discount rate?
   a. A short-term rate established by LIBOR banks for their best customers
   b. A long-term rate to facilitate loans between member banks
   c. A long-term rate to achieve balance of payments
   d. A short-term rate that banks are charged for borrowing from the Federal Reserve

10. Which interest rate is considered the benchmark for determining price and discounting cash flows in regard to commodities?
    a. Federal funds rate
    b. Discount rate
    c. LIBOR
    d. Consumer price index

Commodity Indexes:

A Look inside the Broad-Based Metrics

Commodity indexes track the prices of futures contracts for a select basket of underlying physical commodities. Commodity indexes are much like other financial indexes, such as the S&P 500. Commodity indexes are very useful to investors who want to add commodities to their portfolios without participating in the futures markets by using a passive low-cost method. Another benefit of commodity indexes is that they provide a way to measure the performance of commodities in the aggregate. As investing in commodities continues to gain in popularity, more commodity indexes will be established. With the explosion of exchange-traded funds, there are a number of investable indexes that track very specific commodity classes. In consequence, broad-based commodity indexes are best for investors who do not want to invest with a narrow approach but instead want extensive exposure across multiple markets.

Purposes of Commodity Indexes

Commodity indexes serve three primary roles. The first and most important is that of a *benchmark* by which the performance of commodities as an asset class can be compared with the performance of other asset classes, such as the S&P 500 and real estate investment trusts. The second purpose of a commodity index is that of an indicator by which changes in the index indicate how well or poorly commodities are faring as an asset class and serve as a measure of inflation. Since commodities represent the foundation for an economy, higher commodities prices translate into rising inflation. In the United States, commodity prices are the precursor to producer prices. The third purpose is that of an investable instrument with which investors can gain exposure to commodities through the purchase of the index or an investment that tracks the index.

Characteristics of Commodity Indexes

All commodity indexes have three common criteria for the selection of component commodities: futures availability, commodity deliverability, and market liquidity. For a commodity to be included in a commodity index, a futures contract must be available for trading on an exchange; otherwise, the commodity index will not include that commodity as a component. Without a futures contract there is no way for the index to track the commodity as a pure play. Commodity deliverability refers to the need to select only commodities that have the potential for physical delivery, such as metals and energy; that excludes financials. This means that only hard assets are included in commodity indexes, not intangible financial instruments such as rates and indexes. The third criterion all broad-based commodity indexes employ in selecting component commodities is market liquidity, specifically robust market liquidity. Commodity indexes select only those commodities for which purchases and sales of futures contracts can be executed with relative ease and at current market prices.

In contrast to these common criteria of commodity indexes, there are some characteristics that differentiate one index from the others. These differentiating characteristics include component commodities, allocation (weightings), rebalancing methodology, and contract management.

Most broad-based commodity indexes track all the primary commodity classes: energy, metals (both industrial and precious), agriculture, and livestock. However, commodity indexes do not attempt to track each commodity in the primary commodity classes in an index. For example, the Dow Jones-AIG Commodity Index tracks both gold and silver; the Reuters/Jefferies CRB Index tracks gold, silver, and platinum; and the Goldman Sachs Commodity Index tracks only gold—no silver or platinum. This means that the other commodity indexes are slightly more diversified than the Goldman Sachs. If gold prices increased faster than silver or platinum prices, the Goldman Sachs index would outperform the other two indexes, all else being equal. If gold prices fell faster than prices for silver and platinum, the Goldman Sachs index would experience bigger declines. This is neither good nor bad, just a difference in methodology. The Rogers International Commodities Index includes the greatest number of commodities at 35, whereas the Deutsche Bank index tracks only 6 (gold, aluminum, WTI crude oil, heating oil, corn, and wheat).

The second differentiating characteristic is composition allocation, or the weighting a commodity index establishes for a particular commodity. For instance, although two commodity indexes may include crude oil as a constituent component, one commodity index may overweight crude oil and the other may underweight it. No two commodity indexes have identical composition allocations for all of their constituent commodities. This difference is important when one is evaluating performance and deciding which commodity index to add to a portfolio. For instance, do you want to add a commodity index that is well diversified among the primary commodities or add a commodity index that overweights certain commodities since that index tracks fewer commodities? Finally, some commodity indexes employ diversification constraints in which there are maximum and minimum weightings. The Dow Jones-AIG index includes a 33 percent maximum on individual markets and a 2 percent market minimum.

Rebalancing management is the third differentiating characteristic of commodity indexes. Rebalancing is the act of altering the composition allocations in response to changing market conditions. For instance, if a certain commodity index believed that its composition allocation did not represent current market conditions as it formerly did, it might adjust the compositions to bring the index in line and make it more representative and appropriate. Supply and demand dynamics and changing technologies alter the landscape for commodities over the long term, and commodity indexes make an attempt to incorporate those structural changes. Moreover, commodity indexes do not rebalance at the same time. For example, the Dow Jones-AIG index rebalances annually on a price-percentage basis, whereas the Deutsche Bank index rebalances continuously, based on how far prices deviate from their long-term average.

The fourth differentiating characteristic is contract management, which is the way a commodity index addresses the need to roll off the current month's futures contract for the front month futures contract, which is the next month for trading. Since these two futures contracts have different prices, the commodity index is exposed to what is referred to as roll yield. Commodity indexes also roll at different times during the month. The Reuters/Jefferies CRB index rolls between the first and fourth business days of the month, whereas the Goldman Sachs index rolls between the fifth and ninth business days.

The commodity investing marketplace has five major indexes. Three of those indexes were created after 1990; the oldest is the Reuters/Jefferies CRB index, which was established in 1957 and has had structural revisions made over the years. The five major indexes are the Deutsche Bank Liquid Commodity Index, the Dow Jones-AIG Commodity Index, the Goldman Sachs Commodity Index (GSCI), the Reuters/Jefferies Commodity Research Bureau Index, and the Rogers International Commodities Index (see Figure 7.1).

Figure 7-1. Snapshot of Commodity Indexes

Index Name	Reuters / Jefferies CRB Index	Goldman Sachs Commodity Index	Dow Jones-AIG Commodity Index	Rogers International Commodities Index	Deutsche Bank Liquid Commodity Index
Abbreviation	R/J CRB	GSCI	DJ-AIG	RICI	DBLCI
Year Established	1957	1992	1998	1999	2003
Number of Component Commodities	19	24	19	35	6
Reconstitution	Ad-hoc	Annual, per rules	Annual, per committee	Annual	N/A
Weighting Methodology	Tiered, depends on liquidity	Average quantity of production in the last five years	Liquidity data (two-thirds) and production value (one-third)	Production value	Liquidity
Rebalancing Methodology	Rebalanced monthly	Rebalanced monthly by committee	Rebalanced annually on a price-percentage basis	Rebalanced monthly	Rebalanced continuously based on how current weightings diverge from target weightings
Rollover Date	1st - 4th business each month	5th - 9th business day each month	6th - 10th business day each month	Day prior to the last business day of the month to the first business day of the following month	N/A
Next Futures Contract	Arithmetic average of contract months expiring within six months of current date with two minimum and five maximum	Nearest month with adequate liquidity	Nearest futures contract	Nearest futures contract	Nearest month for metals and agriculture, and following December for energy fuels
Diversification Constraints	N/A	N/A	33% maximum individual sectors and 2% market minimum	N/A	N/A

DEUTSCHE BANK LIQUID COMMODITY INDEX

As the newest index, having been established in 2003, the Deutsche Bank Liquid Commodity Index consists of only six commodities. One of the primary reasons for tracking only six commodities is to reduce rebalancing and rolling costs. Furthermore, in light of the high degree of price correlation among commodities in each market—energy, precious metals, industrial metals, agriculture, and so on—tracking even just one commodity in theory should capture most of the price movements

Figure 7-2. Target Allocations – Deutsche Bank Liquid Commodity Index

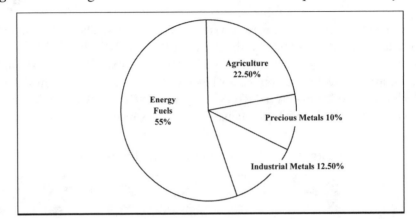

in that commodity market without incurring additional costs in return for negligible results. The six selected commodities are considered the ones with the most liquidity in their respective markets. Energy fuels has the largest weighting in the index at 55 percent, and the smallest weighting is precious metals, as represented by gold, at 10 percent (see Figure 7.2).

Deutsche Bank rebalances the component commodities through the use of two different policies by which energy commodities are rebalanced monthly and nonenergy commodities are rebalanced annually. The aim of this approach is to reduce monthly roll costs. The weightings are set to represent the actual value of commodities produced during the year. Value is defined as the price multiplied by the amount produced. Thus, if crude oil production value increases as a result of higher production or higher prices during the year, the weighting for crude oil will rise. Thus, the weightings of the index track the real-world value of commodities closely rather than subjectively setting weightings.

The Deutsche Bank Liquid Commodity Index does not track livestock, agriculture softs (e.g., cocoa, coffee, sugar), and exotics (e.g., lumber, rubber, silk). Investors can add this commodity index to their portfolios by purchasing the DB Commodity Index Tracking Fund (symbol DBC), an exchange-traded fund offered by Power-Shares that ranks as the tenth largest exchange-traded fund as measured by assets. This exchange-traded fund was the first to track a commodity index.

DOW JONES-AIG COMMODITY INDEX

Established in 1998 and one of the most widely followed indexes, the Dow Jones-AIG Commodity Index is composed of 19 commodities; 33 percent is allocated to energy, 30.1 percent to metals, 29.5 percent to agriculture, and 7.4 percent to livestock (see Figure 7.3). Among the 19 commodities tracked, 3 (aluminum, nickel, and zinc) trade on the London Metals Exchange; the remaining 16 trade on U.S.

Figure 7-3. Target Allocations – Dow Jones-AIG Commodity Index

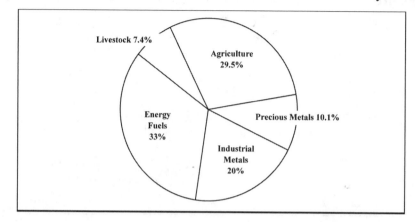

exchanges. To ensure that allocations match target weightings, rebalancing is performed monthly. Target weightings are changed annually by an oversight committee; the commodities with the most liquidity and the highest dollar-adjusted production value are given the highest weightings. One of the aims of the oversight committee is to ensure that the index is highly diversified and that no single commodity dominates it. Thus, no market is permitted to exceed one-third of the total index and no commodity is permitted to exceed 15 percent. In addition, the oversight committee has established a minimum of 2 percent per commodity to ensure no commodity loses its importance. These rules help reduce volatility and control risk.

WTI crude oil is the largest component commodity at 13.2 percent, and cotton and lean hogs are the smallest components at 2.5 percent each. This index provides no exposure to exotics.

Two mutual funds track this index: the PIMCO Commodity Real Return Fund and the Credit Suisse Commodity Return Strategy Fund. In addition, futures contracts on this index are listed on the Chicago Board of Trade, and the iPath Dow Jones-AIG Total Return (symbol DJP) is an exchange-traded note that tracks this index.

GOLDMAN SACHS COMMODITY INDEX

The Goldman Sachs Commodity Index (GSCI), arguably the most widely followed commodity index, was established in 1992 and is composed of 24 commodities. Target weightings are set by a committee each year, but unlike the Dow Jones-AIG Commodity Index, there are no diversification constraints such as floors and ceilings for commodity classes and individual commodities. The committee uses production value over the prior five-year period, a methodology that typically favors the energy sector, specifically crude oil, to establish target allocations. A five-year period is used to ensure that abnormal production in any single year does not result

Figure 7-4. Target Allocations – Goldman Sachs Commodity Index

Energy
Fuels
78.7%

Livestock 3.0%

Agriculture
10.4%

Precious Metals 1.8%

Industrial Metals 6.1%

in unrepresentative target allocations, something that would happen if one-year production periods were used. Liquidity and investability factors are taken into consideration in modifying target allocations.

The energy sector accounts for approximately 78.7 percent, with agriculture at 10.4 percent, metals at 7.9 percent, and livestock at 3 percent. WTI crude oil is the top individual commodity at 30 percent, and the commodity with the smallest allocation is silver at 0.20 percent. Of course, these allocations change each trading day, and rebalancing is done monthly by a committee. Target allocations (see Figure 7.4) are modified annually. Thus, if the price for crude oil declines, lowering the production value, the target allocation to energy will be lowered by the committee.

Investors have a number of alternatives for investing in this index. Futures contracts are listed on the Chicago Mercantile Exchange, and the GSCI Commodity Indexed Trust (symbol GSG) is an exchange-traded fund from iShares. Mutual funds that track this index include the Oppenheimer Real Asset Fund, the Rydex Fund, and the BlackRock Real Investment Fund.

In early 2007, Goldman Sachs sold its index to Standard & Poor's.

REUTERS/JEFFERIES COMMODITY RESEARCH BUREAU INDEX

Established in 1957, the Reuters/Jefferies CRB Index is the oldest commodity index in the world. It has undergone multiple major revisions over the last 50 years and recently increased the number of component commodities from 17 to 19. Before its last restructuring in 2005, the index was known as the Commodity Research Bureau Index. This index is the preferred benchmark among economists for measuring economic activity and inflation.

Unlike the other commodity indexes, the Reuters/Jefferies CRB Index is composed of four tiers, each consisting of different commodities, with each tier given different weightings. Tier 1 is composed of select energy fuels (termed petroleum products by the index) with a weighting of 33 percent based on production value. Tiers 2, 3, and 4 have different fixed weightings within each tier, as shown in Figure 7.5.

Figure 7-5. Reuters/Jefferies CRB Index Tiers and Commodities

Tier 1 Petroleum		Tier 2 Highly Liquid		Tier 3 Liquid		Tier 4 Diversified	
WTI Crude Oil	23.0%	Aluminum	6.0%	Cocoa	5.0%	Lean Hogs	1.0%
Heating Oil	5.0%	Copper	6.0%	Coffee	5.0%	Nickel	1.0%
Unleaded Gas	5.0%	Corn	6.0%	Cotton	5.0%	Orange Juice	1.0%
		Gold	6.0%	Sugar	5.0%	Silver	1.0%
		Live Cattle	6.0%			Wheat	1.0%
		Natural Gas	6.0%				
		Soybeans	6.0%				
Tier 1 Total:	33.0%	Tier 2 Total:	42.0%	Tier 3 Total:	20.0%	Tier 4 Total:	5.0%

Liquidity and production value are the most important factors the index employs in selecting the component commodities in tiers 2 through 4. More specifically, 42 percent of component commodities are considered highly liquid, 20 percent are considered moderately liquid, and 5 percent are considered "diversifying" commodities. Softs represent the largest commodity sector at 21 percent. No other commodity index allocates more than 10 percent to this sector, and this makes the Reuters/Jefferies CRB Index unique. The index does not stop with unconventional target allocations. The livestock sector accounts for approximately 7 percent of the total; nearly 6 percent exposure is derived from live cattle, and 1 percent from lean hogs. Only the Dow Jones-AIG Commodity Index comes close to this. No exposure is given to exotic commodities.

The index is rebalanced monthly, with target allocations adjusted ad hoc. No diversification constraints are used for individual commodities and sectors, although petroleum is fixed at 33 percent of the total. All other commodities are sorted into groups and evaluated as defined by liquidity and diversification considerations (see Figure 7.6).

Futures contracts listed on the New York Board of Trade track this commodity index.

ROGERS INTERNATIONAL COMMODITIES INDEX

Developed by the well-known commodity expert Jim Rogers, the Rogers International Commodities Index (RICI) is by far the broadest and most global commodity index. With 35 component commodities, the RICI attempts to capture the greatest amount of exposure to commodities. To achieve that aim, it tracks exotic commodities such as rubber, silk, and adzuki beans that do not trade on U.S. exchanges. No other broad-based commodity index can make that claim. Furthermore, no other commodity index tracks less popular nonexotic commodities such as palladium, tin, oats, and rice. However, the exposure to those commodities is kept low, whereas

Figure 7-6. Target Allocations – Reuters/Jefferies Commodity Research Bureau Index

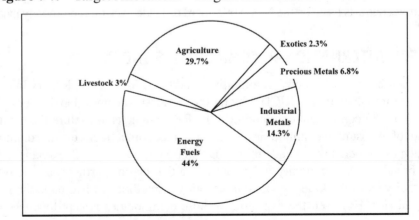

significant exposure is given to more popular commodities such as WTI crude oil, gold, and wheat. WTI crude oil is the largest single commodity tracked at approximately 35 percent of the total index, and wheat is the second largest commodity component at 7 percent. Adzuki beans and wool are the smallest components at 0.25 percent each.

Established in 1998, the RICI is a production-weighted index; that means that commodities are selected on the basis of their production value and importance to global trade (see Figure 7.7). Modifications to the target allocations are made annually on the basis of production value. Rebalancing back to target allocations is performed monthly.

Investing in the RICI can be accomplished by purchasing Rogers TRAKRS (symbol RCI), which is listed on the Chicago Mercantile Exchange.

Figure 7-7. Target Allocations – Rogers International Commodities Index

The components of the commodity indexes discussed in this chapter are listed in Figure 7.8.

Figure 7-8. Commodity Indexes Components

Commodity Year Established	R/J CRB 1957	GSCI 1992	DJ-AIG 1998	RICI 1999	DBLCI 2003
AGRICULTURE					
Adzuki Beans				0.5%	
Barley				0.3%	
Canola				0.7%	
Cocoa	5.0%	0.2%		1.0%	
Coffee	5.0%	0.5%	3.0%	2.0%	
Corn	6.0%	3.1%	5.7%	4.8%	11.3%
Cotton	5.0%	0.7%	2.5%	4.1%	
Oats				0.5%	
Orange Juice	1.0%			0.7%	
Rice				0.5%	
Soybean Meal				0.8%	
Soybean Oil			2.8%	2.0%	
Soybeans	6.0%	1.9%	7.6%	3.0%	
Sugar	5.0%	0.7%	3.2%	2.0%	
Wheat	1.0%	3.4%	4.7%	7.0%	11.3%
Total: Agriculture	**34.0%**	**10.4%**	**29.5%**	**29.7%**	**22.5%**
ENERGY					
Crude Oil	23.0%	55.4%	13.2%	35.0%	35.0%
Heating Oil	5.0%	5.8%	3.8%	3.0%	20.0%
Natural Gas	6.0%	7.2%	12.2%	3.0%	
Unleaded Gasoline	5.0%	10.4%	3.8%	3.0%	
Total: Energy	**39.0%**	**78.7%**	**33.0%**	**44.0%**	**55.0%**
EXOTICS					
Lumber				1.0%	
Rubber				1.0%	
Wool				0.3%	
Total: Exotics	**0.0%**	**0.0%**	**0.0%**	**2.3%**	**0.0%**
LIVESTOCK					
Feeder Cattle		0.3%			
Lean Hogs	1.0%	1.0%	2.5%	1.0%	
Live Cattle	6.0%	1.7%	4.9%	2.0%	
Total: Livestock	**7.0%**	**3.0%**	**7.4%**	**3.0%**	**0.0%**
INDUSTRIAL METALS					
Aluminum	6.0%	2.2%	7.1%	4.0%	12.5%
Copper	6.0%	2.6%	7.0%	4.0%	
Lead		0.3%		2.0%	
Nickel	1.0%	0.6%	2.8%	1.0%	
Palladium				0.3%	
Tin				1.0%	
Zinc		0.4%	3.0%	2.0%	
Total: Industrial Metals	**13.0%**	**6.1%**	**20.0%**	**14.3%**	**12.5%**
PRECIOUS METALS					
Gold	6.0%	1.6%	7.4%	3.0%	10.0%
Silver	1.0%	0.2%	2.7%	2.0%	
Platinum				1.8%	
Total: Precious Metals	**7.0%**	**1.8%**	**10.1%**	**6.8%**	**10.0%**
Total Index	**100.0%**	**100.0%**	**100.0%**	**100.0%**	**100.0%**

Performance and Correlation

Since commodity indexes track different commodities and establish different weightings for those commodities, they do not have the same performance and therefore are not perfectly correlated with one another. Most commodity indexes are highly correlated, with the two most highly correlated being the Deutsche Bank index and the Rogers index. The two indexes with the lowest positive correlation are the Deutsche Bank index and the Reuters/Jefferies CRB index at 59 percent. As can be seen in Figure 7.9, the Reuters/Jefferies CRB Index and Deutsche Bank Liquid Commodity Index have the lowest correlation on average with the other major commodity indexes and the index with the highest correlation on average is the Rogers International Commodities Index.

Figure 7-9. Commodity Indexes Correlations

	CRB	GSCI	DJ-AIG	RICI	DBLCI	Average
CRB	100%	65%	82%	72%	59%	76%
GSCI	65%	100%	89%	92%	92%	88%
DJ-AIG	82%	89%	100%	90%	85%	89%
RICI	72%	92%	90%	100%	96%	90%
DBLCI	59%	92%	85%	96%	100%	86%
Average	76%	88%	89%	90%	86%	86%

Figure 7.10 shows that the two commodity indexes with the highest returns over the period 1991–2004 were the Deutsche Bank Liquid Commodity Index and the Rogers International Commodities Index, both with 10.1 percent annualized returns. However, where there is reward, there is also risk. The Deutsche Bank index experienced the greatest risk during the period with a standard deviation of over 18 percent. One of the principal reasons for the high standard deviation compared with the other indexes is the lack of diversification, with only six constituent commodities. Having fewer

Figure 7-10. Commodity Index Performance

	Annual Return	Standard Deviation	Return to Risk Ratio
CRB	3.3%	8.3%	0.40
GSCI	5.7%	18.1%	0.31
DJ-AIG	7.0%	11.8%	0.59
RICI	10.1%	14.0%	0.72
DBLCI	10.1%	18.5%	0.55
Average	7.2%	14.2%	0.51

commodities means that each one plays a more prominent role in how the index performs. In addition to the constituent commodities, the weightings established affect the index performance. Indexes with higher weightings for energy will rise faster than will indexes with lower weightings when crude oil prices increase, all else held equal. The Reuters/Jefferies CRB Index generated the lowest return over the period but also had the lowest risk. This demonstrates the inescapable relationship between risk and return.

Narrowly Based Commodity Indexes

Although this chapter is devoted to broad-based commodity indexes, that does not mean that narrowly based commodity indexes do not exist. For investors who want to track a more defined market, narrowly based commodity indexes provide a means to do so. The following are three of the more popular narrowly based commodity indexes:

- National Corn Index
- National Soybean Index
- Brookshire International Raw Materials Index

Quiz for Chapter 7

1. All but which of the following are the primary functions commodity indexes serve?
   a. Inflation indicator
   b. Performance benchmark
   c. Investable instrument
   d. Return predictor

2. All commodity indexes are investable.
   a. True
   b. False

3. All but which of the following are characteristics of commodity indexes?
   a. Deliverability
   b. Active management
   c. Market liquidity
   d. Futures availability

4. Which of the following indexes has the smallest number of component commodities?
   a. Dow Jones-AIG Commodity Index
   b. Goldman Sachs Commodity Index

c. Deutsche Bank Liquid Commodity Index

d. Reuters/Jefferies CRB Index

5. Which of the following is the broadest commodity index?

a. Deutsche Bank Liquid Commodity Index

b. Dow Jones-AIG Commodity Index

c. Goldman Sachs Commodity Index

d. Rogers International Commodities Index

6. Which of the following commodity indexes was the first to be established?

a. Dow Jones-AIG Commodity Index

b. Goldman Sachs Commodity Index

c. Reuters/Jefferies CRB Index

d. Rogers International Commodities Index

7. High turnover of component commodities is common with commodity indexes.

a. True

b. False

8. How many component commodities does the Rogers International Commodities Index hold?

a. 5

b. 15

c. 25

d. 35

9. To what factor can a low standard deviation in commodity indexes be attributed?

a. Longer index tenure

b. Greater quantity of component commodities

c. Higher turnover of component commodities

d. Lower turnover of component commodities

10. Target allocations or weightings are fairly consistent from commodity index to commodity index.

a. True

b. False

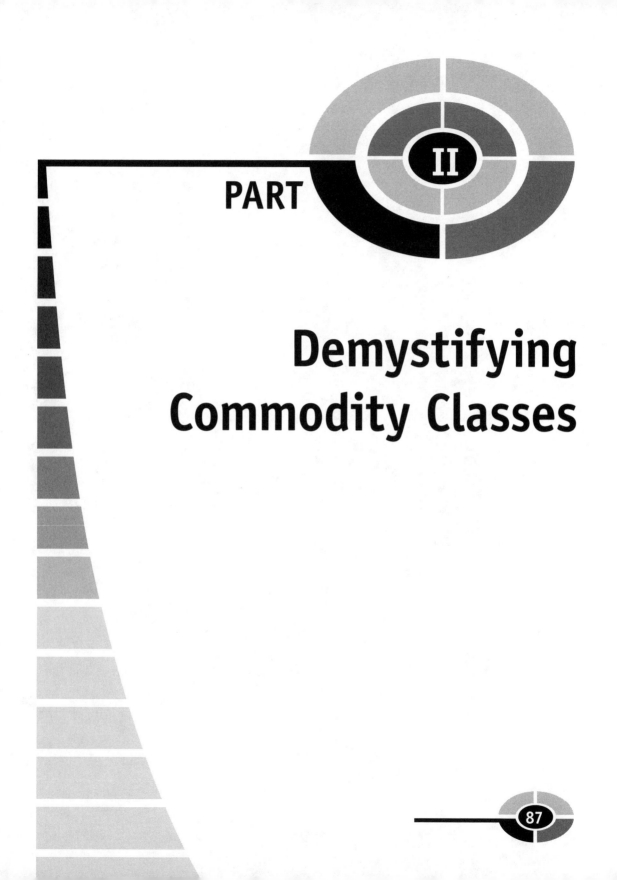

PART

II

Demystifying Commodity Classes

CHAPTER 8

Precious and Industrial Metals:

Strengthening Your Portfolio to Make It Shine

Most precious and industrial metals have been in use for hundreds, if not thousands, of years. As a result, metals have been used in the production of jewelry and coins and have been the foundation for trading for centuries. For investors, there are a number of ways to invest in and trade metals. You can purchase the stock of companies involved in the production of metals, purchase coins or bars, add exchange-traded funds and notes to your portfolio, and trade futures contracts. This chapter discusses precious metals and then industrial metals. Note that industrial metals often are referred to as base metals.

Precious Metals

This section discusses the three primary precious metals: platinum, gold, and silver. Precious metals are defined primarily by their high resistance to corrosion and oxidation, in contrast to industrial metals with their low resistance.

PLATINUM

Platinum—often called the rich person's gold—is one of the rarest metals on earth, significantly less common than gold and silver. Total global annual production of platinum is approximately 130 tons, which is 6 percent of total global annual production of gold and 1 percent of that of silver. The production of an ounce of platinum requires nearly 10 tons of ore, and the extraction process takes six months to complete. Over the history of the world, the total amount of platinum ever produced would not fill an area of 25 cubic feet. Platinum weighs approximately 11 percent more per ounce than gold.

Although gold and silver have been in use for centuries, platinum did not gain favor until the seventeenth century, when the Spanish discovered vast amounts in South America. Since that time, platinum has been sought after for its resistance to corrosion, ability to withstand oxidation from the air, and ideal chemical properties. Although platinum is a highly desirable metal for making jewelry, it also is used in the production of catalytic converters for automobiles and is employed for many industrial processes, such as technology and telecommunications. In fact, platinum has more industrial uses than both silver and gold; more than 50 percent of all platinum production is dedicated to industrial use.

Platinum is more than simply a metal; it is also the name for a group of metals. This group includes traditional platinum, palladium, ruthenium, rhodium, iridium, and osmium. Each of these metals has unique chemical and physical qualities. Palladium is discussed in the industrial metals section because of its significant industrial uses.

Global Platinum Reserves and Production

Unlike other metals and energy fuels, platinum deposits are situated principally in only two countries. South Africa is the dominant player and accounts for nearly 88 percent of world platinum reserves. Russia is second with nearly 10 percent of reserves. That leaves only 2 percent of world reserves of platinum scattered throughout over 100 other countries.

South Africa and Russia also are the two leading producers of platinum. South Africa accounts for nearly 80 percent of total global production, Russia accounts for 11 percent, and North America accounts for 6 percent. Moreover, approximately 90 percent of platinum is produced from four mines: three in South Africa and one in Siberia, Russia.

Global Platinum Consumption

Total production of platinum is approximately 5 million troy ounces per year. Jewelry demands the most platinum at nearly 51 percent of the available supply. The second demand group is automotive catalysts, which consume about 29 percent of the platinum mined. The final large group is petroleum refining and chemicals, which account for 13 percent of annual platinum consumption. Approximately 95 percent of all platinum jewelry demand comes from Japan.

NYMEX Futures Contract Specifications

Trading Unit (1 Contract): 50 troy ounces
Price Quotation: U.S. dollars and cents per troy ounce
Minimum Price Fluctuation: $0.10 per troy ounce or $5.00 per contract
Trading Hours:

- *Open Outcry*: 8:20 a.m. to 1:05 p.m.
- *Electronic*: 6:00 p.m. to 5:15 p.m. via CME Globex; Sunday through Friday *[Note: A 45-minute break occurs each day between 5:15 p.m. (current trade date) and 6:00 p.m. (next trade date).]*

Trading Months: Next 15 months *(Note: Begins with the current month and the next two consecutive months before transitioning to the quarterly cycle of January, April, July, and October.)*
Trading Symbol: PL

GOLD

Gold is the most actively traded precious metal and is one of the rarest commodities in the world. Nearly 15 percent of all gold is recycled each year. Furthermore, most of the gold that has ever been mined is still in use since gold is recycled rather than being discarded. At a rate of 15 percent, all gold is recycled about every seven years. The gold that the Greeks and Romans wore as jewelry is used in modern jewelry.

As with platinum, gold is valued for its high resistance to corrosion and oxidation. There is probably no other metal in the world that receives such high esteem. Many countries throughout the world use gold as a benchmark to value their currencies. Although the United States does not use gold as the standard for valuing the dollar, it is the single largest holder of gold in the world. Gold reserves consist of holdings by governments and by commercial enterprises.

Characteristics of Gold

Gold can be characterized by one of four grades or traits. The first characteristic is its high resistance to oxidation and corrosion. Aside from cyanide, which can dissolve gold, there are nearly no elements that can change the look or feel of gold. The second characteristic is malleability, or the ability to be used in many different ways to create unique works. The more pure the gold, the greater the malleability. Gold often is mixed with other metals (alloyed). The more other metals are mixed with gold, the less purity, and thus flexibility, there is to create a finished product. Malleability is measured by the number of karats in gold; 24 karats is pure gold, and 9 karats is only 37.5 percent gold and 62.5 percent other metals. Figure 8.1 shows the different purities of gold. The other two characteristics are rarity and ductility, a measure of conversion to wire for electric conductivity.

Figure 8-1. Purities of Gold

Karats	Purity
24k	100.0%
22k	91.7%
18k	75.0%
14k	58.3%
10k	41.7%
9k	37.5%

Reasons for Investing in Gold

The major reasons for investing in gold are the following:

- Investing in gold hedges against a weakening U.S. dollar.
- Investing in gold offers safety during uncertain times.
- Investing in gold diversifies a portfolio.
- Investing in gold provides a long-term hedge against inflation.
- Investing in gold protects wealth since gold is the basis for many currencies.

Global Gold Reserves and Production

Of all of the gold ever produced throughout history, nearly 50 percent was sourced from South Africa. Years ago—before increasing challenges to gold extraction—South Africa produced nearly 80 percent of total annual gold supplies. That is surprising because of how global the production of gold actually is. For example, in the United States, approximately two-thirds of the total gold consumed is produced from mines in Nevada and South Dakota. Other areas of large mining operations include the Atacama Desert between Chile and Argentina, Australia, China, Russia, and Peru. Nearly 25 percent of total annual production of gold is estimated to come from small-scale mining operations. In 1980 total global gold production was approximately 1,250 tons. Between 1980 and 1996 annual production increased to nearly 2,500 tons. However, since 1996 the annual production has remained steady with few increases or decreases each year. South Africa now accounts for only about 20 percent of total global annual production.

Global Gold Consumption

The four primary uses of gold are jewelry, electronics, dentistry, and monetary. Jewelry is the single largest use at nearly 70 percent of total consumption. Gold also is used for electronic and other technology equipment because of its robust conductivity of electricity. If you have ever had a cavity, you may have received gold for your filling. Pure gold is not used commonly for this purpose; instead, dentists employ gold alloys that contain a mixture of copper, silver, or platinum. The final use for gold is for monetary products such as gold holdings at central banks. Another monetary use is gold coins, which may or may not be legal tender.

NYMEX Futures Contract Specifications

Trading Unit (1 Contract): 100 troy ounces
Price Quotation: U.S. dollars and cents per troy ounce
Minimum Price Fluctuation: $0.10 per troy ounce or $10.00 per contract
Trading Hours:

- *Open Outcry*: 8:20 a.m. to 1:30 p.m.
- *Electronic*: 6:00 p.m. to 5:15 p.m via CME Globex; Sunday through Friday *[Note: A 45-minute break occurs each day between 5:15 p.m (current trade date) and 6:00 p.m. (next trade date).]*

Trading Months: Current calendar month; next two calendar months; any February, April, August, and October within a 23-month period; and any June and December falling within a 60-month period starting with the current month.
Trading Symbol: GC

SILVER

Silver is the most extensively produced precious metal and has been mined since at least the fourth millennium BC on the islands of the Aegean Sea and in Asia Minor. However, unlike the other precious metals, a large amount of silver is consumed by the industrial sector and thus removed from the market. Most of the silver that is produced is a by-product of mining for gold, copper, lead, and zinc. Much of the earliest silver production was the by-product of lead mining in ancient times. Silver also has been used for monetary purposes throughout history. Judas Iscariot—one of Jesus's disciples—was paid in silver coins for betraying Jesus.

Grades of Silver

There are only two grades of silver, although there are some minor variations. Pure silver is at one end of the spectrum, and sterling silver—standard silver—is at the opposite end. Actually, sterling silver is composed of 92.5 percent silver and 7.5 percent copper and thus is an alloy. Other metals sometimes are used in the alloy, but the standard metal is copper. Copper or another metal is added to provide durability and strength beyond what pure silver can provide. Silver is relatively stable in water and air but is susceptible to tarnishing when exposed to air or water containing ozone or hydrogen. Silver is the whitest metal and also has the highest optical reflectivity.

Global Silver Reserves and Production

The production of silver is diversified, with no one or two countries accounting for the bulk of production. The country with the highest annual production of silver is Peru. Not far behind Peru is Mexico, followed by Australia. From a geographical standpoint, two countries from North America make the top 10 list of the largest silver producers; Central America has one, South America has two, Europe has two, Asia has two, and Australia is one (see Figure 8.2).

Figure 8-2. Top Ten Producers of Silver

Rank	Country	Percentage of Total Global Production
1	Peru	13.7%
2	Mexico	12.3%
3	Australia	10.3%
4	China	8.6%
5	Chile	5.9%
6	Russia	5.6%
7	Poland	5.4%
8	United States	5.2%
9	Canada	4.5%
10	Kazakhstan	3.5%

Global Silver Consumption

Many people believe that the production of jewelry accounts for the largest consumption of silver, but only approximately 27 percent of silver is turned into jewelry; the other 63 percent of consumption is accounted for by the business and industrial sectors. One of the surprising facts about silver is that nearly 20 percent of consumption is accounted for by the photography industry. The amount of silver used by that industry is declining because of the use of digital cameras that do not require silver. The largest group of consumers is related to industrial usage, to which nearly half of all silver demand is allocated. The leading use of silver is in electronics since silver is considered an even better electrical conductor than copper. Pure silver has the highest thermal conductivity of any metal and is second only to diamonds in conductivity. The reason most people think that copper has the highest conductivity is that copper is significantly less expensive than silver and therefore is in greater demand for electrical purposes.

NYMEX Futures Contract Specifications

Trading Unit (1 Contract): 5,000 troy ounces

Price Quotation: U.S. dollars and cents per troy ounce

Minimum Price Fluctuation: $0.05 per troy ounce or $25.00 per contract. Spread, straddle, and settlement determination have other minimums. Check with NYMEX.

Trading Hours:

- *Open Outcry*: 8:25 a.m. to 1:25 p.m.
- *Electronic*: 6:00 p.m. to 5:15 p.m. via CME Globex; Sunday through Friday *[Note: A 45-minute break occurs each day between 5:15 p.m. (current trade date) and 6:00 p.m. (next trade date).]*

Trading Months: Current calendar month; next two calendar months; any January, March, May, and September within a 23-month period; and any July and December falling within a 60-month period starting with the current month.

Trading Symbol: SI

Industrial Metals

There is a great demand for industrial metals as the world economy continues to grow and develop. Countries such as China and India are demanding significant amounts of industrial metals to build their manufacturing infrastructure and manufacture goods that are sold throughout the world. Some people refer to industrial metals as base metals. The four most widely used industrial metals in order of usage are steel/iron, aluminum, copper, and zinc.

PALLADIUM

Palladium is a silver-white metal that is part of the platinum metal group because its chemical structure is similar to that of platinum. Palladium is sought after by the automotive industry for the construction of catalytic converters, which help reduce pollution because of the ability of palladium to absorb 900 times its own volume in gas. It is used instead of platinum because of the cost savings. Future demand for palladium looks strong in light of the importance of reducing greenhouse gases and new laws that require that reduction.

As with platinum, palladium is malleable and highly resistant to corrosion. Palladium is produced not by mining specifically for the metal but by extracting it from copper-nickel ore. As recently as 1803, palladium was discovered in South America and named for the comet Pallas, which had been discovered two years earlier. Palladium not only is the least dense metal but also has the lowest melting temperature of any metal in the platinum group.

Global Palladium Production

Much like platinum, nearly 86 percent of all palladium production is from Russia and South Africa. Russia has a 55 percent market share, and South Africa accounts for 31 percent of total global production. North America—the United States and then Canada—accounts for 11 percent, with the remaining 3 percent produced by the rest of the world. The single largest mine for the production of palladium is the Norilsk-Talnakh, a predominantly nickel deposit. In the United States, Stillwater in Montana is the largest producer of palladium.

An alternative source for the production of palladium is spent nuclear fuel from nuclear reactors. Through a complex synthesis process, some amounts of palladium can be extracted. Although the amount of palladium produced from this source is insignificant compared with the amount produced and demanded, it is interesting to note that not all metals are extracted from ore in the traditional way.

Global Palladium Consumption

As was mentioned above, the automotive industry accounts for the majority of palladium consumption at roughly 48 percent of total demand. Jewelry-related consumption accounts for the second most palladium at 21 percent. Electronics and dentistry are the third and fourth biggest consumers of palladium at 14 percent and 13 percent, respectively. Some of the primary applications of palladium are the following:

- Electronics (multilayer ceramic capacitors, soldering materials, etc.)
- Technology (gas purification, connector plantings, palladium chloride)
- Hydrogen storage
- Jewelry (by itself or as an alloy)
- Photography (platinotype printing process)

NYMEX Futures Contract Specifications
Trading Unit (1 Contract): 100 troy ounces

Price Quotation: U.S. dollars and cents per troy ounce
Minimum Price Fluctuation: $0.05 per troy ounce or $5.00 per contract

Trading Hours:

- *Open Outcry*: 8:30 a.m. to 1:00 p.m.
- *Electronic*: 6:00 p.m. to 5:15 p.m. via CME Globex; Sunday through Friday *[Note: A 45-minute break occurs each day between 5:15 p.m. (current trade date) and 6:00 p.m. (next trade date).]*

Trading Months: 15 months; begins with the current month and the next two consecutive months before transitioning to the quarterly cycle of March, June, September, and December.

Trading Symbol: PA

COPPER

Copper is the third most widely used metal in the world after steel/iron and aluminum. Copper has been produced and used for thousands of years in places such as Egypt, Iraq (Samaria), China, India, and Greece. A copper pendant found in Samaria dates to around 8700 BC, indicating that copper use has been ongoing for 10,000 years. The smelting and refining of copper began around 5000 BC in Anatolia (present-day Turkey). By 2800 BC copper smelting was taking place in China, and by 2000 BC in South America in the Andes region. Archaeological evidence shows that copper smelting was done in western Africa by 900 AD. The Iceman dating to 3200 BC found a few years ago in Switzerland high in the Alps was discovered to have an ax tipped with high-purity copper. In the United States in an area known as the Old Copper Complex in present-day Michigan and Wisconsin, the production of copper began between 6000 BC and 3000 BC.

The Bronze Age would not have begun without copper since bronze is a combination of copper and tin. The Bronze Age was a period of remarkable development and expansion of civilization. Brass is produced from the combination of copper and zinc.

The name for this metal originates from the word *cyprium*, meaning "the metal of Cyprus," the island in the eastern Mediterranean where the Roman Empire mined for copper. The word later was shortened to *cuprum* before becoming the Anglicized *copper*.

Copper Production

In 1900, total global production of copper was about 0.3 million tons. Since that time, the production of copper has increased dramatically with a couple of short periods of declining production. By 1940 total global production was about 2.3 million tons, an increase of 667 percent during the 40 years between 1900 and 1940. Between 1940 and 1950 production was stable, but after 1960 production sharply increased as technology applications became more apparent. By 1980 total global production was at about 8 million tons, and by 2005 production had risen to approximately 15 million tons, an increase of 88 percent over the 25-year period. The United States and Chile (see Figure 8.3) are two of the largest producers of copper; the metal typically is extracted through large-scale open pit mining.

Figure 8-3. Copper Production by Country

Rank	Country	Percentage of Total Global Production
1	Chile	35.8%
2	United States	8.2%
3	Peru	7.0%
4	China	6.0%
5	Australia	6.0%
6	Indonesia	5.5%
7	Russia	4.6%
8	Canada	4.1%
9	Zambia	3.4%
10	Poland	3.3%

SOURCE: Copper Development Association, 2007

Copper Consumption

The construction industry is the leading consumer of copper, accounting for about half of all consumption (see Figure 8.4). The second largest consumer is electrical and electronic products at approximately 20 percent of total consumption. Consumer and general products rounds out the top three largest consumers, accounting for approximately 11 percent. Transportation and miscellaneous consumers account for the remaining consumption. Copper is used in many different applications because it is malleable, a solid conductor of heat, and a good conductor of electricity when pure. Some of the primary applications of copper are the following:

- Architecture (waterproof roofing material, shipbuilding, etc.)
- Biomedical (biostatic surfaces, fungicides, etc.)
- Chemicals (ceramic glazes, glass coloring, musical instruments, textile fabrics, etc.)
- Coinage (pennies, nickels, etc.)
- Electronics (circuit boards, electrical relays, electromagnets, wave guides, etc.)
- Household (doorknobs, frying pans, piping, etc.)

Figure 8-4. Copper Consumption by Industry

Rank	Industry	Percentage of Total Consumption
1	Building Construction	50.7%
2	Electrical and Electronic Products	19.3%
3	Consumer and General Products	10.7%
4	Transportation Equipment	10.5%
5	Industrial Machinery and Equipment	8.9%

SOURCE: Copper Development Association, 2007

NYMEX Futures Contract Specifications

Trading Unit (1 Contract): 25,000 pounds
Price Quotation: U.S. cents per pound
Minimum Price Fluctuation: 0.05¢ ($0.0005) per pound or $12.50 per contract
Trading Hours:

- *Open Outcry*: 8:10 a.m. to 1:00 p.m.
- *Electronic*: 6:00 p.m. to 5:15 p.m. via CME Globex; Sunday through Friday *[Note: A 45-minute break occurs each day between 5:15 p.m. (current trade date) and 6:00 p.m. (next trade date).]*

Trading Months: Current calendar month and the next 23 consecutive calendar months.
Trading Symbol: HG

ALUMINUM

Aluminum has many industrial and commercial uses and is the second most widely used metal in the world, behind steel/iron. Aluminum is popular for its light weight, softness, malleability, and strong resistance to corrosion and oxidation owing to a thin surface layer of aluminum oxide that is formed when aluminum is exposed to air. Aluminum has approximately one-third the strength and density of steel. When they are used in equal weights, aluminum is a more efficient electrical conductor than copper.

Aluminum was used as an astringent for dressing wounds during ancient Greek and Roman times, but its use as a metal did not begin until the nineteenth century in Europe. At one time aluminum was considered a precious metal and was valued more highly than gold.

Aluminum or Aluminium?

The word *aluminum* is used only in the United States and Canada. The rest of the world uses the word *aluminium*. The Canadian Oxford Dictionary prefers *aluminum,* and the Australian Macquarie Dictionary prefers the more common *aluminium*. *Aluminium* is the preferred choice of the International Union of Pure and Applied Chemistry, but in 1993 that organization recognized *aluminum* as acceptable.

Aluminum Production

Total global production of aluminum was 31.9 million tons in 2005, making it the most extensively mined nonferrous metal in the world. In 1990 total production was approximately 19 million tons, representing a 68 percent increase in 15 years. The total amount of aluminum produced in 1980 was about 15 million tons; in 1970 it had been about 10 million tons. The largest producer of aluminum is China, which accounts for nearly 20 percent of the total supply. The other top producers are Russia, Canada, the United States, and Australia. Recycling of aluminum, such as that used in soda pop cans, has become an important aspect of aluminum production. Recycling requires significantly less energy—around 5 percent—to produce aluminum than does the process of producing aluminum from ore. There is a cost with producing aluminum through recycling, however: a greater loss—around 15 percent—of aluminum during the recycling process, resulting in an ashlike material.

Aluminum Consumption

The consumption of aluminum is dominated by three industries: transportation, construction, and packaging. Transportation is the top industry for aluminum consumption, accounting for approximately 26 percent of all demand. Construction and packaging each account for 22 percent of total consumption. The top three industries therefore account for 70 percent of total global aluminum consumption. Figure 8.5 lists the top consumers of aluminum by industry.

Figure 8-5. Aluminum Consumption by Industry

Rank	Industry	Percentage of Total Consumption
1	Transportation	26.0%
2	Packaging	22.0%
3	Construction	22.0%
4	Electrical	8.0%
5	Machinery	8.0%
6	Consumer Durables	7.0%
7	Miscellaneous	7.0%

SOURCE: London Metal Exchange

NYMEX Futures Contract Specifications

Trading Unit (1 Contract): 44,000 pounds
Price Quotation: U.S. cents per pound
Minimum Price Fluctuation: 0.05¢ ($0.0005) per pound or $22 per contract
Trading Hours:

- *Open Outcry*: 7:50 a.m. to 1:15 p.m.
- *Electronic*: 6:00 p.m. to 5:15 p.m. via CME Globex; Sunday through Friday
  [Note: A 45-minute break occurs each day between 5:15 p.m. (current trade date) and 6:00 p.m. (next trade date).]

Trading Months: 25 consecutive months
Trading Symbol: AL

ZINC

Zinc is the fourth most widely used metal in the world today. Historically, the use of zinc can be traced back to ancient times, particularly in India, where zinc production was common before 1000 BC. Zinc—the twenty-third most abundant element in the world—has a low melting temperature point and high chemical reactivity, making it ideal for crafting.

Zinc Production

Some estimates indicate that zinc will be available for less than 50 years. Nevertheless, production of zinc is robust in China, Australia, and Peru. China accounts for nearly 25 percent of total global production of zinc.

Zinc Consumption

The most popular use of zinc is galvanization of metals, which accounts for nearly half of all zinc demand. The production of brass remove at 19 percent is the second most popular, and alloying and miscellaneous account for approximately 15 percent and 14 percent, respectively, of total global consumption of zinc.

LME Futures Contract Specifications

Lot Size: 25 metric tons
Price Quotation: U.S. dollars per ton
Minimum Tick: $0.50 per ton, or $12.50 per contract
Delivery Dates: Monthly contracts out to 15, 27 or 63 months forward
Trading Symbol: LZS

TIN

Tin is a silvery-white metal that is malleable, resistant to oxidation and corrosion, and nontoxic. It also is required, along with copper, for the production of bronze. Another important characteristic of tin is its ability to bond to other metals; it prevents corrosion when applied as a coating to metals such as steel and lead. Tin also is used in the production of tins, in which plating is combined with steel. These tins are used for food preservation and often enhance the presentation of a gift box.

Tin Production

China is the world's largest producer of tin, accounting for over one-third of total supply. China, together with Indonesia, makes Asia the dominant player in the production of tin, accounting for nearly 75 percent of total supply. South America is another major producer of tin.

Tin Consumption

The three primary uses of tin are soldering, tin plating, and alloying with other metals. Soldering is the joining or uniting of the surfaces of metals by fusion of alloys.

LME Futures Contract Specifications

Lot Size: 5 metric tons
Price Quotation: U.S. dollars per ton
Minimum Tick: $5.00 per ton, or $25 per contract
Delivery Dates: Monthly contracts out to 15, 27, or 63 months forward
Trading Symbol: LSN

NICKEL

Nickel is a silvery white metal that has a highly polished look. The use of nickel as an alloy for the production of bronze can be traced back to 3500 BC in what is now Syria. China experimented with nickel as early as 1700 BC, although there is evidence that nickel was mistaken for silver at that time.

Stainless steel is one of the most important applications of nickel. To create stainless steel, steel is alloyed with nickel to create a metal with high resistance to corrosion. Nickel is considered a ferrous metal, or a type of metal that is related to iron.

Nickel Production and Reserves

Australia is the largest producer of nickel in the world at 25 percent of the total global production (see Figure 8.6). Russia and Indonesia fill the second and third spots of producers with slightly less than 13 percent and slightly less than 12 percent, respectively. In terms of individual mines, the Sudbury region in Ontario, Canada, is the leading producer of nickel in the world.

Figure 8-6. Countries with the Largest Nickel Reserves

Rank	Country	Percentage of Total Global Reserves
1	Australia	25%
2	Russia	13%
3	Indonesia	12%
4	New Caledonia	7%
5	Canada	7%
6	Cuba	6%
7	Philippines	5%
8	Papua New Guinea	5%
9	Brazil	4%
10	China	3%

Nickel Consumption

There are four primary uses of nickel. The first is the production of stainless steel, which accounts for nearly two-thirds of total global demand. The second and third most important uses of nickel are nonferrous alloys and ferrous alloys at 12 percent and 10 percent, respectively. Electroplating uses 8 percent of total global consumption.

LME Futures Contract Specifications

Lot Size: 6 metric tons
Price Quotation: U.S. dollars per ton
Minimum Tick: $5.00 per ton, or $30 per contract
Delivery Dates: Monthly contracts out to 15, 27, or 63 months forward
Trading Symbol: LNI

Lead

Known for being very soft, dense, and malleable, lead is a bluish-white metal—although it tarnishes to gray when in contact with air—that is not suitable for electrical conductivity. Highly resistant to corrosion, lead is a primary metal for construction and lead-acid batteries.

Lead has been produced for thousands of years, and many people at one time thought that it was the oldest metal in the world. Compared with other metals, lead is relatively easy to extract and work with. Many lead pipes from the Roman Empire can still be seen. Those pipes were used to transport water for Roman baths. Some of the other former unique applications—now discontinued—of lead are the following:

- As a base for paint
- As a preservative for food and drink in the Roman Empire

- As an additive to gasoline
- As a component of toys

Lead Production

The three leading countries for lead production are Australia, China, and the United States, which together account for more than half of total global production. About 8 million tons of lead is produced each year, half of which comes from recycled scrap metal. Some studies claim that the total global supply of lead could be exhausted in 18 years, but many estimate about 40 years.

Lead Consumption

Lead is used in many different applications, including lead-acid batteries, as a coloring agent for ceramic, as projectiles for weapons, as a base for statues and sculptures, as sheeting for construction and electrical purposes, and as a coolant.

LME Futures Contract Specifications

Lot Size: 25 metric tons
Price Quotation: U.S. dollars per ton
Minimum Tick: $0.50 per ton, or $12.50 per contract
Delivery Dates: Monthly contracts out to 15 months forward
Trading Symbol: LPB

Rare Metals

Although this book does not discuss rare metals, they are mentioned here to present a full and fair picture of the metals markets (see Figure 8.7).

Figure 8-7. Rare Metals

Cadmium	Rhodium
Chromium	Selenium
Cobalt	Silicon
Germanium	Titanium
Magnesium	Tungsten
Manganese	Vanadium
Molybdenum	Wolframite

Quiz for Chapter 8

1. Which of the following metals is significantly rarer than gold and silver?
   a. Aluminum
   b. Copper
   c. Platinum
   d. Zinc

2. The primary metallurgical difference between precious metals and industrial metals is resistance to corrosion and oxidation.
   a. True
   b. False

3. Which of the following countries dominates the mining and production of gold?
   a. Australia
   b. Peru
   c. South Africa
   d. United States

4. About what percentage of all gold is recycled each year?
   a. 5 percent
   b. 15 percent
   c. 25 percent
   d. 35 percent

5. Gold is defined by karats. What exactly do karats represent?
   a. Degree of difficulty of extraction
   b. Density of gold
   c. Life of gold before recycling is needed
   d. Purity of gold

6. All but which of the following are reasons for investing in gold?
   a. Diversify a portfolio
   b. Hedge against inflation
   c. Standard for the U.S. dollar
   d. Safety during uncertain times

7. The photography industry accounts for about 20 percent of total global consumption of silver.
   a. True
   b. False

8. Palladium is part of which of the following groups of metals?
   a. Silver
   b. Platinum

c. Copper

d. Tin

9. Steel/iron is the most widely used metal in the world. Which metal is the second most widely used?

 a. Aluminum

 b. Copper

 c. Tin

 d. Zinc

10. The combination of copper and tin produces what metal?

 a. Aluminum

 b. Nickel

 c. Palladium

 d. Bronze

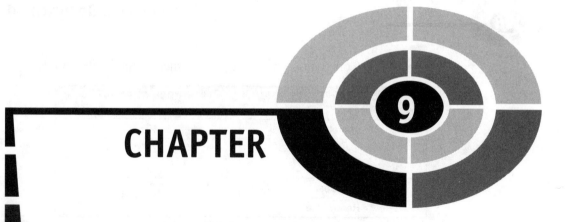

CHAPTER 9

Energy Fuels:

A Powerful Approach to Energizing Your Portfolio

When most people think about investing in commodities, they typically think about energy fuels. Although many investors buy gold as a hedge against inflation, energy fuels are perhaps the most sought after commodities, and for good reason. Unlike precious metals, which historically have generated unfavorable returns on average each year, energy fuels have historically generated much more attractive returns because of the ever-increasing demand for them. Although there are many other energy fuels in the marketplace, such as kerosene and jet fuel, this chapter focuses on the primary energy fuels: crude oil, natural gas, unleaded gasoline, coal, electric power, and uranium ore.

Most authors do not use the term *energy fuels* but instead use *energy*. Thus, natural gas is considered energy. This is only partly true as natural gas is a fuel used to create energy, not the end product. As a result, I have decided to use the term *energy fuel* to represent energy commodities. However, electric power is not a fuel. Nevertheless, I still characterize energy commodities as energy fuels rather than simply as energy. Figure 9.1 shows the composition of the energy used in the United States.

Figure 9-1. Composition of Energy Consumed in the United States

Commodity	Percentage of Total U.S. Energy Consumption
Petroleum	40%
Natural Gas	22%
Coal	23%
Nuclear	8%
Renewable	7%

SOURCE: *Energy Information Administration, Annual Energy Review 2006*

Crude Oil

Crude oil is the dominant commodity and the most frequently followed and news-friendly product in the energy fuels family. This popularity is well deserved since approximately 40 percent of the world's energy supply comes from crude oil. As a result, crude oil is the most widely traded nonfinancial commodity in the world. Many other energy fuel commodities are derived from crude oil, such as gasoline, heating oil, jet fuel, and kerosene. Without crude oil, you would be unable to drive your automobile since you would have no gasoline. Crude oil is not only a necessity to drive an automobile; it is also a necessity for driving the global economy. Without crude oil, much of the global economy would cease to exist. This is a scary thought that is compounded when one considers that much of the global production of crude oil is controlled by an oligopoly called the Organization of the Petroleum Exporting Countries (OPEC).

GRADES OF CRUDE OIL

Crude oil is measured primarily in terms of two classification criteria: sulfur content and density (viscosity), although there are other classifications as well. Density is a measure of how much of other component energy fuels—such as heating oil and Jet fuel—a grade of crude oil will yield. Higher-density crude oils have lower yields of component energy fuels. Conversely, crude oil with lower density typically yields more component fuels. Density is represented by a scale developed by the American Petroleum Institute (API) by which heavy crude oil is characterized by an API score of 20 or below.

The second important classification is sulfur content. The content of sulfur, a corrosive material that affects purity, is a measure of the quality of the crude oil. Crude oil with high levels of sulfur—containing more than 0.5 percent by weight—is referred to as sour, and crude with low levels of sulfur—containing less than 0.5 percent by weight—is referred to as sweet. As a general rule, the higher the sulfur content is, the less desirable crude oil is said to be. Because of its ideal low sulfur content and high component yield, light sweet crude is the standard oil on the market and the basis for all New York Mercantile Exchange futures contracts. One contract on the NYMEX is worth 1,000 barrels of crude oil. There is a trade-off, however, as light sweet crude also commands a premium because of its desirability. Figure 9.2 shows typical yields from a barrel of crude oil.

Figure 9-2. Typical Yields from a Barrel of Crude Oil

Commodity	Percentage of Total Yield
Gasoline	44%
Diesel Fuel / Heating Oil	22%
Miscellaneous / Other	17%
Jet Fuel	9%
Heavy Fuel Oil	4%
Liquid Petroleum Gas	4%

GLOBAL CRUDE OIL RESERVES

Without argument, the country with the largest proven reserves of crude oil is Saudi Arabia at 261 billion barrels (see Figure 9.3). It is followed by Iran, Iraq, and United Arab Emirates with 125, 115, and 101 billion barrels, respectively. The first non–Middle Eastern country to crack the top 10 list is Venezuela at number six with 77 billion barrels of reserves. Russia is the lone European country at number seven with 60 billion barrels. As you can see, Saudi Arabia is king in the crude oil market with nearly twice the proven reserves of second place Iran and over 10 times more than the United States.

In western Canada there is an abundance of what are referred to as oil sands. Crude oil can be extracted from those sands, but the process is difficult, time-consuming, and expensive. A significant amount of natural gas must be used in the process to heat the oil sands to allow for extraction. If the oil sands were included in the list of proven reserves, Canada would rank second on the list with close to 180 billion barrels of oil. This is a far cry from that country's nearly 5 billion barrels of proven conventional crude oil.

GLOBAL CRUDE OIL PRODUCTION

It should be no surprise that the country with the largest proven reserves of crude oil is also the country with the greatest crude oil production. Saudi Arabia produces over 10 million barrels of crude oil every day. Although Russia experienced

Figure 9-3. Countries with the Largest Crude Oil Reserves

Rank	Country	Percentage of Total Global Reserves
1	Saudi Arabia	19.8%
2	Iran	10.0%
3	Iraq	8.5%
4	United Arab Emirates	7.4%
5	Kuwait	7.3%
6	Venezuela	5.7%
7	Russia	5.6%
8	Libya	3.2%
9	Nigeria	2.7%
10	Kazakhstan	2.0%

SOURCE: *CIA World Factbook*

a substantial reduction in crude oil production after the fall of communism in the 1990s, production has increased steadily and stands at approximately 9.5 million barrels per day. That is enough to make Russia number two on the top 10 list. The United States, with perhaps the most mature crude oil production, is number three on the list.

Among the top 10 producers there are five countries that are not represented on the top 10 list of countries with the largest crude oil reserves: United States, Mexico, China, Norway, and Canada. In light of the thirst for crude oil in the United States, it is not surprising that Canada and Mexico make the top 10 list (see Figure 9.4).

Figure 9-4. Countries with the Largest Crude Oil Production

Rank	Country	Percentage of Total Global Production
1	Saudi Arabia	11.8%
2	Russia	11.7%
3	United States	9.5%
4	Iran	5.0%
5	China	4.5%
6	Mexico	4.3%
7	Norway	4.0%
8	Canada	3.9%
9	Venezuela	3.8%
10	United Arab Emirates	3.2%

SOURCE: *CIA World Factbook*

GLOBAL CRUDE OIL CONSUMPTION

The United States is by far the world's largest consumer of crude oil at 20.5 million barrels per day. There is a significant margin between the United States in the top spot and the number two country for crude oil consumption, China, which consumes 6.5 million barrels per day. Among the remaining countries in the top 10 are Japan at 5.4 million barrels, Germany at 2.6 million barrels, and Russia at 2.6 million barrels (see Figure 9.5). Crude oil consumption is expected to increase by nearly 50 percent from 2006 to 2025.

Figure 9-5. Countries with the Largest Crude Oil Consumption

Rank	Country	Percentage of Total Global Consumption
1	United States	25.2%
2	China	7.9%
3	Japan	6.8%
4	Germany	3.2%
5	Russia	3.0%
6	India	3.0%
7	Canada	2.8%
8	South Korea	2.6%
9	Brazil	2.6%
10	France	2.4%

SOURCE: CIA World Factbook

GLOBAL CRUDE OIL EXPORTING AND IMPORTING

The countries with the highest crude oil production also tend to be the countries that export the most crude oil. This is the case with Saudi Arabia, Russia, Iran, Kuwait, and Venezuela. Those countries are included in the top 10 list of the largest oil exporters because their domestic markets do not demand all the crude oil they produce. Other countries that export sizeable amounts of crude oil include the United Arab Emirates, Nigeria, Mexico, and Algeria.

Where does all the exported crude oil go? The vast majority goes to two markets: the United States and Japan at 11.8 million barrels and 5.3 million barrels of daily imports per day, respectively. Imports to those two countries amount to more than the sum of the imports of the remaining eight countries on the top 10 list. Thailand, number 10 on the list of biggest importers, imports approximately 1 million barrels per day, which is less than 10 percent of the crude oil imported by the United States. Figures 9.6 and 9.7 show the top exporting and importing countries, respectively.

Figure 9-6. Top Crude Oil Exporting Countries

Rank	Country	Percentage of Total Global Exports
1	Saudia Arabia	27.0%
2	Russia	20.5%
3	Norway	9.0%
4	Iran	7.8%
5	Venezuela	7.1%
6	United Arab Emirates	7.1%
7	Kuwait	6.8%
8	Nigeria	6.5%
9	Mexico	5.6%
10	Algeria	5.0%

SOURCE: CIA World Factbook

Figure 9-7. Top Crude Oil Importing Countries

Rank	Country	Percentage of Total Global Imports
1	United States	37.5%
2	Japan	16.8%
3	China	9.2%
4	Germany	7.9%
5	South Korea	6.7%
6	France	6.3%
7	Italy	5.4%
8	Spain	5.1%
9	India	4.8%
10	Thailand	3.2%

SOURCE: CIA World Factbook

TOP GLOBAL CRUDE OIL COMPANIES

A number of global companies are involved in the crude oil market. For investors seeking to take an ownership stake in companies, the five largest companies as ranked by market capitalization are ExxonMobil, Total, BP, Shell, and PetroChina. When you invest in individual companies, you are exposed to greater risk but have more return potential. If the increased risk makes you nervous, consider exchange-traded instruments—both funds and notes—or a commodity mutual fund. These investment options are discussed in Part 3 of this book.

NYMEX Futures Contract Specifications

Trading Unit (1 Contract): 1,000 U.S. barrels (42,000 gallons)
Price Quotation: U.S. dollars and cents per barrel
Minimum Price Fluctuation: $0.01 per barrel or $10.00 per contract
Trading Hours:

- *Open Outcry*: 9:00 a.m. to 2:30 p.m.
- *Electronic*: 6:00 p.m. to 5:15 p.m. via CME Globex; Sunday through Friday
  [Note: A 45-minute break occurs each day between 5:15 p.m. (current trade date) and 6:00 p.m. (next trade date).]

Trading Months: 9 years according to a NYMEX schedule
Trading Symbol: CL

Natural Gas

Natural gas is used to heat and cool over half the homes and accounts for approximately 22 percent of total energy consumption in the United States. It is one of the cleanest energy fuels, and demand has grown strongly over the last couple of decades and is forecast to become even greater in the future because of increased use in China and India. Prices for natural gas are nearly five times more volatile than crude oil prices. Unlike crude oil, which is a liquid fossil fuel, and coal, which is a solid fossil fuel, natural gas is a gaseous fossil fuel. It is composed primarily of methane, a hydrocarbon, with the other components being butane, ethane, and propane.

The most heavily traded and therefore most liquid of all natural gas contracts in the United States is the Henry Hub contract. The Henry Hub is not only a contract but also a physical location in Louisiana where most of the natural gas imported into the United States arrives. From the Henry Hub, natural gas flows in pipelines nearly all over the country. Figure 9.8 shows the cost of a unit of energy for residential use.

USES OF NATURAL GAS

There are five major consumers of natural gas in the United States: residential consumers, industrial consumers, commercial consumers, transportation-powered users, and electric generation. By far, industrial entities constitute the largest consumers of natural gas in the United States at nearly 40 percent of all demand. Residential customers are the second largest consumers of natural gas as a group, followed by electric generation, which consists of natural gas–fueled power plants. The other two are commercial consumers and transportation-powered users, which account for 14 percent and 5 percent of all natural gas consumption, respectively (see Figure 9.9).

Figure 9-8. Residential Cost per Unit of Energy (Btu)

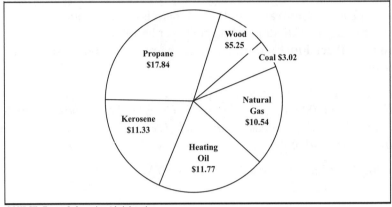

SOURCE: Energy Information Administration

Figure 9-9. Uses of Natural Gas by Consumer

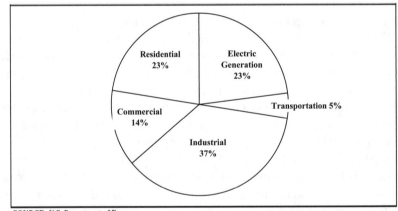

SOURCE: U.S. Department of Energy

NATURAL GAS RESERVES

Global natural gas reserves are highly concentrated, with over 50 percent of all reserves found in three countries: Russia with nearly 28 percent of all reserves followed by Iran and Qatar in the Persian Gulf with approximately 15.50 percent each (see Figure 9.10). After the top three, there is a significant fall in the reserves of other countries. Saudi Arabia holds the world's fourth largest natural gas reserves at approximately 4 percent, but that is nearly four times less than Qatar at number three. The United States with 3 percent of all reserves is the first country in the Western Hemisphere to crack the top 10, and Venezuela is number nine at 2.5 percent of global reserves. As we have seen over the last couple of decades, the political environment in Iran is volatile, as is that of Russia to a lesser degree. That means greater uncertainly for investors in and traders of natural gas, and that uncertainly leads to more risk and greater reward potential.

Figure 9-10. Natural Gas Reserves by Country

Rank	Country	Percentage of Total Global Reserves
1	Russia	27.5%
2	Iran	15.4%
3	Qatar	14.9%
4	Saudi Arabia	3.9%
5	United Arab Emirates	3.5%
6	United States	3.2%
7	Nigeria	2.9%
8	Algeria	2.6%
9	Venezuela	2.5%
10	Iraq	1.8%

SOURCE: CIA World Factbook

GLOBAL NATURAL GAS CONSUMPTION

In 1980, total global consumption of natural gas was 53 trillion cubic feet. Ten years later consumption had risen sharply to 73 trillion cubic feet, an advance of approximately 37 percent. This trend has continued, and in 2007 total global natural gas consumption rose to 108 trillion cubic feet. The U.S. Department of Energy projects that natural gas will experience the greatest increase in demand of all energy fuels over the next 20 years. Coal is second on the list. By 2025, it is projected that 156 trillion cubic feet will be needed to quench the thirst for natural gas throughout the world. This increase of 44 percent, or 48 trillion cubic feet, means opportunities for those brave enough to invest in the natural gas market. Figure 9.11 shows natural gas consumption by country.

Figure 9-11. Natural Gas Consumption by Country

Rank	Country	Percentage of Total Global Consumption
1	United States	22.6%
2	Russia	15.8%
3	Germany	3.6%
4	United Kingdom	3.5%
5	Canada	3.4%
6	Iran	3.0%
7	Japan	3.0%
8	Italy	2.9%
9	Ukraine	2.6%
10	Saudi Arabia	2.3%

SOURCE: CIA World Factbook

GLOBAL NATURAL GAS EXPORTING AND IMPORTING

The countries with the world's largest natural gas reserves also are the largest exporters of natural gas. Russia supplies most of Europe's natural gas needs, although Europe is attempting to diversify by courting Algeria, the country with the eighth largest reserves of natural gas in the world. Iran and Qatar and many other countries with sizable natural gas reserves export their product around the world to places such as the United States and Japan. Before transportation, natural gas is converted into a liquid that is referred to as liquified natural gas (LNG). Without this conversion to liquid form, natural gas could not be transported to far-off places. LNG is loaded into barges and transported to terminals such as the Henry Hub in Louisiana. Once it arrives at a terminal, LNG is piped around the country to residential, industrial, commercial, and transportation and electric generation facilities.

One of the challenges in importing natural gas is the availability of terminals to accept the energy fuel. In late 2007, ExxonMobil announced plans to build a terminal off the coast of Long Island, New York, about seven miles offshore. The idea was to take delivery of LNG at the terminal and then transport the gas in underwater pipes to a station in New Jersey. The placement of the terminal offshore would minimize concerns over environmental damage, avoid aesthetic issues, and lessen terrorist threats since tankers would not come close to populated areas. Even with these grand plans, the project may never get off the drawing board. Figures 9.12 and 9.13 show the top natural gas exporting and importing countries, respectively.

Figure 9-12. Top Natural Gas Exporting Countries

Rank	Country	Percentage of Total Global Exports
1	Russia	26.7%
2	Canada	12.8%
3	Norway	9.3%
4	Algeria	7.5%
5	Netherlands	6.6%
6	Turkmenistan	5.2%
7	Indonesia	4.5%
8	Malaysia	3.6%
9	United States	3.0%
10	Qatar	3.0%

SOURCE: CIA World Factbook

Figure 9-13. Top Natural Gas Importing Countries

Rank	Country	Percentage of Total Global Imports
1	United States	14.8%
2	Germany	11.0%
3	Japan	9.9%
4	Italy	8.3%
5	Ukraine	7.0%
6	France	5.5%
7	Russia	4.5%
8	South Korea	3.5%
9	Spain	3.3%
10	Turkey	2.7%

SOURCE: CIA World Factbook

NYMEX Futures Contract Specifications

Trading Unit (1 Contract): 10,000 million British thermal units (mmBtu)
Price Quotation: U.S. dollars and cents per mmBtu
Minimum Price Fluctuation: $0.001 per mmBtu or $10.00 per contract
Trading Hours:

- *Open Outcry*: 9:00 a.m. to 2:30 p.m.
- *Electronic*: 6:00 p.m. to 5:15 p.m. via CME Globex; Sunday through Friday [*Note: A 45-minute break occurs each day between 5:15 p.m. (current trade date) and 6:00 p.m. (next trade date).]*

Trading Months: Current year and the next five years when a new calendar year is added after termination of trading in the December contract of the current year.
Trading Symbol: NG

Unleaded Gasoline

Since gasoline is a by-product of crude oil, the price of unleaded gasoline is highly correlated with the price of crude oil. That is no surprise to most consumers when they fill up their vehicles with gasoline. However, in the short term the prices of both unleaded gasoline and crude oil can move in somewhat different patterns because of refining operations. Drivers cannot put crude oil in a car and expect it to run; crude oil must be refined into unleaded gasoline and then transported to the local gas station. These extra steps can cause the price of gasoline to rise or fall independently of the price of crude oil. For instance, when there is a significant disruption in refining operations caused by weather—such as Hurricane Katrina in 2005—or equipment breakdowns or accidents, the supply of gasoline will fall and thus drive up prices. In the United States many refiners run at nearly full capacity, and so any shutdown can have a serious impact on the supply of gasoline since other refiners are unable to make up the difference. This is a structural problem that the United States needs to resolve over the next few years. If it does not, there could be multiple future problems. This scenario is positive for traders as it gives them an opportunity to profit from unleaded gasoline.

NYMEX Futures Contract Specifications

Trading Unit (1 Contract): 42,000 U.S. gallons (1,000 barrels)
Price Quotation: U.S. dollars and cents per gallon
Minimum Price Fluctuation: $0.0001 per gallon or $4.20 per contract
Trading Hours:

- *Open Outcry*: 9:00 a.m. to 2:30 p.m.
- *Electronic*: 6:00 p.m. to 5:15 p.m. via CME Globex; Sunday through Friday [*Note: A 45-minute break occurs each day between 5:15 p.m. (current trade date) and 6:00 p.m. (next trade date.)*]

Trading Months: 36 consecutive months on a rolling basis
Trading Symbol: RB

Coal

When people think of energy, they think first of crude oil. However, there is more energy locked inside the total global reserves of coal than there is in all crude oil reserves. Moreover, the coal reserves in the United States alone have more energy potential than all the crude oil reserves in the world. This illustrates the incredible potential coal has to meet energy needs. The major drawback to coal is the substantial amount of climate-changing carbon it emits when burned to generate electric power. The difference between coal and other energy fuels in terms of the emission of carbon is quite significant. Nevertheless, many emerging countries around the world rely on coal to fuel their growing economies. China and India—two countries with sizable coal reserves—are highly dependent on coal to produce energy for their new and expanding factories and technology infrastructure. Unfortunately, cities such as Beijing have incredible amounts of pollution partly caused by the burning of coal. Many countries around the world are responding to the problem of climate change caused by global warming by placing restrictions on the construction of new coal-burning power generation plants. As a result, the future for coal looks mixed at best. If new clean coal

Figure 9-14. Energy Sources for Electric Power Generation in the U.S.

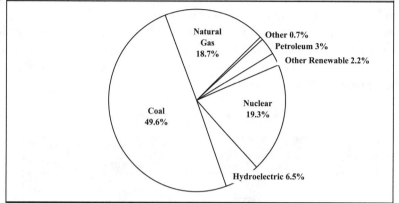

SOURCE: Energy Information Administration, Electric Power Monthly, March 2007

technologies are developed, the awesome potential of coal may be realized. Figure 9.14 lists energy sources for the generation of electric power in the United States.

TYPES OF COAL

There are several different types of coal. The primary differences between coals are the level of sulfur, the amount of ash, and the energy provided per unit. These differences allow coal to be classified into one of four types: lignite, sub-bituminous, bituminous, and anthracite. Lignite is considered the coal with the lowest value because it contains the highest levels of sulfur and ash and the smallest amount of carbon , or energy per unit. The higher the ash and sulfur content, the less desirable the coal. Often referred to as brown coal, lignite is a popular coal for use in electric power generation plants. Sub-bituminous coal is a step up from lignite in that it contains less sulfur and ash and more carbon. This means that sub-bituminous coal is of higher quality and therefore more desirable. The price is higher, reflecting the added desirability. Bituminous coal is found in significant quantities through the United States. Because of its favorable burn temperature and corresponding energy output, bituminous coal is a popular choice for the generation of electric power and for many industrial uses, such as the production of coke needed to make steel. Anthracite coal is by far the preferred choice since it contains the lowest levels of sulfur and ash and the largest amount of energy-generating carbon. Anthracite coal provides the greatest amount of energy per unit of coal.

GLOBAL COAL RESERVES

The United States is home to the world's largest reserves of coal at roughly 27 percent of the total tons. If it were not for this abundant coal supply, the United States

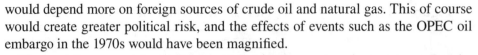

would depend more on foreign sources of crude oil and natural gas. This of course would create greater political risk, and the effects of events such as the OPEC oil embargo in the 1970s would have been magnified.

The next three countries on the top 10 list for the most coal reserves are Russia, China, and India at 17.3, 12.6, and 10.2 percent, respectively. The top four countries control approximately two out of every three tons of coal reserves in the world today (see Figure 9.15).

Figure 9-15. Coal Reserves by Country

Rank	Country	Percentage of Total Global Reserves
1	United States	27.1%
2	Russia	17.3%
3	China	12.6%
4	India	10.2%
5	Australia	8.6%
6	South Africa	5.4%
7	Ukraine	3.8%
8	Kazakhstan	3.4%
9	Poland	1.5%
10	Brazil	1.1%

SOURCE: CIA World Factbook

GLOBAL COAL PRODUCTION

Aside from Russia, the top four countries in the world in terms of coal reserves also are the top producers of coal (see Figure 9.16). Russia is number six in the top 10 list, and Australia rises from number five in total reserves to number three in total production. China leapfrogs the United States and therefore is the number one producer of coal in the world, with the United States in second place. India retains the number four spot, and the smaller European countries Germany and Poland have the eighth and ninth spots. The market in the United States is relatively mature in terms of coal production. In contrast, the markets in China and India are developing to keep pace with expanding economies and the energy needed to fuel their growth.

GLOBAL COAL CONSUMPTION

Decades ago, coal was the standard energy fuel used in electric power–generating plants and in residential homes for heat. Most old homes in the United States have small doors or passageways where coal was delivered. Over the years, natural gas

Figure 9-16. Coal Production by Country

Rank	Country	Percentage of Total Global Production
1	China	36.2%
2	United States	20.8%
3	Australia	7.3%
4	India	6.9%
5	South Africa	5.0%
6	Russia	4.7%
7	Indonesia	3.0%
8	Poland	2.6%
9	Germany	2.0%
10	Kazakhstan	1.6%

SOURCE: CIA World Factbook

was found to be a good substitute for heating homes. In those days, natural gas was more of a nuisance and was burned off during the production of crude oil rather than used as a fuel. Natural gas was a very cost-effective energy fuel when it first came into popular use, and that meant that less coal was needed. However, the popularity of natural gas rose sharply because of its low price and relatively clean burn. Today, natural gas is more expensive, thus driving demand for coal again. The U.S. Energy Administration projects that coal use will rise by almost 40 percent over the next 22 years. If better clean coal technologies are brought to the market, demand could increase even more.

GLOBAL COAL EXPORTING AND IMPORTING

Although there is a global market, coal for the most part is a domestic product because of the excessive transportation costs needed to bring it from the mine to the delivery point at an electric power generation plant. For this reason, most of the coal in the United States and the rest of the world is transported by railroads because of their ability to transport large quantities of coal cheaply. Over time the global market for coal will continue to grow, but it will remain primarily domestic. Europe is slightly different as coal from Germany and Poland can be transported quickly and easily to other European countries by railroads.

NYMEX Futures Contract Specifications

Trading Unit (1 Contract): 1,550 tons of coal
Price Quotation: U.S. dollars and cents per ton
Minimum Price Fluctuation: $0.01 per ton or $15.50 per contract

Trading Hours:

- *Open Outcry*: 9:00 a.m. to 2:30 p.m.
- *Electronic*: 6:00 p.m. to 5:15 p.m. via CME Globex; Sunday through Friday *[Note: A 45-minute break occurs each day between 5:15 p.m. (current trade date) and 6:00 p.m. (next trade date).]*

Trading Months: Current year plus the next three calendar years when a new calendar year is added after the termination of trading in the December contract of the current year.

Trading Symbol: QL

Electric Power

Although electric power is the end product in power generation plants, it is considered a commodity and can be purchased and sold like any other commodity. Electric power—referred to as electricity by consumers and power by those in the commodity trade—is probably the most difficult commodity to trade as there is more to the trading than meets the eye. For instance, there are the issues of congestion and transmission, with both individual components being essential to facilitate the flow of power from one power hub to another. Steering clear of electric power is probably an investor's best approach. Nevertheless, no book on commodities would be complete without at least a brief discussion of electric power.

For experienced traders who are serious about trading electric power, the PJM futures contract on the New York Mercantile Exchange is one of the most heavily traded because of the development of the PJM region. The United States is divided into regions called Regional Transmission Organizations that manage the local electric power grid. The PJM is situated in the upper Midwest and the eastern United States. There are other regions, but the PJM is one of the most mature. Figure 9.17 breaks down energy power production in the United States by commodity.

Figure 9-17. U.S. Electric Power Production by Commodity

Commodity	Percentage of Total Production
Coal	50%
Nuclear	19%
Natural Gas	19%
Hydroelectric	7%
Petroleum	3%
Other Renewables	2%
Other Fuels	1%

NYMEX Futures Contract Specifications

Trading Unit (1 Contract): 40 megawatt hours per peak day (19 to 23 peak days per month), depending on the month. The number of megawatt hours varies between 760 Mwh and 920 Mwh, depending on the number of peak days in the month.

Price Quotation: U.S. dollars and cents per megawatt hour

Minimum Price Fluctuation: $0.05 per megawatt hour

Trading Hours:

- *Open Outcry*: 9:00 a.m. to 2:30 p.m.
- *Electronic*: 6:00 p.m. to 5:15 p.m. via CME Globex; Sunday through Friday *[Note: A 45-minute break occurs each day between 5:15 p.m. (current trade date) and 6:00 p.m. (next trade date).]*

Trading Months: Current year plus the next five calendar years; a new calendar year is added after the termination of trading in the December contract of the current year.

Trading Symbol: JM

Uranium Ore

Uranium ore is the central energy fuel used to run nuclear power plants. In the United States, nuclear power accounts for nearly 20 percent of all electric power production. However, there are some countries in which the use of nuclear power is much greater, especially Japan and France. France generates approximately 79 percent of all its electricity needs from nuclear power. During the 1970s there was a significant global construction of nuclear power plants. Unlike the United States, where production ceased in the 1970s, countries around the world continued to build plants. The construction of new nuclear power plants in the United States was put on hold because of concerns about radiation catastrophes, terrorist threats, and environmental issues concerning depleted nuclear waste rods, a by-product of operating nuclear plants. However, over the last couple of years, as prices for crude oil and natural gas have risen and because the burning of those energy fuels causes climate change, nuclear power plants have come back in vogue. Many nuclear power plants are in the design stage, but it will take several years before any power is generated. This is due to the significant lead time necessary to win regulatory approval and the time needed to construct a plant. The price for uranium ore increased from under $10 per ton in 2002 to over $110 in 2007 as a result of the increased interest in nuclear power. Figure 9.18 shows the use of nuclear power by country.

Figure 9-18. Nuclear Power by Country

Rank	Country	Percentage of Total Power
1	Lithuania	81%
2	France	79%
3	Belgium	56%
4	Slovakia	56%
5	Sweden	51%
6	Ukraine	48%
7	Switzerland	42%
8	Bulgaria	41%
9	Armenia	37%
10	Slovenia	36%

SOURCE: World Development Indicators database

GLOBAL URANIUM ORE RESERVES

Without question, the country with the largest uranium ore reserves is Australia, with approximately one-third of all global uranium ore reserves. The former Soviet republic of Kazakhstan is second on the list, and Canada is number three. The United States enters the list at number eight, but total reserves in the United States are approximately 10 times less than what is found in Australia.

GLOBAL URANIUM ORE PRODUCTION

Canada is king of uranium ore production at approximately 12 million tons per year. Most of the ore mined is transported to the United States since most American utility companies strongly prefer to source ore from Canada. With uranium ore the political stakes are high, and Canada is considered the safest provider for the United States. Second on the top 10 list of global uranium ore producers is Australia, which also is considered a reliable producer. In past years Australia restricted the amount of uranium ore it produced as a way to curtail use of nuclear power. In their judgment, the less uranium ore on the market, the greater the control over the construction and operation of nuclear power plants. This position has changed significantly over the last few years as the impacts to our climate from burning fossil fuels are coming to light. As a result, more favorable provisions regarding the mining of uranium ore are being created.

The two surprises making the top 10 list of the largest global uranium ore producers are Niger and Namibia—both in Africa—at numbers four and six, respectively.

NYMEX Futures Contract Specifications

Trading Unit (1 Contract): 250 pounds of U308
Price Quotation: U.S. dollars and cents per pound
Minimum Price Fluctuation: $0.05

Trading Hours:

- *Open Outcry*: 9:00 a.m. to 2:30 p.m.
- *Electronic*: 6:00 p.m. to 5:15 p.m. via CME Globex; Sunday through Friday
  [Note: A 45-minute break occurs each day between 5:15 p.m. (current trade date) and 6:00 p.m. (next trade date).]

Trading Months: 60 consecutive months
Trading Symbol: UX

Heating Oil

Heating oil is a by-product of crude oil and represents about 25 percent of the yield of a typical barrel, making it the second largest component of crude oil. Heating oil— sometimes called No. 2 heating oil and very similar to diesel fuel—is characterized by its low viscosity and is the preferred energy fuel in building furnaces, commonly called boilers. Most heating oil is transported by delivery truck to consumers in places where natural gas is not available and is stored in above-ground storage tanks (ASTs). However, heating oil is the preferred choice of some consumers even when natural gas is available because the oil produces more energy for the same cost.

NYMEX Futures Contract Specifications

Trading Unit (1 Contract): 42,000 U.S. gallons (1,000 barrels).
Price Quotation: U.S. dollars and cents per gallon.
Minimum Price Fluctuation: $0.0001 per gallon ($4.20 per contract).
Trading Hours:

- *Open Outcry*: 9:00 a.m. to 2:30 p.m.
- *Electronic*: 6:00 p.m. to 5:15 p.m. via CME Globex; Sunday through Friday
  [Note: A 45-minute break occurs each day between 5:15 p.m. (current trade date) and 6:00 p.m. (next trade date).]

Trading Months: 36 consecutive months
Trading Symbol: HO

Quiz for Chapter 9

1. All but which of the following are grades of crude oil?
   a. Sour
   b. Light
   c. Sweet
   d. Harsh

2. Crude oil with lower density typically yields more component fuels.
   a. True
   b. False

3. One NYMEX futures contract for crude oil is worth how many barrels?
   a. 10
   b. 100
   c. 1,000
   d. 10,000

4. Which of the following refers to crude oil with high levels of sulfur?
   a. Sour
   b. Diesel
   c. Sweet
   d. Propane

5. Which country has the largest proven reserves of crude oil in the world?
   a. Iraq
   b. Saudi Arabia
   c. Kuwait
   d. Iran

6. Out of the top 10 countries with the largest proven reserves of crude oil, which is the only European country?
   a. Russia
   b. Spain
   c. Norway
   d. Iceland

7. The Henry Hub in Louisiana is the main point of entry for natural gas imports to the United States.
   a. True
   b. False

8. Over 50 percent of total global natural gas reserves are in three countries. Which of the following is not one of those three?
   a. Russia
   b. Iran
   c. Qatar
   d. Kuwait

9. Which of the following countries has the world's largest reserves of coal?
   a. China
   b. Iran
   c. United States
   d. Russia

10. France generates about what percentage of its electric power needs from nuclear power plants?
    a. 5
    b. 25
    c. 79
    d. 95

CHAPTER 10

Livestock and Agriculture:

MOOving and Growing Your Portfolio

This chapter discusses a set of commodities that are grown and raised rather than mined and extracted. *Livestock* is the term used to describe meat commodities: live cattle, feeder cattle, lean hogs, and pork bellies. Agricultural commodities can be classified either as grains and oilseeds or as softs.

Agricultural and livestock commodities were the first commodities traded and remain the most important because of the need for food. Unlike metals and energy fuels, agricultural and livestock commodities are produced around the world, with typically no market dominated by one or two countries. Moreover, countries have a choice about producing an agricultural or livestock commodity. The same cannot be said for energy fuels or metals, which essentially are or are not found within a country's borders. That is what makes commodities dynamic and the commodities markets complex for investors and traders.

Livestock and Meats

There are four major types of livestock and meats: lean hogs, pork bellies, live cattle, and feeder cattle. The futures contracts that track those commodities are not as popular as those for energy fuels and both precious and industrial metals, but there are opportunities to make money. One of the most important trends in livestock and meats is the increased demand from consumers in countries with increasing economic strength who are improving their lifestyles. However, where there are potential profits, there are potential risks. The most significant drawback to investing in livestock and meats is high volatility and lower liquidity. As a result, investing or trading in these commodities is best for those with high risk profiles.

LEAN HOGS

In 1997 the Chicago Mercantile Exchange established the lean hog futures contract. This contract replaced an older contract that tracked live hogs. The new contract made the market for hogs more efficient since the older contract tracked a commodity—live hogs—that was not really traded. Only the meat of the hog was traded, not the live animal. The new contract did away with the live animal, or preslaughter, and tracks the meat itself, or postslaughter.

Lean hog futures contracts are traded primarily by producers to hedge their exposure to price risk. Most individual investors do not participate in this market. As a result of this dynamic, a lean hogs futures contract is much less liquid than other contracts and therefore exhibits greater price volatility. It does not take a significant volume of trades to move prices.

Global Lean Hog Production

China is far and away the world's largest producer of hogs; the next nine largest producers together do not equal what China produces. However, the demand for pork in China outpaces the supply, and that makes China a net importer of pork. Total global annual hog production is approximately 100 million tons.

The United States is the world's largest exporter of hogs, followed by Denmark, the world's second largest producer of hogs, and then Taiwan. The states with the highest production are Iowa, North Carolina, Minnesota, and Illinois. The biggest market for American lean pork is Japan, with Canada, Mexico, Russia, Hong Kong, Korea, China, and Britain all key export markets. Other major producers of hogs are Brazil, Canada, and Russia.

Hogs generally are sent to slaughter when they reach 250 pounds, a weight that typically takes six to seven months after birth to achieve. On average, a 250-pound hog yields about 90 pounds of lean meat considered good for consumption. Of the lean meat, about 21 percent is ham, 20.3 percent loin, 13.9 percent belly, 10.3 percent picnic, 7.3 percent Boston butt roast and blade steaks, and 3 percent spare ribs. As a result of selective breading, hogs today are roughly 50 percent more lean than were the hogs raised in the 1950s and earlier.

Global Lean Hog Consumption

Although China is the world's largest consumer of pork, it is not the largest consumer on a per capita basis. That honor goes to Denmark. The other four countries that complete the top five list are Spain, Hong Kong, Germany, and Hungary. China is the country with the ninth highest per capita consumption of pork. Canada, the United States, and Britain make the list at numbers 11, 12, and 13, respectively.

CME Futures Contract Specifications

Trading Unit (1 Contract): 40,000 pounds
Price Quotation: U.S. dollars per pound
Minimum Price Fluctuation: $0.0001 per pound ($4 per contract)
Trading Hours (CST): 10:05 a.m. to 2:00 p.m.
Trading Months: February, April, May, June, July, August, October, December
Last Trading Day: Tenth business day of the contract month
Trading Symbol: LH

PORK BELLY (FROZEN)

Pork belly, commonly called bacon, is the underside of a pig and typically weighs 12 pounds. In the United States the underside of a pig is used to make bacon, whereas in most other parts of the world the underside is cut into slabs of meat or steaks. Pork bellies can be frozen and stored for up to 12 months after processing before delivery to customers is made.

The price for pork bellies is dependent on supply and demand for pork and consumer interest in substituting other types of meat for pork.

Pork belly futures contracts were established on the Chicago Mercantile Exchange in 1961 to help processors and storage companies manage volatile hog prices and warehousing risks. Pork belly futures were the first to be based on frozen stored meats. Prices for pork belly futures contracts typically peak in the summer months and bottom in the spring months. Prices are highly susceptible to pork belly inventory in storage and the health-conscious trend among consumers.

CME Futures Contract Specifications

Trading Unit (1 Contract): 40,000 pounds
Price Quotation: U.S. dollars and cents per pound.
Minimum Price Fluctuation: $0.0001 per pound ($4 per contract).
Trading Hours (CST): 9:10 a.m. to 1:00 p.m.
Trading Months: February, March, May, July, August
Trading Symbol: PB

LIVE CATTLE

The Chicago Mercantile Exchange began trading live cattle futures contracts in 1965 to allow cattle producers, meatpackers, consumers, and speculators to hedge and take price risks. Until the introduction of this futures contract, no contract on anything alive existed. Only contracts on energy fuels, metals, and agricultural commodities could be traded.

Cattle are raised for meat, dairy products, leather, and farm work. It has been estimated that there are close to 1.5 billion cattle in the world today. According to a United Nations report from the Food and Agricultural Organization, cattle are responsible for approximately 18 percent of all greenhouse gas emissions from carbon dioxide and methane from feces. Methane is over 20 times more destructive than carbon dioxide.

CME Futures Contract Specifications

Trading Unit (1 Contract): 40,000 pounds
Price Quotation: U.S. dollars per pound
Minimum Price Fluctuation: $0.00025 per pound ($10 per contract)
Trading Hours (EST): 10:05 a.m. to 2:00 p.m.
Trading Months: February, April, June, August, October, December
Last Trading Day: Last business day of the contract month
Trading Symbol: LC

FEEDER CATTLE

Feeder cattle futures contracts were established in 1971 by the Chicago Mercantile Exchange. Feeder cattle are younger cattle that are not ready to make the jump to live cattle status. The typical feeder cow weighs from 650 to 849 pounds; that means that these cattle need fattening before they are slaughtered. To accomplish this, feeder cattle are shipped to feedlots, where they are fattened and made ready for slaughter.

Feeder cattle futures contracts enable livestock producers (ranchers) to hedge their risk exposure with young cattle until they become live cattle. The main risks livestock producers look to hedge are availability of feed, feed costs, weather, shipping costs, conception, and survivability.

Since feeder cattle need time and more feed before they are ready for slaughter, the cost of feed and feeding is an important consideration. If the price for corn rises, the cost for feeder cattle generally increases since it costs more to feed them. However, sometimes the market can have an inverse impact on feed because ranchers sell their feeder cattle at one time, thus flooding the market, to avoid paying higher feed costs.

CME Futures Contract Specifications

Trading Unit (1 Contract): 50,000 pounds
Price Quotation: U.S. dollars per pound
Minimum Price Fluctuation: $0.0001 per pound ($5.00 per contract)
Trading Hours (CST): 9:05 a.m. to 1:00 p.m.
Trading Months: January, March, April, May, August, September, October, November
Last Trading Day: Last Thursday of the contract month (barring holidays)
Trading Symbol: FC

Grains and Oilseeds

This section looks at three of the major agricultural commodities: corn, soybeans, and wheat. Unlike energy fuels and metals, agricultural commodities are very labor intensive and benefit from consumers' increased standards of living, whereas energy fuels and metals depend less on labor and gain from economic and industrial expansion. Agricultural commodities, also referred to as ags, benefit from the long-term trend of population growth and increases in standards of living. Although demand will rise for agricultural commodities, supply is expected not to rise as quickly because of a lack of favorable cropland and the time needed to cultivate and harvest crop yields. The future looks bright for ags.

CORN

Corn, also referred to as maize, is the top agricultural product in the United States in terms of both acres cultivated and total commodity value. Corn originated in Mesoamerica—with most research pointing to southern Mexico—thousands of years ago and quickly was spread to the rest of the world by the Spanish conquistadors in the early sixteenth century. Many countries around the world use the term *maize*. but the United States, Canada, and Australia use *corn* exclusively.

There are four primary uses of corn: as a feedstock, for human consumption, for industrial purposes, and as a source for ethanol fuel. The greatest use of corn is as a feed for livestock, specifically poultry, hogs, and cattle. The second biggest use is for human consumption; corn and corn by-products are found in hundreds of different foods, from cereals to snacks and from sweeteners to bread. Corn by-products are found in many nonfood products as well. However, the use that is experiencing the greatest rise in demand is ethanol production. Many farmers in the United States, especially in the Midwest, are switching to corn to such a degree that water tables in some areas cannot keep pace, and have dropped dramatically.

Corn futures are traded on the Chicago Board of Trade and the Tokyo Grain Exchange. These futures contracts provide farmers, grain processors, ranchers, feedlots, and merchandisers with ways to hedge price risk exposure.

Global Corn Production

Total global production of corn was approximately 692 million tons in 2005. Leading the way was the United States, which accounted for nearly 280 million tons. The next largest corn producer—although producing only half of what the United States produces—was China, accounting for 131 million tons. After China, there is a significant drop to number three, Brazil, which produced about 35 million tons. Other major producers of corn include Mexico, Argentina, India, and Canada (see Figure 10.1).

Figure 10-1. Top Corn Producing Countries

Rank	Country	Percentage of Total Global Production
1	United States	40.5%
2	China	18.9%
3	Brazil	5.1%
4	Mexico	3.0%
5	Argentina	2.9%
6	Indonesia	2.2%
7	France	1.9%
8	India	1.7%
9	South Africa	1.7%
10	Italy	1.6%

SOURCE: United States Department of Agriculture, 2005

Global Corn Consumption

As was mentioned above, there are many uses for corn. As a food product, corn can be consumed as corn on the cob and as cornmeal. Although many countries eat cornmeal, they prepare it slightly differently and use different names. For example, in Italy cornmeal is called *polenta,* whereas in Brazil it is called *angu.* To Americans, eating corn on the cob is a summer tradition, but eating corn on the cob is unheard of in many countries. Figure 10.2 lists the countries that consume the greatest amounts of corn.

Figure 10-2. Top Corn Consuming Countries

Rank	Country	Percentage of Total Global Consumption
1	United States	41.5%
2	China	25.7%
3	Brazil	7.4%
4	Mexico	5.2%
5	Japan	3.2%
6	India	2.5%
7	Canada	2.2%
8	Egypt	2.2%
9	South Korea	1.9%
10	South Africa	1.7%

SOURCE: United States Department of Agriculture

CBOT Futures Contract Specifications

Trading Unit (1 Contract): 5,000 bushels
Price Quotation: U.S. dollars and cents per bushel
Minimum Price Fluctuation: $0.0025 per bushel ($12.50 per contract).
Trading Hours (CST): 9:30 a.m. to 1:15 p.m.
Trading Months: March, May, July, September, December
Last Trading Day: Business day before the fifteenth calendar day of the contract month
Trading Symbol: Open Auction: C; Electronic: ZC

SOYBEANS

Soybeans are native to eastern Asia and thrive in environments with hot summers. Cultivation of soybeans began before the eleventh century BC in eastern China and Korea. Soon afterward soybeans were introduced in many places in Asia, including Japan, Indonesia, Vietnam, Thailand, Malaysia, and the Philippines.

The United States is the world's largest producer of soybeans, accounting for nearly 36 percent of total supply. Soybeans are the third largest crop in the United States behind corn and wheat. Like corn, soybeans are used as a feedstock, for human consumption, for industrial purposes, and as an energy source. As a food source, soy is found in many different foods and is defined by its high protein content of approximately 40 percent. Consequently, many of the foods that contain soy were created to be protein alternatives, such as soy milk and dry soy protein mix. Other food products containing soy are soy burgers, miso, and tofu. Soybeans are used in many industrial products, including soap, ink, solvents, plastics, crayons, and cosmetics. In the United States the consumption of soybean oil exceeds the consumption of all other oils combined.

Soybeans can be classified as vegetables or oils, depending on the extracts produced after processing. The five major postprocessing extracts of soybeans are the following:

- *Soybean meal*: This extract constitutes approximately one-third of the total soybean supply. Most of the soybean meal produced is used in feedlots, but some is processed into soybean flour.
- *Soybean flour*: This extract is made from soybean meal and is the starting material for the production of soy protein isolate because of its 48 percent protein content.
- *Soybean oil*: This extract constitutes about one-fifth of the total soybean supply and sometimes is used to produce ethanol. Soybean oil is used in the production of many culinary products, including cooking oils, mayonnaise, margarine, salad oils, and shortening. Soybean oil consists of 85 percent unsaturated fat and 15 saturated fat. Many liquid industrial products use soybean oil as a base component.
- *Soybean nut butter*: This extract is very similar to peanut butter but uses soybeans as the base component.
- *Infant formula*: Soy is used in infant formula for babies who are lactose-intolerant and allergic to the proteins in cow's milk.

With all the extracts produced from natural soybeans, investors will find futures contracts on soybeans, soybean meal, and soybean oil. The existence of more defined futures contracts on soybeans gives producers and speculators an opportunity to hedge or take price risk.

Global Soybean Production

After the United States, Brazil is the largest producer of soybeans, accounting for roughly 27 percent of total global production (see Figure 10.3). This means that the United States and Brazil dominate the production of soybeans with 63 percent of total supply. Not surprisingly, the United States produces significantly more soybeans than it consumes and therefore exports about one-third of its soybean production.

Figure 10-3. Top Soybean Producing Countries

Rank	Country	Percentage of Total Global Production
1	United States	36.2%
2	Brazil	27.4%
3	Argentina	17.9%
4	China	8.3%
5	India	3.7%
6	Paraguay	2.1%
7	Canada	1.2%
8	Bolivia	1.0%
9	Indonesia	0.4%
10	Russia	0.2%

SOURCE: Production Estimates and Crop Assessment Division, FAS, USDA

Global Soybean Consumption

Although soybeans originated in eastern Asia, they are a basic staple in many countries around the world. The biggest consumer of soybeans is China owing to its huge population and tradition of consuming soybeans. Because of the high protein content and strong health benefits of soy, soybean consumption is expected to increase.

Soybeans: CBOT Futures Contract Specifications

Trading Unit (1 Contract): 5,000 bushels
Price Quotation: U.S. dollars per bushel
Minimum Price Fluctuation: $0.0025 per bushel ($12.50 per contract)
Trading Hours (CST): 10:30 a.m. to 2:15 p.m.
Trading Months: January, March, May, July, August, September, November
Last Trading Day: Business day before the fifteenth calendar day of the contract month
Trading Symbol: Open Auction: S; Electronic: ZS

Soybean Oil: CBOT Futures Contract Specifications

Trading Unit (1 Contract): 60,000 pounds
Price Quotation: U.S. dollars and cents per pound
Minimum Price Fluctuation: $0.0001 per pound ($6.00 per contract)
Trading Hours (CST): 9:30 a.m. to 1:15 p.m.
Trading Months: January, March, May, July, August, September, October, December
Last Trading Day: Business day before the fifteenth calendar day of the contract month
Trading Symbol: Open Auction: BO; Electronic: ZL

Soybean Meal: CBOT Futures Contract Specifications
Trading Unit (1 Contract): 100 tons
Price Quotation: U.S. dollars and cents per ton
Minimum Price Fluctuation: $0.10 per ton ($10 per contract)
Trading Hours (CST): 9:30 a.m. to 1:15 p.m.
Trading Months: January, March, May, July, August, September, October, December
Last Trading Day: Business day before the fifteenth calendar day of the contract month
Trading Symbol: Open Auction: SM; Electronic: ZM

WHEAT

Wheat, along with barley, was one of the first two cereals to be domesticated. Its origins can be traced by archaeological evidence to the Fertile Crescent, present-day Iraq and Turkey, around 10,000 years ago. Wheat cultivation quickly expanded to India, Ethiopia, Spain, and the British Isles, and sometime around 2000 BC wheat cultivation reached China.

Wheat is produced for three primary reasons: as a feedstock (approximately 45 percent of use), for human consumption (approximately 41 percent), and for industrial purposes (approximately 14 percent). In terms of human consumption, the top use for wheat is the production of flour.

Wheat is a popular cash crop for three important reasons. First, it grows well in mild environments even when the growing season is relatively short. Second, wheat produces an ample yield per acre. Third, wheat yields quality flour—wheat flour—that is essential for many popular baking products. However, for the first time in history, acreage devoted to wheat cultivation is declining—even though yields are rising owing to new technologies—as a result of declining population growth rates.

The primary classifications of wheat traded in the United States are hard red spring (primarily used for bread and hard baked goods), hard red winter (primarily used for bread and hard baked goods and as an adjunct to other flour), soft red winter (primarily used for cakes, pie crusts, biscuits, and muffins), hard white (primarily used for bread and brewing), and soft white (primarily used for pie crusts and pastries). Since hard wheats are more difficult to process and red wheats may need bleaching, soft and white wheats typically are priced higher than hard and red wheats.

Investors can purchase futures contracts on wheat on the Kansas City Board of Trade (hard red winter wheat), Minneapolis Grain Exchange (hard red spring wheat), and Chicago Board of Trade (soft red winter wheat), the exchange with the most widely traded wheat futures contracts. Each exchange sets its own rules and has its own contract specifications.

Global Wheat Production

Wheat production is dominated by the top 10 producing nations, which account for over two-thirds of total global production (see Figure 10.4). However, no one or two countries control the entire trade. China is the leading producer of this commodity with over 22 percent of total global production. The next two biggest producers are India and the United States, which produce 17 percent and 16 percent, respectively. The top three producers account for over one-third of total global production. Rounding out the top 10 are Russia, Australia, Canada, Pakistan, Turkey, Argentina, and Kazakhstan. Asia accounts more than 40 percent of total global production, and the leading exporter of wheat is the United States, which accounts for over one-third of all global exports.

Figure 10-4. Top Wheat Producing Countries

Rank	Country	Percentage of Total Global Production
1	China	22.3%
2	India	17.1%
3	United States	16.3%
4	Russia	8.7%
5	Australia	6.1%
6	Canada	5.6%
7	Pakistan	4.7%
8	Turkey	4.4%
9	Argentina	3.5%
10	Kazakhstan	3.1%

SOURCE: United States Department of Agriculture

Global Wheat Consumption

The two nations that consume the most wheat per year are China and India, which have populations of over a billion people each. Next on the list are Russia, the United States, Pakistan, Turkey, Egypt, Brazil, and Ukraine. On a per capita basis, China and India do not make the top 10. At the top of that list is Australia, where the average person eats an amount equal to 110 gallons of wheat per year. Rounding out the top 10 are Russia, Turkey, Canada, Ukraine, Algeria, Iran, Morocco, Egypt, and Pakistan. The United States is eleventh on this list from the U.S. Department of Agriculture.

CBOT Futures Contract Specifications

Trading Unit (1 Contract): 5,000 bushels
Price Quotation: U.S. dollars and cents per bushel
Minimum Price Fluctuation: $0.0025 per bushel ($12.50 per contract)

Trading Hours (CST): 9:30 a.m. to 1:15 p.m.
Trading Months: March, May, July, September, December
Last Trading Day: Business day before the fifteenth calendar day of the
    contract month
Trading Symbol: Open Auction: W; Electronic: ZW

Softs

The commodities that constitute softs are diversified. Softs are defined by seasonal growing patterns—most soft commodities can be grown only during specific times of the year—and are limited to certain geographical areas for cultivation. Many softs, such as coffee, cocoa, sugar, and orange juice, are grown in warm climates and sometimes are referred to as *tropical commodities*. The term *fiber commodity* sometimes is used for cotton.

COCOA

Cocoa is a partially fermented and dried seed from the cacao tree, which grows best within 20 degrees north and south of the equator. Cacao trees, from which cocoa beans are harvested, are indigenous to South America in the Andes region. Research shows that the Mayans, Toltecs, and Aztecs introduced cacao trees to Central America. Cocoa beans were used not only for consumption but also for monetary purposes. Once the Spanish conquistadors arrived, they brought cacao trees back to Europe, the Philippines, and the West Indies, where chocolate was made. Cocoa is traded in both New York—which emphasizes cocoa from Southeast Asia—and London—which emphasizes cocoa from West Africa. Cocoa beans are harvested from the trunks and branches of cacao trees once they have ripened.

Cocoa comes in three different varieties: Forastero, Criollo, and Trinitario. Forastero is the most widely produced cocoa bean in the world with nearly 95 percent of total production. Criollo is considered by many to be the premium cocoa.

Global Cocoa Production

Cocoa is the world's smallest softs commodity market. Today, over 3.5 million tons of cocoa are grown each year worldwide. Although cocoa is indigenous to South America, African countries are now the top producers, with a 70 percent share of total global production (see Figure 10.5). The top producer of cocoa is Ivory Coast in West Africa, accounting for 1.3 million tons each year. Ghana and Indonesia are in the second and third places with 0.72 and 0.44 million tons produced annually, respectively. Cocoa butter and cocoa powder are two of the products derived from cacao trees.

Figure 10-5. Top Cocoa Producing Countries

Rank	Country	Percentage of Total Global Production
1	Ivory Coast	37.4%
2	Ghana	20.7%
3	Indonesia	12.7%
4	Cameroon	5.0%
5	Nigeria	4.6%
6	Brazil	4.5%
7	Ecuador	3.4%
8	Columbia	1.6%
9	Mexico	1.4%
10	Dominican Republic	1.4%

SOURCE: International Cocoa Organization

Global Cocoa Consumption

The top two countries in the world for consumption are the Netherlands and the United States. By far the most popular product from cocoa is chocolate. The emperor of the Aztecs, Montezuma II, is said to have demanded 50 pitchers of cocoa a day.

NYBOT/ICE Futures Contract Specifications

Trading Unit (1 Contract): 10 metric tons (22,046 pounds)
Price Quotation: U.S. dollars per ounce
Minimum Price Fluctuation: $1.00 per ton ($10 per contract)
Trading Hours (EST): 8:00 a.m. to 11:50 a.m.
Trading Months: March, May, July, September, December
Last Trading Day: Eleven business days before the last business day of the delivery month
Trading Symbol: CO or CC

COFFEE

Coffee was discovered in the highlands of Kaffe, Ethiopia, during the ninth century and quickly became one of the most widely consumed beverages in the world. The production of coffee is centered on two different types of coffee beans: Arabica (*Coffea arabica*) and Robusta (*Coffea canephora*). Arabica is the most widely produced coffee bean in the world and is considered the premium bean, making it more expensive than Robusta. Nearly 60 percent of all coffee bean production is accounted for by Arabica. Robusta is not grown as widely but is the bean of choice for coffee companies because of its lower price. Robusta is easier to cultivate than Arabica, can be grown in areas where Arabica does not thrive, and contains approximately 45 percent more caffeine than Arabica. Coffee beans also can be categorized by the regions where they are produced, such as Kona from Hawaii, Java from Indonesia, and Columbian. Other types of coffee beans include *Coffea liberica* and *Coffea esliaca*, both grown in Africa.

Global Coffee Production

Many countries rely so heavily on producing and exporting coffee beans that it has become the top agricultural export for 12 countries (see Figure 10.6). Brazil is by far the world's largest producer and supplies more than two times as much coffee as the second largest producer, Vietnam. Columbia is the third largest producer of coffee, ahead of number four Indonesia. For the most part, Arabica coffee beans are grown principally in Latin America, Arabia, western Africa, and select parts of Asia. Robusta coffee beans are grown in southeastern Asia, western and central Africa, and select areas in Brazil.

Figure 10-6. Largest Coffee Producing Countries

Rank	Country	Percentage of Total Global Production
1	Brazil	28.8%
2	Vietnam	13.6%
3	Colombia	10.6%
4	Indonesia	6.0%
5	Ethiopia	4.9%
6	India	4.1%
7	Mexico	3.7%
8	Guatemala	3.4%
9	Honduras	3.0%
10	Peru	2.7%

SOURCE: International Coffee Organization

Global Coffee Consumption

Four companies dominate the coffee trade and often are referred to in the industry as the Big Four. Accounting for over 50 percent of the coffee trade, these companies are Kraft, Nestlé, Sara Lee, and Procter & Gamble. The Big Four companies prefer Robusta coffee beans because of its lower price. Smaller companies focus on the high-end coffee trade and therefore typically offer Arabica coffee beans.

On a per capita basis, Norway is the largest consumer of coffee; the average person there consumes nearly 11 kilograms per year. Next on the list are the Scandinavian countries Finland, Denmark, and Sweden. The first non-European country to make the list of top coffee consumers per capita is the United States at number 12, where the average person consumes about 3 kilograms per year.

NYBOT/ICE Futures Contract Specifications

Trading Unit (1 Contract): 37,500 pounds
Price Quotation: U.S. dollars per pound
Minimum Price Fluctuation: $0.0005 per pound ($18.75 per contract)
Trading Hours (EST): 8:30 a.m. to 12:30 p.m.
Trading Months: March, May, July, September, December
Last Trading Day: Eight business days before the last business day of the delivery month
Trading Symbol: KC

COTTON

Cotton, the most widely used natural fiber for clothing, is a soft staple fiber that has been used by people throughout the world for over 7,000 years and traded for over 3,500 years. Cotton use can be traced back 7,000 years in the Americas and 6,000 years in India, from which it later spread to Mesopotamia. Although cotton was cultivated in both regions of the world, different varieties were produced independently of one another.

The preferred varieties—*Gossypium hirsutum* and *Gossypium barbadense*—of cotton originated in the Americas and have longer and stronger fibers. Today most of the cotton cultivated around the world consists of the American varieties. Cotton is a relatively easy commodity to cultivate since it can grow nearly everywhere as long as two conditions are met: The cotton must be in an environment with 200 frost-free days per year, and water must be available as cotton is a very thirsty crop.

Natural cotton is highly dependent on pesticides to safeguard against destruction by pests and weeds. Unfortunately, pesticides are expensive and bad for the environment. As a result, genetically modified cotton was developed and is now the leading type of cotton cultivated in the United States, although it is still the minority cotton in the world. Genetically modified cotton requires over 75 percent less pesticide than does natural cotton. Organic cotton is natural cotton produced without the application of pesticides.

Global Cotton Production

Over 75 countries produce cotton to some degree, with total global annual production of $12 billion. The top producers of cotton are China, the United States, India, and Pakistan. China consumes most its harvest of cotton, whereas India produces cotton as an export commodity. The largest exporter of cotton is the United States, which accounts for approximately $5 billion in annual supply. This figure is somewhat misleading since the cotton trade is subsidized in the amount of $2 billion per year. The South Plains area of the United States is the largest continuous cotton-cultivating area in the world. Texas, Arkansas, Georgia, and Mississippi are the major producing states in that order. Other leading exporters of cotton include Brazil and Turkey (see Figure 10.7).

Figure 10-7. Largest Cotton Producing Countries

Rank	Country	Percentage of Total Global Production
1	China	29.0%
2	United States	19.9%
3	India	14.2%
4	Pakistan	9.5%
5	Brazil	5.0%
6	Turkey	4.8%
7	Greece	1.9%
8	Syria	1.5%
9	Australia	1.5%
10	Mali	1.2%

SOURCE: United States Department of Agriculture

Global Cotton Consumption

Most cotton is consumed by the textile industry to produce clothing and household products. Some of the major products created from cotton are denim, terrycloth, chambray, and corduroy. Other applications include paper printing, coffee filters, and livestock feed.

Synthetic fibers have been slowing the appetite for natural and genetically modified cotton. Nylon, acrylic, and polyester are the major synthetic fibers that have caused the demand—and therefore the production—of cotton to slow. Not all countries in the textile trade are involved in the production of cotton. Many countries import the cotton they need. Some of the major nonproducing countries that import cotton are Taiwan, Bangladesh, and Indonesia.

NYBOT/ICE Futures Contract Specifications

Trading Unit (1 Contract): 50,000 pounds
Price Quotation: U.S. dollars per pound
Minimum Price Fluctuation: $0.0001 per pound ($5 per contract)
Trading Hours (EST): 10:30 a.m. to 2:15 p.m.
Trading Months: March, May, July, October, December
Last Trading Day: Seventeen business days before the end of the spot month
Trading Symbol: CT

ORANGE JUICE

Oranges are widely grown in most warm climates throughout the world and are the primary fruit crop in the United States. Oranges are thought to have originated in southern China, Vietnam, or India. The main varieties are Persian, Valencia, navel, and blood.

Oranges have been consumed for hundreds of years, but only as a fresh fruit because they are perishable and difficult to transport. As a result, the solution of creating frozen concentrated orange juice (FCOJ) was developed in 1945 in Florida. There are two futures contracts that track frozen concentrated orange juice: the FCOJ-A contract for Brazil and the United States and the FCOJ-B contract for the rest of the world. The two major commodities exchanges for trading FCOJ are the New York Board of Trade and the Brazilian Mercantile and Futures Exchange.

As with other agricultural commodities, FCOJ prices are influenced by weather conditions. Freezing temperatures and hurricanes can have drastic impacts on Florida orange crops and can cause prices to shoot up nearly overnight. Consequently, investors need to remain cautious and vigilant to safeguard their investments in FCOJ.

Global Orange Production

The largest producer of oranges is Brazil, accounting for twice the production of the number two producer, the United States. In the United States, the state of Florida is the leading producer of oranges, although a sizable amount comes from California. Brazil produces approximately 18 million tons annually, and the United States produces about 8.3 million tons. Other top producers include Mexico, India, Italy, China, and Spain. Since nearly all the oranges harvested in the United States are consumed domestically, Brazil is the dominant player in the export trade, accounting for about 80 percent of supply.

Global Orange Consumption

Oranges are eaten fresh, canned, and squeezed for juice to produce frozen concentrated orange juice and canned orange juice. Over 70 percent of oranges are processed into orange juice in the United States. Other uses include sweet orange oil, orange blossom honey, and marmalade. Once it is thawed, frozen concentrated orange juice is mixed with water to create reconstituted juice; it is the most widely consumed form of orange juice in the world.

NYBOT/ICE Futures Contract Specifications

Trading Unit (1 Contract): 15,000 pounds
Price Quotation: U.S. dollars per pound

Minimum Price Fluctuation: $0.0005 per pound ($7.50 per contract)
Trading Hours (EST): 6:00 a.m. to 12:30 p.m.
Trading Months: January, March, May, July, September, December
Last Trading Day: Fourteenth business day before the last business day of the month
Trading Symbol:

- FCOJ-A (Florida/Brazil): OJ
- FCOJ-B (World): OB

SUGAR

The production of sugar started many thousands of years ago in southeastern Asia and quickly spread throughout the world, including the New World during the early stages of colonization. Throughout history, sugar has been used as a food sweetener and for medicinal purposes. The word *sugar* is derived from the Sanskrit *sharkara*, and sugar is considered a basic food carbohydrate.

There are two primary sources of refined sugar—sugarcane and sugar beets—and three types of sugar: sucrose, lactose, and fructose. Sugar is also present in maple syrup (sugar maple) and sorghum. Sugarcane is cultivated more widely than sugar beets and accounts for about 70 percent of global supply. The cultivation of sugar beets is more recent than the cultivation of sugarcane, which can be traced as far back as 12,000 years ago. In contrast, beet roots were found to hold sugar in the eighteenth century.

The single largest cost component of producing and refining sugar is energy. To increase sugar harvests and reduce labor costs, many producers rely on mechanical equipment, which increases energy cost risk exposure. Sugar is also one of the leading sources for the production of ethanol fuel, with corn being the other major source.

Investors have two futures contracts alternatives for making an investment in sugar. The first futures contract is the Sugar #11 contract, which emphasizes world sugar, and the second is the Sugar #14 contract, which emphasizes U.S. sugar. The Sugar #11 contract is more widely traded on the New York Board of Trade, and the Sugar #14 contract typically is traded at a higher price.

Global Sugar Production

Most sugarcane is grown in India, Cuba, and Brazil—the world's largest sugar producer—and sugar beets are grown principally in Asia, Europe, and Australia. Both sugar beets and sugarcane are produced in the United States, where most sugarcane is cultivated in Hawaii, Florida, and Louisiana, whereas sugar beets are cultivated in California.

As was mentioned previously, the largest producer of sugar in the world is Brazil, accounting for nearly 28 million tons. However, not far behind Brazil is India, which produces approximately 26 million tons per year. After India there is a significant drop-off in production—about 50 percent—to the number three producer, China, at 12.7 million tons and the United States at 11 million tons. Many developing countries place tariffs on the importation of sugar or subsidize domestic production. Total global production of sugar was about 223 million tons in 2005.

Global Sugar Consumption

Sugar is consumed in nearly every country, and on average, approximately 70 percent of the sugar produced in any country is consumed in that country. Sugar derived from sugarcane and from sugar beets is essentially indistinguishable. However, sugar from beets typically is used as an industrial fermentation feedstock or an animal feed. The more pleasant-tasting sugar from sugarcane is used for human consumption.

China and India are the top two consumers of sugar. However, Brazil tops the per capita sugar consumption list because of its use of sugar-based ethanol to fuel automobiles. Mexico, Australia, and Russia complete the list of the top consumers of sugar on a per capita basis. There is a strong positive correlation between sugar consumption and per capita income. Countries with higher per capita incomes tend to have higher per capita sugar consumption because sugar is a nonstaple food and is considered more of a luxury item. Addressing basic food needs is more pressing for people with lower incomes.

NYBOT/ICE Futures Contract Specifications

Trading Unit (1 Contract): 112,000 pounds
Price Quotation: U.S. dollars per ounce
Minimum Price Fluctuation: $0.01 per pound ($11.20 per contract)
Trading Hours (EST): 8:10 a.m. to 12:30 p.m.
Trading Months:

- Sugar #11 (World): March, May, July, October
- Sugar #14 (USA): January, March, May, July, September, November

Last Trading Day: Last business day of the month before delivery month
Trading Symbol:

- Sugar #11 (World): SB
- Sugar #14 (USA): SE

Quiz for Chapter 10

1. All but which of the following are types of livestock futures contracts?
   a. Lean hogs
   b. Pork bellies
   c. Live cattle
   d. Fattened hogs

2. Increasing living standards around the world will result in greater demand for livestock and meats.
   a. True
   b. False

3. Which of the following countries is the largest exporter of lean hogs in the world?
   a. Argentina
   b. United States
   c. Australia
   d. China

4. According to the United Nations report from the Food and Agricultural Organization, about what percentage of total greenhouse gases is attributed to the feces from cattle?
   a. 1
   b. 2
   c. 18
   d. 38

5. The term *ags* refers to which of the following?
   a. Aggregate global supply
   b. Agricultural commodities
   c. Eggs destined for human consumption
   d. Grain and oilseed commodities only

6. Which of the following is the top agricultural crop in the United States?
   a. Wheat
   b. Corn
   c. Soybeans
   d. Oranges

7. Human consumption is the leading use for corn in the United States.
   a. True
   b. False

8. Which of the following commodities can be processed into other tradable commodities, namely, oil and meal?
   a. Soybeans
   b. Wheat
   c. Corn
   d. Oats

9. The top country for the production of coffee produces two times more coffee than does the second biggest producer. What country is the top producer?
   a. Columbia
   b. Jamaica
   c. Brazil
   d. Kenya

10. Which of the following commodities is the largest fruit crop in the United States?
    a. Cocoa
    b. Coffee
    c. Sugar
    d. Oranges

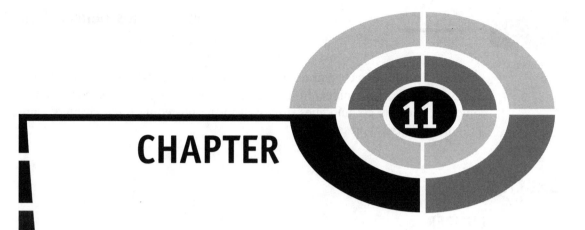

CHAPTER 11

Exotics and Financials:

Unordinary Commodities for Portfolio Profits

As the final entry in this part of the book, this chapter covers commodities that do not fall within the other markets or are traded thinly because of lower demand or because they are relatively new to the market. Nevertheless, some of the less known commodities are presented to ensure that all the major world commodities are discussed. At the end of this chapter there is a discussion of financials such as currencies and indexes. Some authors of books on commodities omit financials since they are not hard assets or raw materials. They are included in this book since commodity exchanges trade them and they are important financial instruments. In addition, the fact that a commodities exchange trades a financial product is evidence of that product's importance.

The first part of this chapter discusses exotic commodities, and then the chapter covers financial commodities. In light of the lower interest in exotic commodities compared with the commodities discussed in the preceding three chapters, only short discussions are presented.

Exotics

LUMBER

The demand for lumber and other wood products is highly correlated with economic activity. When the economy is growing, the demand for lumber is strong. Conversely, when the economy is weakening, the demand for lumber is weak. There is no better measure of demand than the strength in new residential construction since finished lumber is a major component of any housing project. Unfinished lumber is considered more of a raw material that needs refining before becoming a finished product. Furniture making is one industry that requires unfinished lumber. Finished lumber that is cut to standardized width and depth specifications often is called dimensional lumber, and that category can be divided into softwoods (southern yellow pine, Douglas fir, ponderosa pine, and true firs), hardwoods, engineered lumber (laminated veneer, finger-jointed, manufactured trusses, etc.), and non–North American sizes. Most lumber produced in the United States is softwood.

To invest in lumber, one can purchase Random Length Lumber Futures contracts on the CME or purchase shares of stock in companies involved in the lumber industry. Three of the largest companies are Weyerhaeuser Company (symbol WY), Rayonier (symbol RYN), and Louisiana-Pacific (symbol LPX). All these companies have significant market capitalizations and pay favorable dividends.

The United States is the world's largest producer of lumber, followed by Canada and Russia. Note that lumber sometimes is referred to as timber in some parts of the world.

> **Exchange:** Chicago Mercantile Exchange
> **Trading Unit (1 Contract):** 110,000 board feet
> **Price Quotation:** U.S. dollars
> **Trading Symbol:** LB

RUBBER

Although the bulk of rubber is now produced in Asia, the Para rubber tree is native to Central and South America. The Aztecs and the Maya extracted rubber and used it for many purposes, including rubber balls for competitive games. Other uses by Mesoamericans included rubber shoes, padding, and waterproof clothes.

Today over 70 percent of rubber is produced in three Asian countries: Indonesia, Malaysia, and Thailand. Those three countries, together with other Asian countries such as India, account for over 90 percent of total global rubber production, which was approximately 21 million tons in 2005. The largest consumers are the United States at 14 percent of consumption, Japan at 10 percent, and Germany and France, which together account for 7.5 percent.

There are many household and industrial applications of rubber, with tires and tubes accounting for over 50 percent of total consumption. The remaining demand is divided into many miscellaneous applications, including automobile engine parts, gloves, balloons, rubber bands, textiles, and adhesives.

The four primary exchanges that trade rubber are the Osaka Mercantile Exchange (OME), the Shanghai Futures Exchange (SHFE), the Tokyo Commodity Exchange (TOCOM), and the Singapore Commodity Exchange.

Exchange: Tokyo Commodity Exchange
Trading Unit (1 Contract): 5,000 kilograms
Price Quotation: Japanese yen per kilogram
Trading Symbol: JN

ETHANOL

Ethanol is a flammable and colorless liquid that has many applications. The most widely known application is drinking alcohol. However, the application for ethanol that has been shaking up the energy industry is its use as a fuel, specifically for automobiles. Over the last couple of years, as crude oil prices have risen, interest in ethanol as a fuel has increased sharply because it can reduce energy costs.

Today, many countries around the world are racing to use more ethanol as an energy fuel. Brazil is by far the leader is ethanol fuel; in that country nearly half of all automobiles can run on 100 percent ethanol. To accomplish this, an automobile must have an ethanol-only engine or have a flex engine, which allows it to run on 100 percent ethanol, 100 percent gasoline, or a combination of the two.

The most widely used agricultural products for producing ethanol are sugar and corn. Sugar is the preferred choice since it generates about 10 times more energy than does an equivalent unit of corn. For this reason Brazil is the leader in ethanol fuel. Brazil, together with the United States, accounts for nearly 70 percent of total global production, which was 13.5 billion gallons in 2006.

Unfortunately, there is much speculation among energy experts about how much of a benefit there is from producing and using ethanol. According to the U.S. Department of Agriculture in a report titled *The Energy Balance of Corn Ethanol*, the energy returned—energy supplied minus energy required to produce ethanol—from corn ethanol is about 34 percent. This means that for every $1 in energy costs to produce a unit of ethanol, $1.34 in energy is produced. As was mentioned above, sugar produces a much higher amount of energy. Note that some experts claim that it takes more energy to produce one unit of ethanol than that unit supplies.

For investors looking to add ethanol to their portfolios, investing via the CBOT is the preferred alternative. Other ways to profit from this growing trend include investing in companies involved in growing corn, such as Archer Daniels Midland, and investing in professionally managed funds.

Exchange: Chicago Board of Trade (CBOT)
Trading Unit (1 Contract): 29,000 gallons
Price Quotation: U.S. dollars
Trading Symbol: Open Auction: AC; Electronic: ZE

WOOL

Australia is the world's leading producer of wool, accounting for about 29 percent of total supply. China and New Zealand are the second and third largest producers at 16 percent and 11 percent, respectively. The United States is a relatively small producer of wool; the largest three states for wool production are Texas, New Mexico, and Colorado.

With the introduction of synthetic fibers, production of wool has declined over the last 50 years. By the late 1960s, wool production had experienced a sizable reduction of over 40 percent. Nevertheless, investing in wool is possible through the Australian Securities Exchange, Sydney Futures Exchange, Chubu Commodity Exchange, Osaka Mercantile Exchange, and Tokyo Commodity Exchange.

Exchange: Sydney Futures Exchange (SFE)
Trading Unit (1 Contract): 25,000 kilograms
Price Quotation: Australian dollars
Trading Symbol: OL

SILK

Much like wool, silk is a commodity that is not followed by most investors. However, for those who wish to add more exotic commodities to their portfolios, the option to invest in the silk trade is available. Most silk is produced in Asia, with China accounting for nearly 69 percent of total supply. The two other Asian countries that produce silk in significant quantities are India and Japan, each accounting for a little over 11 percent of total global supply. The largest importers of silk are Italy, Japan, India, and South Korea. Italy accounts for approximately 14.5 percent of total global demand.

Raw silk is traded on the Kansai Agricultural Commodities Exchange (KANEX) in Japan. Dried cocoons are traded on the Chuba Commodity Exchange (CCE) in

Japan. Raw silk is scheduled to trade on the National Commodity and Derivatives Exchange in India and the Shanghai Futures Exchange in China.

Financials

EMISSIONS ALLOWANCE CREDITS

Carbon dioxide (CO_2) is responsible for much global warming and climate change. Most experts agree that without a reduction in greenhouse gases, climate change will go from theory to fact. Carbon dioxide measurements taken at Mauna Lau in Hawaii have confirmed the buildup of CO_2 over the last 45 years. According to measurements, in 1960 atmospheric carbon dioxide stood at about 305. Since that time the reading steadily increased to 375 in 2005.

There are two ideas for limiting and eventually reducing the amount of carbon dioxide emissions released into the atmosphere. The first idea is to place hefty taxes on companies that emit more CO_2 gases than they are permitted to. The hope is that companies will be motivated to control their CO_2 emissions to ensure they are not hit with the penalty tax. Unfortunately, this plan has a major flaw because companies could consider the tax a part of doing business and pay it instead of installing emissions reduction equipment. As a result, CO_2 emitted in the air may not decline as companies simply pay the tax and avoid the costs associated with capital improvements to reduce emissions.

The second and significantly more intelligent plan is to employ what can be referred to as a cap and trade system. Under this system there is a ceiling on the amount of CO_2 that an entire country can emit. Companies are given individual emissions limits and credits that permit the release of gases. If a company does not emit as much gases as it has credits for, it can sell those credits to companies that are emitting more than they have credits to emit. If there are more companies that need to buy credits because they are emitting over their allowance, the price for credits increases, and that will motivate some companies to reduce emissions to enable the selling of credits, whereas others would be forced to cut emissions since they could not afford the high credit price. A cap and trade system is ideal for limiting the amount of CO_2 and would foster an efficient market in which companies attempt to reduce emissions to meet their allowance or free up credits to sell on the open market.

This market is still relatively young, and there will be growing pains over the next few years. In the United States a market has developed in Chicago called the Chicago Climate Exchange (CCX). The CCX is entirely voluntary at this time, but the buying and selling of credits can be executed on the exchange in anticipation that the government one day will require a cap and trade system.

Exchange: Chicago Climate Exchange (CCX)
Trading Unit (1 Credit):

- Vintage 2009 and earlier: 1 ton, or 2,000 pounds
- Vintage 2010 to 2014: 0.5 ton, or 1,000 pounds

Price Quotation: U.S. dollars

CURRENCIES

The Chicago Mercantile Exchange was the first exchange to create currency futures, having done so in 1972 after fixed exchange rates were abandoned together with the gold standard. A currency futures contract is an agreement between two parties to exchange one currency for another currency at a preestablished exchange rate with a defined settlement date. Settlement dates are the third Wednesday in March, June, September, and December, and most contracts have an average term of three months. If a futures contract is held to settlement, delivery of each currency to the other counterparty is made. Any gain or loss on the exchange rate between the two currencies is embedded in the currencies and thus is received at settlement. However, most currency futures do not settle physically but are closed with an off-setting currency futures contract. The typical futures contract is inclusive of interest amounts.

In 2005 the total notional value of currency futures traded each day was over $40 billion. Today there are many options for investors and traders to participate in the foreign exchange market. Figure 11.1 lists select currencies on which futures can be traded on the Chicago Mercantile Exchange.

Figure 11-1. Foreign Currency Futures

Listed on the Chicago Mercantile Exchange	
Australian Dollar	Korean Won
Brazilian Real	Mexican Peso
British Pound	New Zealand Dollar
Canadian Dollar	Norwegian Krone
Czech Koruna	Polish Zloty
Euro FX	Russian Ruble
Hungarian Forint	South African Rand
Israeli Shekel	Swedish Krona
Japanese Yen	Swiss Franc

Exchange: Chicago Mercantile Exchange (CME)
Trading Unit (1 Contract): Depends on the currency
Price Quotation: U.S. dollars

INDEXES

If you watch CNBC or Bloomberg TV in the morning, you most likely hear the morning journalists talk about futures trading up and futures trading down. Online news sites report the same numbers. What exactly are they talking about? The journalists are talking about futures contracts on the major indexes, specifically the Dow Jones Industrial Average (DJIA), Standard & Poor's 500, and NASDAQ–100. These indexes serve as the underlying exchanges for futures contracts, which represent a legally binding agreement between two parties to pay or receive the difference between the expected price for the underlying index when the trade was executed and the actual price at contract expiration.

Index futures contracts trade with a multiplier that increases the value of the contract and adds leverage to the trade. The multiplier depends on the index futures contract; the DJIA is $10, the NASDAQ–100 is $100, and the S&P 500 is $250. Thus, for every 1-point change in the DJIA, the futures contract will change by $10. Likewise, for every 1-point change in the S&P 500 and NASDAQ, the futures contracts will change by $250 and $100, respectively. As for the notional value of a total futures contract, if the Dow was at 13,000, one contract would equate to $130,000 (13,000 × $10, the multiple).

The DJIA futures contract is traded on the Chicago Board of Trade, with trading beginning at 8:20 a.m. Eastern Standard Time (EST). Both the S&P 500 and the NASDAQ–100 futures contracts trade on the Chicago Mercantile Exchange, with trading beginning at 8:30 a.m. EST. Since trading for all three futures contracts begins a good hour before the equities market opens for trading, investors are able to get a better perspective on how the market is going to open: higher, lower, or flat.

The primary differences between purchasing the index outright and purchasing a futures contract on an index are the following:

- Futures contracts owners do not have to invest the full amount of the position, whereas purchasing the index outright requires full payment or partial payment along with borrowing.
- Futures contracts are naturally leveraged and do not charge interest, whereas a partial purchase of the index outright will cause interest to be charged on the borrowed funds.
- Futures contracts do not participate in cash dividends, whereas owning the stock does allow for the receipt of cash dividends.

DJIA Futures Contract

Exchange: Chicago Board of Trade (CBOT)
Multiplier: $10 is common, but a $5 (mini) and a $25 (BIG) also exist
Trading Unit (1 Contract): $10 × DJIA index
Contract Months: March, June, September, and December
Price Quotation: U.S. dollars
Trading Symbol: Open Auction: DJ; Electronic: ZD

S&P 500 Futures Contract

Exchange: Chicago Mercantile Exchange (CME)
Multiplier: $250
Trading Unit (1 Contract): $250 × S&P 500 stock price index
Contract Months: Eight months in the March quarterly cycle; March, June, September, December
Price Quotation: U.S. dollars
Trading Symbol: SP

NASDAQ–100 Futures Contract

Exchange: Chicago Mercantile Exchange (CME)
Multiplier: $100
Trading Unit (1 Contract): $100 × NASDAQ–100 index
Contract Months: Five months in the March quarterly cycle
Price Quotation: U.S. dollars
Trading Symbol: ND

In addition to the S&P 500 and NASDAQ–100 futures contracts, the Chicago Mercantile Exchange trades the following index futures contracts:

- MSCI Emerging Markets Futures
- S&P 500 MidCap 400
- S&P 600 SmallCap 600
- Russell 2000
- Nikkei 225
- S&P Asia 50 (E-mini)
- NASDAQ Biotechnology (E-mini)

RATES

Rates, otherwise known as interest rates, are one of the most widely traded commodities. Rates are interest rate futures in which the underlying security is a debt instrument, for example, long-term instruments such as T-bonds and T-notes and short-term instruments such as Fed funds and eurodollars. The Chicago Board of Trade emphasizes long-term interest rate futures, and the Chicago Mercantile Exchange emphasizes short-term interest rate futures.

The first interest rate futures contract—a GNMA (Government National Mortgage Association, or Ginnie Mae)—was developed in 1975 by the Chicago Board of Trade to enable individuals and institutional investors to manage fixed-income risk and optimize fixed-income performance. Since their establishment, interest rate futures have grown in complexity and gained in popularity.

The value of an interest rate futures contract is dependent on prevailing interest rates. When interest rates rise in the marketplace, the value of interest rate futures contracts will fall. Likewise, interest rate futures contracts will rise when prevailing interest rates fall. Interest rate futures and prevailing interest rates have an inverse relationship. As a trader, if you believe prevailing interest rates will fall, you will purchase, or go long, an interest rate futures contract. If prevailing rates fall as anticipated, you will gain. However, if prevailing rates rise, you will lose money. Institutional investors with large holdings of fixed-income securities are concerned about interest rates rising because that will cause the market prices for fixed-income securities to drop. To hedge this risk exposure, institutions can go short interest rate futures contracts. As a result, if prevailing interest rates rise, a loss will occur in the fixed-income holdings but a gain will occur in the futures position since you are short—rather than long—the futures contract. The aim is to offset the loss on the holdings with a gain in the futures contract.

Some of the leading interest rate futures contracts are listed below. You can investigate the websites for both the CBOT and CME for contract specifications.

- Chicago Board of Trade
  - 30-year U.S. Treasury bonds
  - 10-year U.S. Treasury notes
  - 5-year U.S. Treasury notes
  - 2-year U.S. Treasury notes
  - 30-year interest rate swaps
  - 10-year interest rate swaps
  - 5-year interest rate swaps
  - 30-day federal funds
- Chicago Mercantile Exchange
  - 13-week T-bills
  - Swap rate futures
  - Eurodollars
  - Euroyens
  - LIBOR
  - Credit Index event contracts

Quiz for Chapter 11

1. The Para rubber tree is native to what part of the world?
   a. West Africa
   b. Middle East
   c. Central and South America
   d. East Indies

2. The demand for lumber and wood products is directly correlated with economic activity.
   a. True
   b. False

3. Which country is the largest producer of ethanol fuel?
   a. Saudi Arabia
   b. France
   c. United States
   d. Brazil

4. Which of the following countries is the leading producer of wool?
   a. New Zealand
   b. Britain
   c. Australia
   d. Argentina

5. Which country accounts for approximately 69 percent of total global production of silk?
   a. Japan
   b. China
   c. Vietnam
   d. Indonesia

6. CO_2 is an acronym for which greenhouse gas?
   a. Carbon oxidation
   b. Carbon dioxide
   c. Methane
   d. Centrifuge elements

7. The New York Board of Trade is the leading commodity exchange in the United States for emissions allowance credits.
   a. True
   b. False

8. What was the catalyst that made trading foreign currencies possible?
   a. OPEC demanded more dollar purchasing power.
   b. Central banks needed easy access to dollars.
   c. Fixed exchange rates were abandoned with the gold standard.
   d. The World Bank required all members to adopt fixed exchange rates.

9. All but which of the following are the leading indexes for futures contracts trades?
   a. NASDAQ–100
   b. Dow Jones Industrial Average
   c. New York Stock Exchange Total Market
   d. Standard & Poor's 500

10. All but which of the following are financial commodities?
    a. Treasury bonds
    b. Interest rate swaps
    c. Eurodollars
    d. Collateral mortgage obligations

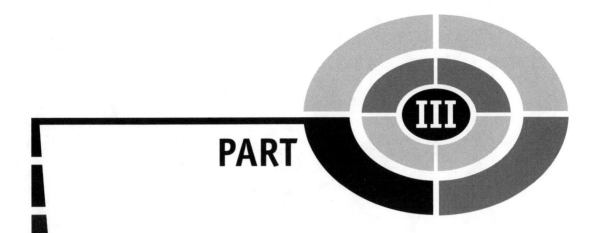

PART

III

Demystifying Commodity Investing and Trading

CHAPTER 12

Mutual Funds:

Using a Conventional Approach to Invest in Commodities

Mutual funds offer investors a conventional approach for adding commodities to their portfolios. With mutual funds, investors do not have to worry about picking individual stocks or becoming knowledgeable about futures and options on futures, two of the more difficult investing instruments in the financial marketplace today. Mutual funds offer diversification and instant exposure to the commodities market an investor is targeting. Investing in mutual funds that target the commodities market makes sense for many investors, particularly those who want to entrust the management of their accounts to others because of lack of expertise, minimal time to do research and place trades, or little desire to manage their own portfolios. Mutual funds can be the right approach for many investors looking to add commodities to their portfolios rather than trade commodities outright.

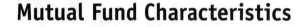
Mutual Fund Characteristics

There are two types of mutual fund categories you should know about: traditional commodity mutual funds and index-based commodity mutual funds. There are four primary differences between the two categories:

- Investment management style (active versus passive)
- Investment holdings (stocks versus futures)
- Costs (higher versus lower)
- Risk-return profile (higher versus lower)

INVESTMENT MANAGEMENT STYLE

The most important difference between traditional commodity mutual funds and index-based commodity mutual funds is investment management style. Traditional mutual funds employ an active style, which means the fund managers focus on security selection—stock picking—and market timing. The aim of active management is to pick stocks at the right times that will generate returns that outperform an appropriate benchmark index. In contrast, index-based commodity mutual funds employ a passive style, which means that no decision making is done in an attempt to outperform the benchmark index. Instead, the fund tracks a certain index and generates a return that mirrors that benchmark.

INVESTMENT HOLDINGS

Traditional mutual funds buy and sell stocks of commodity-related companies much like any other non-commodities-related mutual fund. Conversely, index-based commodity mutual funds do not hold stocks but instead hold futures and options on futures. Although the holdings may differ, each type of fund provides investors with exposure to and a means to invest in commodities.

COSTS

This is another area in which the two types of mutual funds differ greatly. Because of their active investment management style, traditional commodity mutual funds charge approximately two to three times the fees that index-based commodity mutual funds charge. Index-based funds use computers to track their indexes, whereas actively managed funds have a full staff of mutual fund managers and research analysts who command top compensation.

RISK-RETURN PROFILE

Traditional mutual funds typically have more risk than index-based funds, but they have a higher return potential. Traditional mutual funds exist only because they offer the potential to outperform the market. At the same time, they have higher risk than index-based funds since they are actively managed, and that means you must depend on the skills of the manager rather than simply earning the return of the market. The higher risk and the higher return potential are both a benefit and a drawback, but more on that below.

Benefits of Mutual Funds

Investing in mutual funds provides six primary benefits not available to those who purchase individual stocks of companies involved in the commodities trade: instant exposure to commodities in the market the fund is targeting, diversification, better asset allocation, professional management, the ability to make an initial investment with a minimal amount, and greater access to opportunities in the commodities markets.

INSTANT EXPOSURE

When you purchase a commodity mutual fund, you buy a proportional share of every company held by that fund regardless of the number of companies. Thus, if the mutual fund holds 25 commodity-related companies, you automatically and instantly became an equity owner of each of those companies. For this reason, you gain instant exposure to a broad spectrum of companies, from energy to precious metals and from industrial metals to transportation companies. Furthermore, when you make subsequent investments in the mutual fund, you increase your ownership of each company and gain an even bigger foothold in the commodities markets in which each company operates.

DIVERSIFICATION

One of the key benefits of investing in a mutual fund is the diversification of your commodity investment. Most research shows that diversification typically is achieved when you hold 15 or more companies. When you invest in individual companies, you are exposed to two types of risk: company-specific risk and non-company-specific risk. Company-specific risk arises from specific actions of management that are unique to a firm, such as what capital projects to undertake, how much debt to assume, what accounting treatment to employ, and how to advertise the company's products. When things go badly at a company, such as management fraud, the entire company can cease operations; Enron is a real-world example.

These are the risks investors do not want to assume when they invest in commodities. As a result, investing in many companies minimizes the risk that any one company will have a negative impact on your investment. Diversification among your holdings helps minimize your company-specific risk, or the risk inherent in any particular company. The best portfolios not only minimize company-specific risk but for all intents and purposes eliminate it. Unfortunately, investors are typically unable to minimize non-company-specific risk through diversification since investing in multiple companies does nothing to control the ways in which the market can affect a portfolio. There are strategies that many hedge funds employ to control market risk, such as selling short a market index fund. Nonetheless, diversification is very important with commodities investing, and mutual funds offer this benefit.

BETTER ASSET ALLOCATION

Not to be confused with diversification, which deals only with companies in a single sector such as energy, asset allocation is about dividing your investment among the different commodities markets. Thus, if you invest in a mutual fund that holds only energy companies, your investment will be diversified but not properly allocated since you will have omitted other commodities markets, such as precious metals and industrial metals. The more commodities markets you invest in, the better your asset allocation and the more ideal your risk and return profile. Since you never know which type of commodity is going to outperform or underperform, investing in multiple commodities markets is often the best decision an investor can make. Over time, one commodity market will perform well while another market does not. Often, however, commodities markets move together, either increasing or decreasing. Nevertheless, investing in more commodities markets will give your portfolio better asset allocation.

PROFESSIONAL MANAGEMENT

When you invest in commodities, you can use the do-it-yourself approach, in which you do all the research and make all the decisions, or employ professionals who have expertise in this area. Investing in commodities companies is not the same as investing in blue-chip companies. You must be more skilled and spend more time researching companies, markets, and trends when you invest in commodities companies. This self-directed approach will save you money since you will not have to pay someone else to do it for you, but it is not for everyone. For the typical investor who simply wants to gain extra exposure to commodities, using a professional manager or index investment is the preferred approach. Mutual funds offer professional management in which the managers are skilled at determining what is occurring in the commodities markets and which companies are best positioned to benefit from opportunities. Managers have contacts in the field and have vast amounts of information available to them. Of course professional management can be both a benefit and a drawback, depending on the manager. The drawback of professional management is discussed in the following section. All the same, employing the help of a professional manager or investing in an index investment is best for most commodities investors.

INVESTOR-FRIENDLINESS

Most commodity mutual funds have initial investment minimums under $5,000, which is quite manageable. For some investors $5,000 may be prohibitive; however, investing in commodities is not for everyone, especially those with small portfolios. Investors with limited investable capital should consider traditional investments such as an S&P 500 index fund before they invest in commodities. Each mutual fund company has its own minimum requirements, which often vary from $1,000 to $5,000. These minimum amounts are in sharp contrast to most other professionally managed portfolios, specifically hedge funds, managed futures funds, and separately managed accounts (SMAs), which can have minimums of $1 million or more. For investor-friendly provisions, mutual funds are very difficult to beat.

GREATER ACCESS TO INVESTMENT OPPORTUNITIES

When you pool your money with other investors, you gain access to some investments that you would not be able to purchase if you invested by yourself. Some of these opportunities include initial public offerings (IPOs) and structured debt. Although this benefit is more important with noncommodity mutual funds, there are some circumstances in which it can be a nice bonus. This benefit is something to keep in mind when you are trying to decide between mutual fund investing and do-it-yourself investing.

Drawbacks of Mutual Funds

Unfortunately for investors, mutual funds have drawbacks. The most important ones are the fees and expenses incurred by investing in a mutual fund. Since these investments are actively managed by a money manager, high fees are charged to the investors. The average traditional mutual fund charges an annual expense ratio of over 1 percent, whereas the average index-based fund or exchange-traded fund assesses about half that amount. As long as performance offsets the higher expenses, investors need not worry. However, when performance is lower than that of a low-cost passive investment, investors should wonder what they are paying for. The following are the major drawbacks of mutual funds.

HIGH FEES

The biggest knock against mutual funds is the high fees they charge investors for professionally managing their money. Many commodities mutual funds assess an annual fee in excess of 1.00 percent or 1.50 percent. Thus, if you earn 10 percent in a mutual fund that charges a 1.40 percent fee, you pay 14 percent of your gain for investing in that fund. Let's take this example further. If you earned 2.80 percent in your fund, you are given a bill for 50 percent of the earnings you have made. Note that if your fund losses money, you still have to pay the fee. Taking a loss in your account and paying someone on top of that for poor performance is an obvious problem inherent in mutual funds. Many investors and financial advisors do not invest in mutual funds because of the high fees and instead employ index-based mutual funds or exchange-traded instruments such as exchange-traded funds (ETFs) and exchange-traded notes (ETNs). With mutual funds, there is one rule that you must be aware of and consider before you invest: A mutual fund must demonstrate its worth by beating an appropriate benchmark after taking into consideration fees and early capital gains distributions. If a mutual fund can accomplish this objective, it is adding value. However, if it is not accomplishing this objective, you should pass on making an investment and seek out another mutual fund or invest in a commodity index.

CAPITAL GAINS

Investors in mutual funds and other pooled investments are exposed to capital gains in one of two ways. First, when investors sell a portion or the full mutual fund position at a gain, they are responsible for capital gains on the difference between the sales price and the cost basis. Thus, if you sell a position for $125,000 with a cost basis of $90,000, you will be required to pay taxes on the gain of $35,000. The second way investors are exposed to capital gains occurs when mutual funds distribute capital gains to their shareholders at the end of the year. During the course of the year, mutual funds purchase and sell stock. If a mutual fund sells a position that has had a gain, capital gains distributions must be made to the shareholders. Mutual funds are required to make distributions of capital gains and losses since these are considered pass-through investments. If mutual funds did not distribute capital gains and losses, they would be taxed on their capital gains and losses.

Mutual funds make these distributions at the end of the year—typically in December—to shareholders of record as of a certain date before the distribution date. Therefore, if you held a certain mutual fund as of the date of record, you would receive any capital gains or losses that mutual fund distributed. Nearly all mutual funds attempt to minimize capital gains distributions by offsetting against capital losses or transferring the stock to another mutual fund within the same mutual fund family rather than selling it outright. Transferring accomplishes the goal of eliminating the position from the mutual fund without selling it and incurring a capital gains consequence. When investors receive capital gains distributions, they receive them in cash that is paid into their accounts or reinvested in the fund. The price for the mutual fund adjusts for the cash distributed; thus, there is no opportunity for investors to purchase the fund simply to obtain the cash distribution.

Index mutual funds and exchange-traded instruments generally do not generate capital gains consequences the way traditional mutual funds do. Since a dollar is worth more today than it is worth tomorrow, deferring capital gains tax consequences is highly desirable. Because of their operational structure, exchange-traded instruments—namely, exchange-traded notes—offer the best way to avoid capital gains tax consequences from annual distributions. Before you invest in any mutual fund, investigate the fund's turnover as this is an indication of how much in capital gains will be distributed. The higher a fund's turnover, the greater the probability that a fund will generate capital gains and distribute those capital gains to shareholders at the end of the year.

MARKET UNDERPERFORMANCE

If you had two choices of investments, option A, which generated a return of 10 percent and assessed an annual fee of 1.25 percent, and option B, which generated a return of 11 percent and assessed an annual fee of 0.50 percent, which one would you select? The obvious answer is option B. With this example, option A is a typical mutual fund and option B is an equivalent index fund. Much research has been done on money managers and how well they perform against an appropriate benchmark. Most research has concluded that the majority—approximately 80 percent—of money managers do not outperform their benchmarks. Furthermore, money managers who do outperform their benchmarks in any specific year have a lower probability of outperforming that benchmark the next year. Over any holding period there will be some money managers who outperform their benchmarks, but most will not. The number of money managers who outperform the market will be no greater than predicted by standard mathematical probability. It is simply the law of large numbers accompanied by statistical outliers.

So what does this mean to you as a potential commodities investor? It means that you need to do your homework about each mutual fund before you invest. Secondarily, it means that you should consider whether investing in a mutual fund is the smart choice or whether you should invest by using an index-based mutual fund or exchange-traded fund or note.

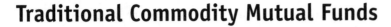
Traditional Commodity Mutual Funds

Traditional commodity mutual funds are the same as any other mutual fund, with one obvious difference. The difference is the types of stocks a commodity mutual fund holds: commodity companies exclusively. By investing in a traditional commodity mutual fund, you gain instant exposure to the commodity sector you are targeting, diversification across that sector, and professional management in an area that requires unique knowledge of the markets and the companies that operate in those markets.

There are three primary types of traditional commodity mutual funds available to investors: natural resources funds, precious metals funds, and energy fuels funds.

NATURAL RESOURCE FUNDS

Unlike precious metals funds and energy fuels funds, natural resource mutual funds do not target a specific commodity sector. These funds can invest in energy fuels companies, precious metals companies, or any other company that is directly or indirectly involved in commodities. As a result, a natural resource fund offers investors a means to participate in other commodities, such as grains, softs, livestock, and lumber. This means a more balanced approach to commodities investing with less risk but a lower return potential compared with a more narrowly defined energy fuels and precious metals funds. However, many natural resource funds hold considerable positions in energy fuels and some have positions in precious metals, albeit lower. Consequently, investigate a fund's holdings before investing. Some of the leading natural resources funds are listed in Figure 12.1.

Figure 12-1. Natural Resources Mutual Funds

Fund	Ticker Symbol	Minimum Investment	Expense Ratio	Assets
BlackRock All-Cap Global Resources Inv A	BACAX	$1,000	1.31%	$460 M
Fidelity Select Natural Resources	FNARX	$2,500	0.85%	$3.01 B
Franklin Natural Resources A	FRNRX	$1,000	1.03%	$837.07 M
Ivy Global Natural Resources A	IGNAX	$500	1.31%	$6.12 B
Jennison Natural Resources A	PGNAX	$2,500	1.19%	$2.09 B
Putnam Global Natural Resources A	EBERX	$500	1.23%	$671 M
T. Rowe Price New Era	PRNEX	$2,500	0.63%	$8.2 B
U.S. Global Investors Global Resources	PSPFX	$5,000	0.94%	$1.69 B

PRECIOUS METALS FUNDS

For investors looking to invest in precious metals without gaining more exposure to energy companies through a diversified natural resources fund, a precious metals fund could be the answer (see Figure 12.2). Although there are a number of funds to choose from, they come with a drawback: fewer commodities for the mutual fund to invest in. The difference is small but is something to be aware of. Most precious metals funds invest only in gold, silver, platinum, and other precious metals, whereas some include industrial metals.

Figure 12-2. Precious Metals Mutual Funds

Fund	Ticker Symbol	Minimum Investment	Expense Ratio	Holdings
Vanguard Precious Metals and Mining	VGPMX	$10,000	0.35%	39
American Century Global Gold Inv	BGEIX	$2,500	0.67%	83
U.S. Global Investors World Precious Mineral	UNWPX	$5,000	0.99%	258
Tocqueville Gold	TGLDX	$1,000	1.50%	83
USAA Precious Metals and Minerals	USAGX	$3,000	1.21%	61
Rydex Precious Metals Inv	RYPMX	$2,500	1.26%	27
AIM Gold & Precious Metals Inv	FGLDX	$1,000	1.41%	34
U.S. Global Inv Gold and Precious Metals	USERX	$5,000	1.28%	79
Fidelity Select Gold	FSAGX	$2,500	0.87%	110

ENERGY FUELS FUNDS

Energy fuels mutual funds (see Figure 12.3) provide investors with considerable exposure to energy companies that are directly or indirectly involved in commodities. These funds allow investors to take advantage of anticipated bull markets in the energy sector. As with other traditional commodity mutual funds, before you make an investment, make sure that a fund's historical performance is worth the extra costs over a low-cost passive index investment such as index-based funds or exchange-traded instruments such as ETFs.

Figure 12-3. Energy Fuels Mutual Funds

Fund	Ticker Symbol	Minimum Investment	Expense Ratio	Holdings
AIM Energy Inv	FSTEX	$1,000	1.17%	43
Fidelity Select Energy	FSENX	$2,500	0.89%	88
Fidelity Select Energy Services	FSESX	$2,500	0.88%	58
Fidelity Select Natural Gas	FSNGX	$2,500	0.89%	71
Guinness Atkinson Global Energy	GAGEX	$5,000	1.45%	40
ICON Energy	ICENX	$1,000	1.17%	69

Index-Based Commodity Mutual Funds

Unlike traditional commodity mutual funds, index-based commodity mutual funds do not employ active management. Instead, they tie the performance of their funds to one or more commodity indexes, whether broad-focused or narrowly focused. The first index-based mutual fund was established in 1997 by Oppenheimer as the Oppenheimer Real Asset Fund. It took nearly five years before the next index-based fund was established: the PIMCO Commodity Real Return Fund in 2002. Since that time additional money managers have entered the business and established their own index-based mutual funds, such as the Credit Suisse Commodity Return fund and the ProFunds Short Precious Metals fund.

In response to a recent IRS ruling, some money managers now employ structured notes instead of financial swaps to gain exposure to the commodity indexes they track. In the judgment of the IRS, financial swaps are not technically securities and therefore are not "qualifying income" but instead are financial agreements to exchange, or swap, money at a future date given either a fixed or a variable payment schedule.

The following section provides a list of index-based commodity mutual funds. If you are interested in investing in commodities through a passive indexed approach, you should investigate exchange-traded instruments. The most popular of these instruments are exchange-traded funds and exchange-traded notes. Chapter 13 provides a detailed discussion of this approach to investing in commodities.

AVAILABLE INDEX-BASED COMMODITY MUTUAL FUNDS

Credit Suisse Commodity Return Strategy (Symbol CRSAX)

This index-based commodity mutual fund tracks the Dow Jones-AIG commodity benchmark index, using commodity-linked derivatives and fixed-income securities.

Direxion Commodity Bull 2X (Symbol DXCLX)

This index-based commodity mutual fund is designed to move twice as fast as the index it tracks, the Morgan Stanley Commodity Related Index. Thus, when that index is up 1 percent, the mutual fund will be up 2 percent. The opposite is true when the index is down 1 percent. The index mutual fund is composed of over-the-counter derivates and exchange-traded funds.

DWS Commodity Securities (Symbol SKNRX)

This index-based commodity mutual fund tracks three different indexes to create a more diversified and balanced fund: the Goldman Sachs Commodity Index, the

MSCI World Materials Index, and the MSCI World Energy Index. Half the fund is allocated to the GSCI, and the remaining 50 percent is allocated evenly between the two MSCI indexes.

Oppenheimer Real Asset (Symbol QRAAX)

This index-based commodity mutual fund primarily tracks the Goldman Sachs Commodity Index but also attempts to gain additional exposure to individual commodities through futures and options trading. It also employs leverage to enhance the returns of the GSCI.

PIMCO Commodity RealReturn Strategy (Symbol PCRAX)

This index-based commodity mutual fund tracks the performance of the Dow Jones-AIG index and uses Treasury Inflation Protected Securities and other fixed-income securities to manage its collateral.

ProFunds Short Oil & Gas (Symbol SNPIX)

This index-based commodity mutual fund tracks the inverse performance of the Dow Jones U.S. Oil & Gas Index. That means that the fund will experience a gain when the index is down and experience a loss when the index is up. The strategy of the fund is to deliver a 100 percent inverse correlation to the index fund.

ProFunds Short Precious Metals (Symbol SPPIX)

Similar to the ProFunds Short Oil & Gas fund, this index-based commodity mutual fund tracks the inverse performance of the Dow Jones U.S. Precious Metals Index. That means that the fund will experience a gain when the index is down and a loss when the index is up. Its strategy is to deliver a 100 percent inverse correlation to the index fund.

Evaluating Commodity Mutual Funds

If you have decided that investing in commodities through mutual funds is your preferred choice, how can you identify the proper fund? There are several key considerations you should investigate before making the initial investment. Because of the popularity and regulation of the mutual fund industry, finding information on any specific fund is relatively quick and easy. Some of the best websites for obtaining information are Yahoo Finance and Morningstar, but there are others as well. The following are the important considerations to investigate before investing in a specific commodity mutual fund.

OBJECTIVE

All mutual funds have a stated objective, such as to invest in out-of-favor S&P 500 stocks or invest in real estate investment trusts with high dividend yields. With commodities, some mutual funds may have the objective of investing in a broad basket of commodities companies, whereas others may have the objective of investing only in a narrowly defined basket of commodities companies, such as precious metal miners. Knowing what you are investing in is the first step with any type of investing program.

HOLDINGS AND DIVERSIFICATION

Once you have made sure the mutual fund's objective is a good fit with your goals and objectives, reviewing the latest holdings will provide some insight into how well the fund adheres to its objective and how well diversified it is. If the objective calls for a broad-based diversified approach to commodities investing but the data show a significant bias toward energy companies, the fund is straying from its stated objective. If there are few holdings compared with other mutual funds, perhaps the fund is not as diversified as it should be.

FUND MANAGER TENURE

As a rule of thumb, longer fund manager tenures are better than short tenures. All else being equal, you want a manager who has experience investing in the fund's target objective market and is knowledgeable about the holdings in the fund. Some studies have concluded that manager tenure and fund performance are correlated. Thus, the longer the fund manager's tenure, the better the prospects for good performance.

FEES AND EXPENSES

One of the significant drawbacks of mutual funds is the fees and expenses shareholders must pay. The most significant expense a shareholder pays when investing in a mutual fund is the management fee. This fee is assessed to compensate the fund manager for his or her professional management services. A fund's expense ratio captures the management fee plus a couple of smaller expenses, such as the 12b–1 fees that are paid to financial advisors as compensation for investing their clients' money. Another significant fee is the up-front or deferred sales loads that "loaded" funds charge, which can be anywhere from 1 percent to 5.50 percent. Many fund families charge one-time account fees to shareholders as well. All else being equal, avoid funds with high fees and seek out funds with low fees, specifically targeting no-load funds.

MANAGER'S STRATEGY

Although mutual funds typically have one objective, there are many different strategies a fund manager can employ to accomplish that objective. For example, a mutual fund may have a high-yield dividend objective, whereas each of 10 different managers will have his or her own strategy to meet that objective. Identifying a manager's strategy is not an easy task, but you can get some information by reading the fund's prospectus.

SHARE CLASS

The typical mutual fund offers multiple share classes. This means that although you will invest in the same fund, you have extra options for how you want to pay fees and expenses. Each share class is identical to the others except for the expense structure. The A share class charges an up-front load or commission, and the B share class charges a back-end or deferred sales load for early redemption. Share class C is sold by financial advisors to enable them to put more of your money in their pockets, whereas the remaining shares are less popular and typically are targeted to institutional investors. If you are investing in a load mutual fund, be careful about selecting the right share class. Personally, I would exercise extreme caution with investing in both A and C share classes.

PERFORMANCE

One of the most important considerations in investing with a money manager is performance, both relative and absolute. Relative performance is used to measure how well or poorly a money manager is doing against his or her competition. Thus, when a money manager is generating returns of 10 percent and industry peers are generating returns of 3 percent, that money manager is considered to have strong relative performance. However, absolute performance does not measure a money manager against industry peers. Instead, money managers are measured by their frequency of generating positive returns. For example, over a three-year period money manager A generates returns of 6 percent, 8 percent, and 1 percent and money manager B generates returns of 22 percent, 3 percent, and −17 percent. Money manager A clearly has better absolute performance since all three years of returns are positive. Although money manager B demonstrates strong performance in years 1 and 2, year 3 is a disaster. Often it is better to experience lower positive performance than to have strong and weak performances in consecutive years.

TURNOVER

Turnover measures how often the composition investments in a mutual fund are purchased and sold during the year. Turnover creates capital gains tax consequences when investments with gains are sold. Thus, high-turnover mutual funds typically have more chances to sock you with a capital gains tax bill than does a mutual fund with low turnover. Low turnover does not mean you will earn a higher return on your investment; it simply means that all else being equal, it is generally more advantageous to invest in a mutual fund with low turnover than one with high turnover.

MINIMUM INVESTMENT REQUIREMENT

Many mutual funds require a certain minimum investment from shareholders to invest in their funds because each shareholder, regardless of the amount invested, adds new costs to the mutual fund, such as monthly statements and postage to mail prospectuses. The fact that someone invests $1 million with a mutual fund does not mean that the costs to service that shareholder are 10 times higher than those for a shareholder who invests $100,000. As a result, mutual funds establish a minimum investment to ensure that each shareholder invests enough to cover those expenses. The minimums are actually quite low and should not present problems for the vast majority of investors.

SIZE

One of the primary drawbacks to investing in mutual funds is the potential problem of having too much money in a fund and not being able to invest it properly. Over time as more and more investors commit money to a particular mutual fund, that fund becomes too big to generate the returns it earned when it was smaller and more nimble and could take advantage of investment opportunities with relative ease. One of the best examples of this dilemma is the Magellan Fund from Fidelity Investments. Managed by the legendary money manager Peter Lynch, this fund generated strong performance when fund assets were at a manageable level. Once investors recognized the strong returns the fund was generating, they began to invest in Magellan at increasing rates. Many financial experts say those capital inflows were too much for the fund to handle, and the returns the investors were accustomed to earning no longer were generated. Why does this occur? The reason is that funds get too large and cannot put the money to work in the same manner or with the same strategy they traditionally used. That is not to say that the opportunities disappeared completely, only that the opportunities are only so large and even a modest investment from a titanic fund will exploit that opportunity fully.

Quiz for Chapter 12

1. All but which of the following are considered primary mutual fund characteristics?
   a. Investment management style
   b. Investment holdings
   c. Costs
   d. Performance incentive fees

2. Traditional mutual funds employ active management rather than passive management.
   a. True
   b. False

3. All but which of the following are considered benefits of commodity mutual funds?
   a. Low cost
   b. Instant exposure to commodity classes
   c. Diversification
   d. Professional management

4. All but which of the following are considered drawbacks to commodity mutual funds?
   a. Year-end capital gains distributions
   b. High fees
   c. Diversification
   d. Only for high-net-worth investors

5. All but which of the following are types of commodity mutual funds?
   a. Natural resource funds
   b. Precious metals funds
   c. Livestock funds
   d. Energy fuels funds

6. Which of the following commodity classes typically is overweighted in commodity mutual funds?
   a. Agricultural and livestock
   b. Energy fuels
   c. Precious metals
   d. Exotics

7. Commodity mutual funds typically hold futures contracts on commodities rather than stocks of commodity companies.
   a. True
   b. False

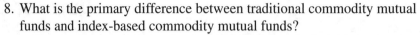

8. What is the primary difference between traditional commodity mutual funds and index-based commodity mutual funds?
   a. Index-based mutual funds provide less exposure to commodities.
   b. Index-based mutual funds track the performance of a commodity index, whereas traditional mutual funds do not.
   c. Establishing traditional mutual funds no longer is permitted by the SEC.
   d. Traditional mutual funds have lower turnover of holdings.

9. All but which of the following are important considerations in evaluating a commodity mutual fund?
   a. Objective
   b. Fees and expenses
   c. Performance
   d. Margin provisions

10. Absolute performance is used to measure the performance of one mutual fund manager against his or her peer group.
    a. True
    b. False

CHAPTER 13

Exchange-Traded Instruments:

The ABCs of ETFs, ETNs, and CEFs

This chapter discusses three ways investors can invest in commodities by using a passive management approach: exchange-traded funds (ETFs), exchange-traded notes (ETNs), and closed-end funds (CEFs). Each has advantages and disadvantages, but all offer unique benefits: stocklike tradability, low costs, high tax efficiency, favorable diversification, and immediate asset class exposure. This means, all else being equal, that you will maximize the performance of your portfolio while controlling and managing risk and will keep more of your money rather than pay unnecessary management fees and face unfavorable tax consequences.

The majority of this chapter covers exchange-traded funds because of their popularity and importance for building optimal portfolios. Exchange-traded notes are a newer investment product and therefore are emphasized less. Closed-end funds have been around much longer than the other two investment instruments but are not used as widely. Finally, the chapter provides brief introductions to two other types of exchange-traded instruments HOLDRS (holding company depositary receipts) and TRAKRS (total return asset contracts).

Exchange-Traded Funds

Exchange-traded funds are stocks that trade on organized stock exchanges such as the American Stock Exchange (AMEX) with the aim of generating a return that mirrors a predetermined index such as the Goldman Sachs Commodity Index. ETFs can be purchased and sold like any stock during trading hours, can be purchased using leverage, and can be sold short. Exchange-traded funds track nearly all the indexes in the marketplace today, including many you may not have heard about. Many investors believe so strongly in the power and benefits of ETFs that they build their entire portfolios with them and avoid individual company stocks. For a commodities investor, ETFs can be a smart way to gain exposure to commodities markets through a low-cost and high-tax-efficiency approach. There are many broadly focused ETFs that track the overall commodities market without differentiating among energy fuels, agriculture, and metals, and there are many narrowly focused ETFs that target specific commodities markets such as silver and gold. Figure 13.1 lists the largest ETF providers.

Figure 13-1. Largest ETF Providers

Asset Manager	ETF Series
Barclays Global Investors	iShares
Powershares Capital Management	Powershares XTF
Vanguard Funds	VIPERS
State Street Global Advisors	streetTracks
Merrill Lynch	HLDRS

DIFFERENCES BETWEEN COMMODITY MUTUAL FUNDS AND EXCHANGE-TRADED FUNDS

Commodity mutual funds and exchange-traded funds appear to be quite similar in that both try to track a certain segment of the commodities market, such as energy or basic materials. In addition, there are enough types of both commodity mutual funds and exchange-traded funds for an investor to gain exposure to nearly every corner of the commodities markets. However, there are some important differences between the two investments that may make you decide to use exchange-traded funds rather than mutual funds. The three most important differences are the following:

- Stocklike tradability
- Low cost
- High tax efficiency

Note that these are only three of the primary benefits of exchange-traded funds, with the other two being ideal diversification and immediate asset class exposure. Exchange-traded funds provide ideal diversification since each share typically represents every product or company operating in that market.

STOCKLIKE TRADABILITY

The most important difference and the selling point for exchange-traded funds over mutual funds is their stocklike tradability. With mutual funds, an investor places an order to buy or sell shares of the fund and the transaction is executed at the end of the day, when the markets are closed and the fund is valued with revised prices from its collective investments. The same is not true of exchange-traded funds, which can be transacted any time the market is open. The six attributes of stocklike tradability are as follows:

- Intraday trade executions
- Selling short
- Purchasing on margin
- Employing options
- Market price transparency
- Types of execution orders

Intraday Trade Executions

As was mentioned above, exchange-traded funds permit investors to buy or sell an investment any time the markets are open. Thus, if you wish to add an energy ETF to your portfolio at the ringing of the opening bell, you have that ability. Furthermore, you can sell the ETF whenever you want and therefore do not have to wait for the market close, when the selling price may not be what you thought, as sometimes happens with mutual funds.

Selling Short

This attribute refers to the option investors have to borrow shares of an ETF and then sell them in the open market. Afterward the investor will purchase an equal number of shares of the ETF—preferably at a lower price—and return them to satisfy the borrowing. This means that investors can profit when the price of an ETF is falling since they essentially sell high and then buy low. This is not possible with mutual funds.

Purchasing on Margin

For investors looking to purchase more of a particular ETF without investing more capital, purchasing on margin provides an alternative. When you purchase on margin, you are borrowing money from your brokerage firm and using that money to buy more shares of stock. As long as the return on the stock is higher than the interest charged on the borrowed money, you benefit. However, if the stock falls in value or does not generate a return at least as high as the borrowing costs, you lose money. Leveraging is another term for purchasing on margin. The stakes go up when you purchase on margin, but so does the potential reward.

Employing Options

Options provide investors with more investing alternatives, and that is always a good thing. Although options do not trade on mutual funds, they do trade on ETFs. These options can be used to hedge or speculate, depending on the side of the market on which you are. Options can increase portfolio risk but also can generate nice returns. Unless you are familiar with options, it is best not to get involved with them and instead use the other alternatives at your disposal.

Market Price Transparency

One of the biggest knocks against mutual funds is their inherent limited market price transparency. In other words, investors do not know with confidence what price they will receive when they purchase or sell their shares since prices are not established until the market is closed and valuation work is performed. ETF investors do not face that challenge; market prices are known through the day since ETFs are traded on organized exchanges. This means that when you decide to execute a transaction, you will receive confirmation quickly about the price at which you purchased or sold the shares and the total cost or proceeds.

Types of Execution Orders

With mutual funds, you can place purchase or sale orders; it does not get any more complex than that. With ETFs, you can place many different types of orders just as you can with stocks. For instance, if you want to place a limit order, a stop order, or a good-till-canceled order, you can do that. If you are a more sophisticated investor and like placing stop limit orders, you can do that with ETFs. What does this mean to you and other investors? It means that you have more options for getting the best execution for your purchase or sale order, and that typically means money saved.

LOW COST

Most mutual funds charge a fee whenever investors purchase or sell them. This transaction fee is front-loaded, meaning the charge is assessed when you purchase the fund, or back-end-loaded or deferred, meaning the charge is assessed if you sell the fund within a certain period, commonly five years. These fees commonly are referred to as loads and can range from 1 percent to 5 percent or even more. Exchange-traded funds do not charge these fees, and therefore the investor is assessed only the commission on the transaction. This commission ranges but typically is not too high because of the availability of discount brokers. Some mutual funds do not charge loads and thus are called no-load funds. If you decide to invest in a mutual fund, you should consider no-loads first.

A second type of fee that investors in mutual funds and exchange-traded funds incur is investment management fees, commonly expressed as expense ratios. These fees are assessed on a pro rata basis each trading day and are used to compensate for the active or passive management of the investment. On balance, mutual funds typically charge higher investment management fees than do exchange-traded funds. Always keep in mind that small differences in fees can add up to big money over the years. Figure 13.2 shows expense ratios for ETFs.

Figure 13-2. Exchange-Traded Funds Expense Ratios

Asset Class	Average ETF Expense Ratio	Number of ETFs
Broad Market	0.39%	26
Commodity	0.70%	17
Currency	0.45%	14
Emerging Markets	0.63%	20
Fixed-Income	0.20%	27
Global and International	0.51%	80
Large Cap	0.37%	49
Mid Cap	0.35%	27
Small Cap	0.39%	31

SOURCE: Yahoo.com

TAX EFFICIENCY

Capital gains taxes can have a significant impact on a portfolio and its performance. All else being equal, it is better to defer taxes to future years than to pay them in today's dollars. The reason for this is that the present value of $1 today is more than the value of that dollar in the future as a result of inflation and loss of purchasing power.

Mutual funds are notorious for their poor tax efficiency. When a mutual fund sells a collective investment, any gain generated from that sale must be distributed to shareholders in the form of capital gains tax consequences. At tax time, investors have to pay taxes to Uncle Sam, thus reducing their investment performance. Even if you did not sell your investment in a mutual fund, you can incur capital gains tax consequences from the passing down of gains from the fund. This rarely happens with exchange-traded funds because of their tax-friendly structure. When an ETF redeems shares of a collective investment, those shares are considered to be sold to another investor in the ETF instead of being sold outright and creating a taxable event. An ETF can create capital gains tax consequences when it is forced to alter the composition of its collective holdings because of a change in the index it is tracking, as occurs when one company is dropped from an index and replaced with another company. This ideal tax efficiency gives exchange-traded funds a nice advantage over most mutual funds.

Types of Commodity Exchange-Traded Funds

Commodity exchange-traded funds can be divided into four primary groups, depending on which indexes they track. Some ETFs track broadly focused markets such as the Goldman Sachs Commodity Index, but the vast majority track narrowly focused markets such as U.S. energy. The more broadly focused an ETF is, the greater the exposure to all commodities you will receive. Furthermore, more broadly focused ETFs have less risk than their narrowly focused counterparts, although with less return potential. You cannot separate risk from return.

COMMODITY FUTURES INDEX ETFS (BROADLY FOCUSED)

PowerShares DB Commodity Index Tracking Fund (Symbol DBC)

This ETF tracks the Deutsche Bank Liquid Commodity Index, which is composed of 55 percent energy, 22.5 percent agriculture, and 22.5 percent metals. This ETF holds futures positions in the collective investments and invests the collateral in short-term bonds.

iShares GSCI Commodity-Indexed Trust (Symbol GSG)

This ETF tracks the Goldman Sachs Commodity Index, which is composed of 78.7 percent energy, 10.4 percent agriculture, 6.1 percent industrial metals, 3.0 percent livestock, and 1.8 percent precious metals.

COMMODITY STOCK INDEX ETFS (NARROWLY FOCUSED)

Vanguard Energy ETF (Symbol VDE)

This ETF tracks the Morgan Stanley Capital International (MSCI) U.S. Investable Market Energy Index, an index of stocks of U.S. companies within the energy sector.

Vanguard Materials ETF (Symbol VAW)

This ETF tracks the Morgan Stanley Capital International (MSCI) U.S. Investable Market Materials Index, which consists of companies in the metals, mining, chemical, paper/forest, and construction materials fields.

Select SPDR Materials (Symbol XLB)

This ETF tracks the S&P Materials Select Sector Index, which is composed of S&P 500 companies involved in the production of chemicals, construction materials, containers and packaging, mining products, and paper/forest products.

Select SPDR Energy (Symbol XLE)

This ETF tracks the return of the companies in the S&P 500 involved in the exploration and production of oil, natural gas, energy-related equipment, and energy-related services.

iShares Dow Jones U.S. Energy (Symbol IYE)

This ETF tracks the Dow Jones Oil & Gas Index, which is composed of companies involved in the production of oil and natural gas and companies involved in oil equipment, oil services, and distribution.

streetTRACKS SPDR Metals & Mining (Symbol XME)

This ETF tracks the S&P Metals & Mining Select Industry Index, which is composed of a diversified group of mining companies.

streetTRACKS SPDR Oil & Gas Exploration & Production (Symbol XOP)

This ETF tracks the S&P Oil & Gas Exploration & Production Select Industry Index.

streetTRACKS SPDR Oil & Gas Equipment & Services (Symbol XES)

This ETF tracks the S&P Select Oil & Gas Equipment & Services Index.

i Shares S&P North American Natural Sector Index (Symbol IGE)

This ETF tracks the Goldman Sachs Natural Resources Sector Index, which is composed of companies involved in the production of energy fuels, timber, paper/pulp, mining products, and plantation products.

iShares S&P Global Energy (Symbol IXC)

This ETF tracks the S&P Global Energy Sector, which is composed of companies engaged in oil exploration, oil production, oil refining, and the provision of oil equipment and services.

iShares Dow Jones U.S. Basic Materials Sector Index Fund (Symbol IYM)

This ETF tracks the Dow Jones U.S. Basic Materials Index, which is composed of companies involved in mining, forestry, and the production of chemicals and paper.

iShares Dow Jones U.S. Oil & Gas Exploration & Production Index (Symbol IEO)

This ETF tracks the Dow Jones U.S. Oil & Gas Index, which is composed of companies involved in the exploration and production of oil and natural gas.

iShares Dow Jones U.S. Oil Equipment & Services Index Fund (Symbol IEZ)

This ETF tracks the Dow Jones U.S. Oil Equipment & Services Index, which is composed of companies involved in the manufacture and sales of equipment and services to oil companies.

PowerShares Dynamic Oil & Gas Services Portfolio (Symbol PXJ)

This ETF tracks the Oil & Gas Services Intellidex, a proprietary index created by PowerShares, an investment company that offers multiple exchange-traded funds, that includes 30 companies involved in oil and natural gas services. This index emphasizes companies with strong fundamentals and takes into consideration timeliness, valuation, and risk.

PowerShares Dynamic Energy Exploration Production Portfolio (Symbol PXE)

This ETF tracks the Energy Exploration & Production Intellidex Index, another proprietary index from PowerShares, which consists of companies involved in the exploration and production of oil and natural gas.

Market Vectors Gold Miners ETF (Symbol GDX)

This ETF tracks the AMEX Gold Miners Index, which is composed of companies listed on the AMEX that have market capitalization of at least $100 million and are involved in the mining of gold and silver.

Market Vectors Steel ETF (Symbol GDX)

Much like the Market Vectors Gold Miners ETF, this ETF tracks the AMEX Steel Index, which is composed of companies listed on the AMEX that are involved in the production of steel.

Market Vectors Agribusiness ETF (Symbol MOO)

This ETF tracks the DAXglobal Agribusiness Index, which is composed of 40 ADRs (American Depositary Receipts) of global companies involved in agricultural products, equipment, livestock, chemicals, and ethanol/biodiesel. This ETF has a reasonable 0.65 percent annual expense ratio.

SINGLE-COMMODITY ETFS (NARROWLY FOCUSED)

iShares COMEX Gold Trust (Symbol IAU)

This ETF tracks the price of gold bullion and derives its exposure to gold by holding gold in vaults.

iShares Silver Trust (Symbol SLV)

This ETF tracks the price of silver and, like the COMEX Gold Trust, gains exposure to silver through the storage of silver in vaults. One share of this ETF is equal to 10 ounces of silver; thus, when the price of the silver changes, so does the value of the ETF.

streetTRACKS Gold Trust (Symbol GLD)

This ETF tracks the price of gold bullion but differs from other gold ETFs because it stores the gold bullion in the investment managers' own vaults. This does not mean that this ETF is a better investment than other gold ETFs; it only makes it different.

United States Oil Fund (Symbol USO)

This ETF tracks the price of West Texas Intermediate (WTI), a light sweet crude oil that is considered the standard for oil.

COMMODITY CURRENCY ETFS (NARROWLY FOCUSED)

Rydex CurrencyShares Canadian Dollar Trust (Symbol FXC)

This ETF tracks the price strength of the Canadian dollar and thus provides a hedge to U.S. companies that export products to or import products from Canada. For instance, companies that import goods from Canada can buy this ETF to offset the appreciation of the Canadian dollar. Additionally, this ETF provides not only opportunities to hedge but also opportunities to speculate on the direction of the Canadian dollar.

Other CurrencyShares ETFs

There are several other CurrencyShares ETFS:

- CurrencyShares Australian Dollar Trust (symbol FXA)
- CurrencyShares British Pound Sterling Trust (symbol FXB)
- CurrencyShares Euro Trust (symbol FXE)
- CurrencyShares Japanese Yen Trust (symbol FXY)
- CurrencyShares Mexican Peso Trust (symbol FXM)
- CurrencyShares Swedish Krona Trust (symbol FXS)
- CurrencyShares Swiss Franc Trust (symbol FXF)

Figure 13.3 lists select commodity ETFs.

Figure 13-3. Select Commodity Exchange-Traded Funds

Name	Ticker	Asset Class	Exp Ratio	Holdings
Claymore MACROshares Oil Down Tradeable Shares	DCR	General	1.60%	-
Claymore MACROshares Oil Up Tradeable Shares	UCR	General	1.60%	-
Claymore/Clear Global Timber Index	CUT	General	0.65%	27
Claymore/LGA Green	GRN	Natural Resources	0.60%	180
Claymore/SWM Canadian Energy Income	ENY	Natural Resources	0.00%	31
Energy Select Sector SPDR	XLE	Energy	0.26%	35
First Trust Energy AlphaDEX	FXN	Energy	0.70%	54
First Trust ISE Water	FIW	Natural Resources	0.60%	36
First Trust ISE-Revere Natural Gas	FCG	Energy	0.60%	29
First Trust NASDAQ Clean Edge US Liquid	QCLN	Natural Resources	0.60%	53
iShares COMEX Gold Trust	IAU	Precious Metals	0.40%	1
iShares Dow Jones US Energy	IYE	Energy	0.60%	87
iShares Dow Jones US Oil & Gas Ex Index	IEO	Energy	0.48%	59
iShares Dow Jones US Oil Equipment Index	IEZ	Energy	0.48%	53
iShares S&P GSCI Commodity-Indexed Trust	GSG	General	0.75%	12
iShares S&P GSSI Natural Resources	IGE	Natural Resources	0.50%	132
iShares Silver Trust	SLV	Precious Metals	0.50%	1
Market Vectors Coal ETF	KOL	Energy	0.65%	-
Market Vectors Environmental Services ETF	EVX	Natural Resources	0.55%	25
Market Vectors Gold Miners ETF	GDX	Precious Metals	0.55%	34
Market Vectors Steel ETF	SLX	Industrial Metals	0.55%	30
Oil Services HOLDRs	OIH	Energy	0.00%	17
PowerShares Cleantech	PZD	Natural Resources	0.60%	48
PowerShares DB Agriculture	DBA	Agriculture	0.91%	18
PowerShares DB Base Metals	DBB	Industrial Metals	0.78%	10
PowerShares DB Commodity Index Tracking Fund	DBC	General	0.83%	20
PowerShares DB Energy	DBE	Energy	0.78%	12
PowerShares DB Gold	DGL	Precious Metals	0.54%	7
PowerShares DB Oil	DBO	Energy	0.54%	5
PowerShares DB Precious Metals	DBP	Precious Metals	0.79%	7
PowerShares DB Silver	DBS	Precious Metals	0.54%	5
PowerShares Dynamic Energy	PXI	Energy	0.60%	61
PowerShares Dynamic Energy Exploration & Production	PXE	Energy	0.66%	30
PowerShares Dynamic Oil & Gas Services	PXJ	Energy	0.64%	30
PowerShares FTSE RAFI Energy	PRFE	Energy	0.75%	52
PowerShares Water Resources	PHO	Natural Resources	0.67%	35
PowerShares WilderHill Clean Energy	PBW	Natural Resources	0.71%	42
PowerShares WilderHill Progressive Energy	PUW	Energy	0.60%	48
Rydex S&P Equal Weight Energy	RYE	Energy	0.50%	35
SPDR S&P Metals & Mining	XME	General	0.36%	26
SPDR S&P Oil & Gas Equipment & Services	XES	Energy	0.36%	23
SPDR S&P Oil & Gas Exploration & Production	XOP	Energy	0.36%	37
streetTRACKS Gold Shares	GLD	Precious Metals	0.40%	1
United States 12 Month Oil	USL	Energy	0.66%	-
United States Natural Gas	UNG	Energy	0.60%	-
United States Oil	USO	Energy	0.65%	3
Vanguard Energy	VDE	Energy	0.25%	154

Exchange-Traded Notes

Similar to ETFs, exchange-traded notes are debt instruments that track the return of a single currency, commodity, or index. ETNs are established with 30-year maturities and are senior, unsecured, unsubordinated debt of Barclays Bank. ETNs are not stocks or index funds but resemble them in many ways, such as trading on an exchange and having the ability to be shorted. Unlike ETFs, ETNs employ an arbitrage strategy by which market prices are linked closely to the intrinsic value of the benchmarks each ETN tracks. The primary advantage of exchange-traded notes is their favorable tax treatment, in which positions held for at least one year are taxed as long-term capital gains and thus are subject to lower tax rates. This is especially important for investors who hold taxable portfolios and wish to gain exposure to specific sectors of the commodities market. No dividend or interest payments are made with ETNs.

Investors who hold exchange-traded notes have three ways to liquidate their investments:

- Sell their positions in the secondary market as one can do with any other stock.
- Redeem the shares with Barclays for cash (typically only for large shareholders).
- Hold to maturity and receive the market value of the position in cash from Barclays.

Figure 13.4 lists the differences between commodity ETFs and commodity ETNs.

TYPES OF EXCHANGE-TRADED NOTES

iPath GSCI Total Return (Symbol GSP)

This ETN tracks the Goldman Sachs Commodity Index much as the ETF version does. However, it tracks the actual index, whereas the ETF version tracks the GSCI Excess Return Index. Regardless of the tracking method, both instruments are of equal value.

iPath Dow Jones-AIG Total Return (Symbol DJP)

This ETN tracks the Dow Jones-AIG Total Return Index, one of the most diversified and broadly focused commodity indexes in the marketplace today.

Figure 13-4. Differences between Commodity ETFs and ETNs

Characteristic	Commodity ETFs	Commodity ETNs
Ability to Sell Short?	Yes	Yes
Composition of Instrument	Portfolio of Securities	Issuer Credit
Continuous Pricing and Trading Throughout the Day?	Yes	Yes
Distribution of Dividends?	Yes	No
Have a Maturity Date?	No	Yes
Have a Net Asset Value (NAV)?	Yes	No
Marginable?	Yes	Yes
Method of Registration and Regulation	Investment Company Act of 1940	Securities Act of 1933
Purchased Through a Traditional Brokerage Account and IRA?	Yes	Yes
Quantity Available	Significant	Few
Risks to Investment	Market Risk	Market Risk and Issuer Credit Risk
Tax Treatment	60 percent long-term capital gains treatment and 40 percent short-term capital gains treatment	Similar to stocks where positions held for longer than one year qualify for long-term capital gains treatment

iPath Goldman Sachs Crude Oil Total (Symbol OIL)

This ETN tracks the return of West Texas Intermediate crude oil futures traded on the New York Mercantile Exchange (NYMEX). It uses the Goldman Sachs Commodity Index as its foundation and thus is considered a subindex.

iPath CBOE S&P 500 BuyWrite (Symbol BWV)

This ETN tracks the return of a hypothetical buy-write, or covered call strategy, on the S&P 500 Index Fund. The aim of a covered call strategy is to provide income from writing the call that offsets any loss caused by the S&P 500 declining in value. Historically, this ETN has generated a return comparable to the return of the S&P 500, but with much less risk. This ETN is considered a financial instrument commodity.

Figure 13.5 provides a select list of commodity ETNs.

Figure 13-5. Select List of Commodity Exchange-Traded Notes

Name	Ticker	Expense Ratio
iPath Dow Jones-AIG Agriculture Total Return Sub-Index	JJA	0.75
iPath Dow Jones-AIG Commodity Index Total Return	DJP	0.75
iPath Dow Jones-AIG Copper Total Return Sub-Index	JJC	0.75
iPath Dow Jones-AIG Energy Total Return Sub-Index	JJE	0.75
iPath Dow Jones-AIG Grains Total Return Sub-Index	JJG	0.75
iPath Dow Jones-AIG Industrial Metals Total Return Sub-Index	JJM	0.75
iPath Dow Jones-AIG Livestock Total Return Sub-Index	COW	0.75
iPath Dow Jones-AIG Natural Gas Total Return Sub-Index	GAZ	0.75
iPath Dow Jones-AIG Nickel Total Return Sub-Index	JJN	0.75
iPath EUR/USD Exchange Rate	ERO	0.40
iPath GBP/USD Exchange Rate	GBB	0.40
iPath JPY/USD Exchange Rate	JYN	0.40
iPath S&P GSCITM Crude Oil Total Return Index	OIL	0.75
iPath S&P GSCITM Total Return Index	GSP	0.75

Closed-End Funds

Closed-end funds, like mutual funds, are collective investments in which investors pool their money in one fund that owns multiple different securities and, in the case of commodities, multiple commodities. It is a misconception that closed-end funds are closed to new investors in the manner of a closed mutual fund. Instead, closed-end funds do not issue new shares of a fund once the initial shares are sold to investors. This means that shares of closed-end funds trade on the secondary market, with their prices dictated by supply and demand forces. As a result, closed-end funds trade at discounts or premiums to their net asset value, thus adding a unique element to owning this investment. For instance, if a closed-end fund with a net asset value of $25 per share is trading at $22 per share, there is a $3 discount. If that fund is trading at $27 per share, there is a $2 premium. Some investors make purchase and sale decisions solely on the basis of the amount of the premium and discount and the way that premium or discount is changing over time. Furthermore, some investors seek out closed-end funds that they believe will experience narrowing in the discount to net asset value. These investors do not necessarily care about changes in the net asset value since they attempt to make money on the change in the discount. For example, an investor purchases a certain closed-end fund for $19 when the net asset value is $23. If the discount narrows from $4 to $3, given a $1 change in price, the investor will make $1 regardless of how the net asset value changes. Most closed-end funds trade with discounts that range from 15 to 25 percent of net asset value; these sizable discounts make closed-end funds more price-volatile than mutual funds.

Regardless of the presence of discounts or premiums, closed-end funds offer an alternative way for investors to gain exposure to commodities. If you want to know more about closed-end funds, the Closed-End Fund Association, a national trade association of approximately two dozen fund managers, has a website at www.cefa.com. Figure 13.6 provides a select list of commodity closed-end funds.

Figure 13-6.   Select List of Commodity Closed-End Funds

Name	Symbol
BlackRock Global Energy & Resources	BGR
Central Fund of Canada	CEF
DWS Global Commodities	GCS
Gabelli Global Gold Natural Resources	GGN
ING Risk Managed Natural Resources	IRR
Kayne Anderson Energy	KYE
Kayne Anderson Energy Development	KED
Kayne Anderson MLP	KYN
Macquarie Global Infrastructure	MGU
Petroleum & Resources	PEO
Tortoise Energy Cap Corp	TYY
Tortoise Energy Inf Corp	TYG
Tortoise NA Energy Corp	TYN

HOLDRS

HOLDRS are very much like ETFs in that you purchase a fund that tracks a certain index or market. However, HOLDRS are not actually funds. HOLDRS may resemble ETFs, but there are some differences. HOLDRS, a product of the financial services firm Merrill Lynch, represent a pool of 20 stocks that are held in a grantor trust owned by the investment company. Over time the 20 stocks in the trust can decline as companies are acquired or merged with other companies. No additions are made to the trust when a company is removed, however. HOLDRS provide unique benefits that ETFs do not, including the ability to receive proxies and vote directly on issues involving the companies held in the trust, such as voting for the board of directors. Owners of HOLDRS also are entitled to receive dividends directly from the companies held in the trust and pay no management fees. Owners are assessed an annual custody fee of $0.08 per HOLDRS for cash dividends and distributions. The downside to HOLDRS is that investors must purchase and sell shares in blocks of 100, in contrast to ETFs, in which an the investor can purchase as little as 1 share.

OIL SERVICE HOLDRS (SYMBOL OIH)

This HOLDRS tracks the performance of 18 companies involved in providing services to oil exploration and production companies.

TRAKRS

Another Merrill Lynch instrument, TRAKRS provide investors with yet another way to invest in commodities by using a commodity-traded instrument. The aim of TRAKRS is to provide small investors with the ability to gain commodity exposure in their portfolios without purchasing futures or employing margin. TRAKRS initially are priced at $25 minus offering expenses and change in value with changes in the market price of the underlying commodity. One of the unique benefits of TRAKRS is their favorable tax treatment; TRAKRS are taxed as ordinary stocks instead of futures contracts and even qualify for long-term capital gains treatment after 6 months instead of the 12 months for stocks and bonds. TRAKRS trade on the Chicago Mercantile Exchange's Globex platform and require the financial advisor on the brokerage account to preregister with the National Futures Association. Figure 13.7 provides a select list of commodity TRAKRS.

Figure 13-7. Select List of Commodity TRAKRS

Name	Symbol
LMC II TRAKRS	LMC
Rogers TRAKRS	RCI
BXY TRAKRS	TBX
PIMCO CommodityRealReturn TRAKRS	PCT
PIMCO StocksPLUS TRAKRS	PST

Quiz for Chapter 13

1. All but which of the following are considered exchange-traded instruments?
   a. Exchange-traded funds
   b. Closed-end funds
   c. Open-end funds
   d. Exchange-traded notes

2. Exchange-traded funds and exchange-traded notes can be sold short and purchased on margin.
   a. True
   b. False

3. All but which of the following are advantageous characteristics of exchange-traded instruments?
   a. Low costs
   b. Favorable diversification
   c. Stocklike tradability
   d. Ability to outperform the underlying index

4. Stocklike tradability includes all but which of the following attributes?
   a. Intraday trade execution
   b. No dividends permitted
   c. Market price transparency
   d. Selling short

5. What is the single most important difference between exchange-traded funds and exchange-traded notes?
   a. Exchange-traded notes are debt instruments, whereas exchange-traded funds are equity instruments.
   b. Exchange-traded notes do not track the broadly based commodity indexes.
   c. Exchange-traded funds do not pay dividends, whereas exchange-traded notes do.
   d. Exchange-traded funds have low turnover, whereas exchange-traded notes have high turnover.

6. Which of the following exchange-traded instruments present issuer credit risk in addition to market risk?
   a. Exchange-traded funds
   b. Exchange-traded notes
   c. Closed-end funds

7. Similar to traditional mutual funds, exchange-traded instruments typically charge loads to purchase and sell.
   a. True
   b. False

8. From what do closed-end funds obtain their name?
   a. Closed to new fund holdings
   b. Closed to new investors
   c. Closed to market price impacts
   d. Closed to new shares

9. What is the primary advantage of exchange-traded notes over exchange-traded funds?
   a. Favorable tax treatment
   b. Lower expense ratios
   c. Higher distribution of dividends
   d. No market risk

10. Exchange-traded notes have stated maturity dates?
    a. True
    b. False

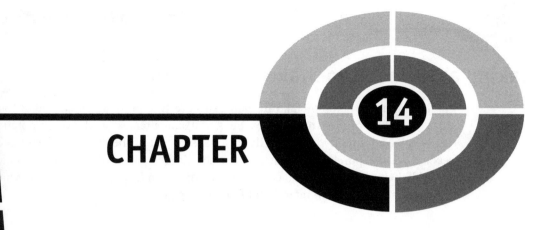

CHAPTER 14

Stocks and Partnerships:

Taking an Ownership Stake in Commodities Companies

For those who want to get started investing in commodities, taking an ownership stake in a publicly traded company or master limited partnership will accomplish that aim. Taking an ownership stake in a commodities-related company is no different from taking an ownership interest in any other company. As long as you have an online brokerage account or an account with a financial advisor, you can purchase stock or partnership units (master limited partnership) with relative ease. Deciding which companies to purchase is a more difficult task as buying ownership stakes in individual companies is far more risky than investing in commodities mutual funds or commodities exchange-traded funds. However, where there is added risk, there is added return potential. If you have decided to take an ownership stake, there are three primary approaches.

Taking an Ownership Stake

Purchasing an ownership stake to gain exposure to commodities can be accomplished with one of three approaches. First, you can purchase stock in a corporation that is involved directly or indirectly in some segment of the commodities market. Second, you can purchase an interest in master limited partnerships, some of which are publicly traded. Third, you can purchase American Depositary Receipts, which are essentially ownership interests in foreign companies.

PUBLICLY TRADED CORPORATIONS

The traditional approach to taking an ownership stake is to purchase the stock of a publicly traded corporation. There are many corporations to choose from, and each has its own risk and reward profile. One of the key decisions you will have to make if you go this route is whether to purchase the stock of a corporation that is directly involved or indirectly involved.

Direct-Involvement Corporations

Direct-involvement corporations are companies that are engaged in the early phase of commodity production, such as mining companies and oil and natural gas exploration and production companies. These corporations present an elevated degree of risk but also provide a higher reward potential. Unfortunately, some corporations cannot be defined as either direct-involvement or indirect-involvement since they have business operations that span the spectrum from production to service. These corporations are generally very diversified conglomerates in which profits rise and fall with the prices of commodities.

Indirect-Involvement Corporations

Indirect-involvement corporations are companies that are not involved in the initial stage of exploration and procurement but provide critical equipment and services to direct-involvement corporations. One of the best known of these corporations is Transocean. Although this corporation does not explore for oil and natural gas, it sells offshore exploratory equipment and related services. When prices for oil rise, oil exploration companies pursue more projects to extract oil, and that means increased demand for exploratory equipment. Other examples of indirect-involvement corporations are transportation companies, storage companies, and distribution companies.

Indirect-involvement corporations do not provide the high-risk–high-reward potential of direct-involvement corporations, but they provide a solid way for investors to capitalize on the growing need for support equipment and services that has resulted from rising commodities prices.

MASTER LIMITED PARTNERSHIPS

Also referred to as publicly traded partnerships (PTPs), master limited partnerships are public companies that trade on public stock exchanges—principally the New York Stock Exchange—just as common stocks do. However, instead of purchasing shares of stock, investors purchase what are called units and therefore are referred to as unit holders rather than shareholders. This difference in wording is purely semantic and has no impact on the investor's ownership interest. The chief differences between master limited partnerships and publicly traded corporations are the following:

- Ownership structure
- Tax treatment
- Tax reporting

A master limited partnership is composed of a general partner or partners and limited partners. General partners are responsible for both establishing and managing the partnership. They assume 100 percent liability for claims against the partnership in case of financial hardship. In contrast, limited partners are responsible for claims against the partnership only up to the amount of their investment. For this reason, limited partners have limited risk and can lose only what they invest in the partnership. General partners are held to a higher standard and can be held personally responsible for losses over and above their investment.

The second difference and the principal reason for investing in master limited partnerships over publicly traded corporations is favorable tax treatment. With corporations, income is subject to double taxation by which the corporation pays taxes on income earned and the shareholder pays taxes on the same income received through the distribution of dividends. Double taxation does not occur with a master limited partnership as long as the partnership gets at least 90 percent of its income from activities involving the exploration, production, distribution, and transformation of commodities. For master limited partnerships that qualify for this tax-exempt treatment, only the income received by a partner is subject to taxation on the personal level. Master limited partnerships do not distribute dividends as corporations do but provide for a "flow-through" of income in which each partner receives a proportionate share of the gains or losses generated by the partnership and declares that income on his or her tax return. For investors in master limited partnerships, single taxation on the personal level means less money paid in taxes and therefore more money in their pockets.

The third difference between master limited partnerships and publicly traded corporations involves tax reporting. Investors (shareholders) in publicly traded companies receive 1099s that show the income they received in the form of dividends and capital gains or losses. Investors (partners) in master limited partnerships do not receive 1099s but instead receive K-1 tax forms that illustrate the proportionate amount of income received by the partner and earned by the partnership. Federal law requires that 1099s be mailed before the end of January, whereas K-1s typically are not received until late in the tax filing season. Some investors in partnerships must file for extensions because of the time needed to receive their K-1s.

Three of the biggest master limited partnerships that trade on the New York Stock Exchange are Enbridge Energy (symbol EEP), which participates in energy pipelines; Enterprise Products (symbol EPD), which participates in storage, drilling platforms, and oil and natural gas pipelines; and Kinder Morgan (symbol KMP), which participates in the transportation, storage, and distribution of various energy fuels.

AMERICAN DEPOSITARY RECEIPTS

American Depositary Receipts provide ownership in a foreign company that is not listed on an American stock exchange. Some foreign companies decide not to list their stocks in the United States for reasons that range from burdensome regulatory requirements to added costs. As a result, many money center banks in the United States purchase shares of stock in foreign companies on foreign stock exchanges and then offer to sell the rights to those shares in the form of depositary receipts. Thus, owners of American Depositary Receipts hold ownership rights to shares of stock of a particular foreign company. American Depositary Receipts provide for appreciation when the foreign stock rises and provide for income when the foreign company pays a stock dividend. Owners of American Depositary Receipts face added risks, particularly geopolitical and foreign exchange risk. For investors looking to own stock in a foreign company involved in commodities that is not listed on an American stock exchange, American Depositary Receipts can be an ideal investment. American Depositary Receipts often are referred to as ADRs.

Commodities Companies

The following section is a comprehensive but not exhaustive list of companies involved either directly or indirectly in the commodities markets. The companies are divided by commodity, and a short description of each one, with its stock symbol, is provided. For more information on a company, visit Finance.Yahoo.com, one of the leading websites for company information and stock data.

ENERGY FUELS

Coal

- *Arch Coal, Inc. (NYSE: ACI):* This company is involved in mining for coal, producing about 130 million tons of coal a year, with operations in nearly two dozen mines in the western United States and central Appalachia. This company also operates the Arch Coal Terminal near the Ohio River.
- *Peabody Energy Corporation (NYSE: BTU):* This company, established in 1883, is the largest coal producer in the world, with operations in more than 40 mines and processing facilities in the United States and Australia. Peabody Energy produces about 250 million tons of coal annually and has 10 billion tons in reserve. Other activities include coal trading and brokering, coal bed methane production, the development of coal-based generating plants, and transportation-related services.
- *Rio Tinto Group (NYSE: RTP; an ADR):* This company is involved in mining for copper, iron, uranium, gold, diamonds, and of course coal, which accounts for about 20 percent of its sales. As one of the world's largest mining companies, Rio Tinto operates primarily in Australia and North America, which together account for about 80 percent of its operations.
- *Burlington Northern Santa Fe Corporation (NYSE: BNI):* This Fort Worth–based company that was founded in 1849 provides freight rail transportation services through North America. A few of the commodities transported are coal, diesel fuels, wheat, corn, soybeans, lumber, and liquefied petroleum gas. Burlington Northern Santa Fe operates over 30,000 route miles in 28 states and two provinces in the United States and Canada.

Crude Oil and Natural Gas

- *Total, S.A. (NYSE: TOT; an ADR):* This French company is involved in exploration, production, refining, and distribution of crude oil and related products. With operations in over 100 countries, Total is a truly global oil and gas company.
- *BP, plc (NYSE: BP; an ADR):* This London-based company is involved in exploration, production, refining, and distribution of crude oil, gasoline, and related energy fuel products, with operations in Europe, Africa, the Middle East, and the Americas. BP, the new name for what was once British Petroleum, operates the Trans-Alaska pipeline and has enormous reserves of oil and natural gas.
- *ConocoPhillips Company (NYSE: COP):* This American company is involved in exploration, production, refining, and distribution of crude

oil and natural gas in the United States and Canada. ConocoPhillips participates in the extraction of oil from oil sands in western Canada. The company nearly was acquired by a Chinese company before American political pressure torpedoed the deal.

- *ExxonMobil Corporation (NYSE: XOM):* This Houston-based company is involved in exploration, production, refining, and distribution of crude oil and natural gas, with operations in over 200 countries and territories around the world. ExxonMobil claims to be the largest nongovernmental marketer of natural gas in the world.
- *Royal Dutch Shell (NYSE: RDS'A; an ADR):* This well-known global company is involved in exploration, production, refining, and distribution of both crude oil and natural gas. This Dutch and British company also operates pipelines in the United States and Canada.
- *Chevron Corporation (NYSE: CVX):* This California-based company is involved in both the crude oil and natural gas markets, with operations in the United States, Australia, Africa, and the Gulf of Mexico.
- *Petroleo Brasileiro S.A. (NYSE: PBR; an ADR):* This Brazilian company from Rio de Janeiro, together with the companies it invests in, is involved in the supply, transportation, and distribution of crude oil and natural gas, primarily in Brazil.
- *Statoil, ASA (NYSE: STO; an ADR):* This Norwegian company is involved in exploration and production of crude oil and natural gas. Many of the operations are off the coast of Norway in the North Sea; there are other operations in Africa, South America, Asia, and other parts of Western Europe.
- *Enterprise Products Partners, L.P. (NYSE: EPD):* This American company based in Houston, Texas, is involved in the production and processing of natural gas and propane. Operations are principally in the United States, and the company is registered as a limited partnership rather than a corporation.
- *Transocean (NYSE: RIG):* This company provides offshore exploratory equipment and services to oil exploration and production companies involved in the extraction of new deposits.
- *Ultra Petroleum (NYSE: UPL):* This company is involved in oil and natural gas exploration and production principally in Green River Basin, Wisconsin, and Bohai Bay, China.
- *Noble Corporation (NYSE: NE):* This company is one of the oldest drilling contractors in the world, serving oil exploration and production companies all over the world.
- *Baker Hughes International (NYSE: BHI):* This company is a diversified provider of services to oil companies throughout the world. Its product line is extensive.

- *GlobalSantaFe (NYSE: RIG):* This company is involved in offshore drilling, specifically contracted drilling services, direct broad-service drilling services, and project engineering services. GlobalSantaFe was acquired by Transocean in the second half of 2007.
- *Knightsbridge Tankers Limited (NASDAQ: VLCCF):* This company is involved in the transportation of crude oil via oil tankers from producing and exporting nations to importing nations such as the United States.

Electric Power

- *Dynegy, Inc. (NYSE: DYN):* This Houston-based company is involved in the generation and distribution of electric power in the United States. The primary energy fuels used to generate electric power are coal, natural gas, and crude oil.
- *American Electric Power Company, Inc. (NYSE: AEP):* This is one of the largest companies for the generation and distribution of electric power in the United States. With a transmission network of approximately 39,000 miles, AEP is also a big player in the wholesale energy business, where it markets and trades electricity, natural gas, and other commodities and has interests in independent power plants. Its product line is rounded out with natural gas transportation, storage, and processing; barge transportation; and telecommunications infrastructure services.
- *Duke Energy Corporation (NYSE: DUK):* In 2006 this company acquired Cinergy for $9 billion in stock, making it one of the largest electric power companies in the world. After the completion of the deal, Duke had 3.9 million electric customers in the American South and Midwest, with a sizable commercial power unit and foreign operations.

Ethanol

- *Aventine Renewable Energy Holdings, Inc. (NYSE: AVR):* This American company, which began trading publicly in 2006, is involved in the production and marketing of ethanol, making it one of the leading companies for that fuel product. Aventine's production facilities are situated in Illinois and Nebraska, two of the leading corn-growing states.

Solar Power

- *SunPower Corporation (NASDAQ: SPWR):* This company is involved in the production of solar cells and solar panels. Other products include imaging and infrared detectors manufactured through a thin-wafer process. SunPower is majority owned by Cypress Semiconductor.

Uranium Ore

- *Cameco Corporation (NYSE: CCJ):* This company, the world's leading producer of uranium ore, is involved in the mining and enriching of uranium ore used to fuel nuclear power plants. Cameco, the producer of 20 percent of the world's uranium output, has the world's largest known deposit of high-grade uranium in Canada. Aside from Canada, countries where other operations are situated include the United States, Mongolia, and Kyrgyzstan, the later two through a controlling interest in Centerra Gold.
- *AREVA Group (Euronext: CEI):* This French company mines and enriches uranium ore and builds and services nuclear reactors. Other services include treating and recycling used nuclear fuel and electric power transmission and distribution equipment.

AGRICULTURE

Coffee

- *Starbucks Corporation (NASDAQ: SBUX):* This company is the leading specialty coffee retailer in the world, with more than 13,000 coffee shops in over 30 countries. Seattle's Best Coffee is owned by Starbucks. Other products include tea, roasted beans, and coffee accessories.

Corn and Wheat

- *Archer Daniels Midland Company (NYSE: ADM):* This company is involved in the production of corn, wheat, and oilseeds, with operations around the world. Its refined products include durum flour, syrups, citric and lactic acids, sweeteners, and ethanol.

Soybean Products

- *Archer Daniels Midland Company (NYSE: ADM):* This diversified food company based in Illinois is involved in growing, harvesting, processing, and distribution of many agricultural products, including soybeans, which are processed into oils and meals for the feed and food industries.
- *Bunge Limited (NYSE: BG):* This company is involved in many different agricultural products, including soybean oils and meal, grains, livestock, and poultry. Based in New York, its operations span the production, processing, and storage segments, making it a very diversified commodities company.

Sugar

- *Imperial Sugar Company (NASDAQ: IPSU):* This company is involved in the production and distribution of refined sugar to food-related manufacturers and distributors throughout the United States. Imperial Sugar is headquartered in Texas.

LIVESTOCK

Pork

- *Seaboard Corporation (AMEX: SEB):* This diversified livestock and agricultural company sells pork, flour, and sugar to over 25 countries around the world. It also is involved in shipping services, power plants, flour mills, commodity trading, and the refining of sugarcane.
- *Smithfield Foods, Inc. (NYSE: SFD):* This company is the world's largest hog producer and pork processor. Smithfield sells meat products in over 40 countries around the world and purchased Premium Standard Farms, a pork producer, in 2007.

Poultry and Beef

- *Tyson Foods, Inc. (NYSE: TSN):* This company is one of the largest chicken producers in the United States and the single largest meat-producing company in the world; that status was accomplished after its acquisition of IBP Fresh Meats. Through its 53 meat-processing plants, Tyson sells products in over 80 countries. Other product lines include frozen prepared foods and precooked meats.
- *Pilgrim's Pride Corporation (NYSE: PPC):* This company is involved in the breeding, hatching, raising, processing, distributing, and marketing of turkey and chicken. Prepared poultry is another principal product line sold under the Pilgrim's Pride and Country Pride names.

PRECIOUS METALS

Gold

- *Anglo American Plc (NASDAQ: AAUK; an ADR):* This Britain-based company is involved in mining and is one of the leading gold-producing companies in the world. It also mines for platinum, diamonds, and coal.
- *Barrick Gold Corporation (NYSE: ABX):* This Canadian company is involved in mining for gold in Australia, Africa, and North and South America. Barrick has over 80 million ounces of proven and probable gold and mineral reserves.

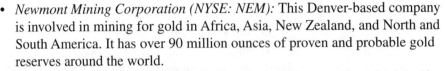

- *Newmont Mining Corporation (NYSE: NEM):* This Denver-based company is involved in mining for gold in Africa, Asia, New Zealand, and North and South America. It has over 90 million ounces of proven and probable gold reserves around the world.
- *AngloGold Ashanti Ltd (NYSE: AU; an ADR):* This company, which is 42 percent owned by Anglo American, is involved in mining for gold around the world.
- *GoldCorp, Inc (NYSE: CG):* This Vancouver-based company with operations principally in Australia and North and South America is involved in mining for gold. It has over 25 million ounces of proven and probable gold reserves.

Platinum

- *Anglo Platinum Limited (a subsidiary):* Majority-owned by Anglo American, Anglo Platinum is the largest producer of platinum in the world, accounting for about 38 percent of total global production, with mining, sheltering, and refining operations concentrated in South Africa. It also is involved in the production of palladium and rhodium and has more than 220 million ounces of reserves.
- *Impala Platinum Holdings Limited (Pink Sheets: IMPUY; an ADR):* This company is the second largest platinum producer in the world, with principal operations in South Africa and Zimbabwe. Other metal products produced are palladium, rhodium, and ruthenium, which are all part of the platinum metal group.

Silver

- *Silver Wheaton Corp. (NYSE: SLW):* This Vancouver, Canada–based company is involved in the purchase and distribution of silver procured from Central and South America as well as Sweden. Silver Wheaton is a subsidiary of GoldCorp.
- *Pan American Silver Corporation (NASDAQ: PAAS):* This company is involved in mining for silver in Central and South America, with an emphasis on Mexico and Peru. It is based in Vancouver, Canada.
- *Silver Standard Resources, Inc (NASDAQ: SSRI):* Based in Vancouver, this company is involved in silver exploration in Australia and the Americas, principally Mexico, Argentina, and the United States.
- *Apex Silver Mines Limited (AMEX: SIL):* This Cayman Islands–based company is involved in the production of silver in South America, principally in Bolivia.

- *Hecla Mining Company (NYSE: HL):* This Idaho-based company is involved in the production of silver in the United States, Mexico, and Venezuela. Its Idaho headquarters is in the town of Coeur d'Alene.

INDUSTRIAL METALS

Aluminum

- *Alcoa, Inc. (NYSE: AA):* This well-known company is involved in the production of aluminum and fabricated products used in many diversified final products. New York–based Alcoa has operations in Australia, Russia, Brazil, and the United States.
- *Alcan, Inc. (Toronto: AL):* This Montreal-based company is involved in the mining, refining, and finishing of bauxite and alumina in the United States, Europe, and Asia. Alcan is the world's third largest aluminum producer, behind former parent Alcoa (split in 1928) and Rusal (a Moscow, Russia–based private company). After a failed takeover bid by its competitor Alcoa, Alcan announced a friendly merger deal with Rio Tinto that would create the world's largest aluminum company, named Rio Tinto Alcan.
- *Kaiser Aluminum (NASDAQ: KALU):* This American company is involved in the production of aluminum ingots and fabricated products used in many transportation products, such as automobiles.
- *Maxxam, Inc. (AMEX: MXM):* The owner of approximately 60 percent of Kaiser Aluminum, Maxxam is engaged primarily in real estate and lumber production.

Copper

- *Freeport-McMoRan Copper & Gold (NYSE: FCX):* This company is involved in mining for copper, gold, and silver. Copper, in the form of concentrates and refined products, accounts for the majority of sales. In 2007, Freeport-McMoRan acquired Phelps Dodge in a transaction valued at $26 billion. The resulting combined company was the second biggest copper-producing company in the world. This company has approximately 35 billion pounds of copper and about 35 million ounces of gold in proved and probable reserves.
- *Southern Copper Corporation (NYSE: PCU):* This company is involved in the mining and extraction of copper, with principal operations in Mexico and Peru. Based in Phoenix, Arizona, Southern Copper is a subsidiary of the Americas Mining Corporation.

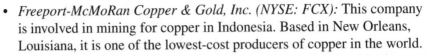

- *Freeport-McMoRan Copper & Gold, Inc. (NYSE: FCX):* This company is involved in mining for copper in Indonesia. Based in New Orleans, Louisiana, it is one of the lowest-cost producers of copper in the world.
- *Ivanhoe Mines, Ltd. (NYSE: IVN):* This company is involved in the mining of copper in remote areas around the world, specifically Myanmar, Mongolia, and Australia.
- *Corporación Nacional del Cobre de Chile (Codelco):* This company is the leading producer of copper in the world and controls 20 percent of the world's known copper reserves. Unfortunately, investors are unable to make investments in Codelco since the company is owned by the Chilean government.

Nickel

- *Vale Inco Limited (NYSE: Rio; an ADR):* This Toronto-based company is involved in mining for copper but is known principally for the mining of nickel. Inco is the world's number two producer of nickel (after the Russian giant Norilsk Nickel), supplying approximately 33 percent of all nickel demand. Operations are in Canada and Indonesia. Acquired in 2006, Vale Inco Limited (formerly CVRD Inco and before that Inco Limited) is a wholly owned subsidiary of the Brazilian mining company Companhia Vale do Rio Doce.

Palladium

- *North American Palladium* (AMEX: PAL): This Toronto-based company is involved in mining for gold, copper, nickel, and platinum, its principal metal.
- *Stillwater Mining Company (NYSE: SWC):* This company is involved in refining palladium, platinum, and other related minerals. Most of its operations are in Montana.

Zinc

- *Boliden AB (Pink Sheets: BDNNF):* This European company is involved in the mining and smelting of zinc and copper, with operations in the Scandinavian countries. Other metal products produced are lead, tin, and some precious metals.
- *Horsehead Holding Corporation (NASDAQ: ZINC):* This company is involved in the production of zinc, zinc oxide, and zinc products from zinc-containing dust, such as dust from electric-arc furnaces at steel mills and residue from the galvanizing of metals. Horsehead has operations in Texas, Illinois, Oklahoma, Tennessee, and Pennsylvania.

OTHER COMMODITIES

Lumber

- *Weyerhaeuser Company (NYSE: WY):* This company is involved in the growing, harvesting, and distribution of timber. Additional operations include the manufacture of timber-related products, such as construction materials, used in the United States. Weyerhaeuser is based in the state of Washington and has operations in approximately 20 countries around the world.
- *Rayonier, Inc. (NYSE: RYN):* This Jacksonville, Florida–based company is involved in the growing and distribution of timber in properties stretching from the United States to Australia and New Zealand. The manufacture of timber-related products is also done.
- *Louisiana-Pacific Corporation (NYSE: LPX):* This company is involved in the provision of timber-related products to many home outlet companies and distributors throughout Asia, Europe, and the United States, its principal base of operations.
- *Universal Forest Products, Inc. (NASDAQ: UFPI):* This Michigan-based company is involved in the production and distribution of lumber and related products to wholesalers and general construction contractors.

Cotton

- *Delta and Pine Land Company (NYSE: DLP):* This Mississippi-based company is involved in the growing, harvesting, and distribution of cotton throughout the world, principally from operations in Turkey, South Africa, Costa Rica, and Australia.

Final Thoughts

Although taking an ownership stake in a commodities-related company is as easy as purchasing shares of stock in any other company, there are additional risks unique to each company that must be addressed. These company-specific risks include the following:

- *Business risk*: the risk attributed to a company's operations, particularly those involving sales and income.
- *Financial risk*: the risk attributed to a company's financial stability and structure, namely, the company's use of debt to leverage earnings.
- *Industry risk*: the risk attributed to a group of companies within a particular industry. Investments tend to rise and fall on the basis of what a company's peers are doing.

- *Liquidity risk*: the risk that an investment cannot be purchased or sold at a price at or near market prices.
- *Call risk*: The risk attributed to an event in which an investment may be called before maturity.
- *Regulation risk*: the risk that new laws and regulations will affect the market value of an investment negatively.

As a result of the greater risk inherent in investing in individual companies, you will need to use additional due diligence to ensure that you are investing in a company with sound fundamentals and strong long-term prospects. If you do that, you have the potential to generate very attractive returns for your portfolio.

Quiz for Chapter 14

1. All but which of the following are approaches to taking an ownership stake in companies involved in the commodities trade?
   a. Purchasing shares of stock of a publicly traded corporation
   b. Purchasing units of a master limited partnership
   c. Investing in American Depositary Receipts
   d. All of the above

2. Direct-involvement companies present higher risk and higher reward potential than do indirect-involvement companies.
   a. True
   b. False

3. All but which of the following are considered direct-involvement companies?
   a. Mining companies
   b. Farming companies
   c. Railroad companies
   d. Drilling companies

4. Master limited partnerships differ from publicly traded corporations in all but which of the following ways?
   a. Reward potential
   b. Ownership structure
   c. Tax treatment
   d. Tax reporting

5. Which of the following documents do master limited partnership unit holders receive for tax reporting purposes?
   a. W-2
   b. 1099

    c. W-4

    d. K-1

6. Which of the following is not subject to double taxation?

    a. Publicly traded companies

    b. Master limited partnerships

    c. American Depositary Receipts

    d. International commodity corporations

7. American Depositary Receipts represent ownership in American corporations and trade on international stock exchanges.

    a. True

    b. False

8. What percentage of income from production-related activities must be distributed to unit holders to eliminate double taxation and provide for a flow-through of gains and losses?

    a. 5%

    b. 25%

    c. 50%

    d. 90%

9. Where are the largest master limited partnerships listed for trading?

    a. New York Board of Trade

    b. New York Mercantile Exchange

    c. New York Stock Exchange

    d. Pink sheets

10. What type of security underlies an American Depositary Receipt?

    a. Shares of stock in a foreign corporation

    b. Investment-grade bonds issued by a foreign corporation

    c. Preferred stock of foreign drilling companies

    d. Shares of foreign mutual funds not available in the United States

15 CHAPTER

Commodity Hedge Funds:

An Alternative Approach for the Accredited Investor

For investors who are looking to gain a performance edge, commodity hedge funds can be the answer. Hedge funds are a powerful way to build wealth, but what exactly is a hedge fund? In simple terms, a hedge fund is an actively managed private investment fund that attempts to generate attractive positive returns. To accomplish that goal, hedge funds employ many different strategies, financial instruments, and tools of the trade. Some of the strategies are aggressive, and some are conservative. Hedge funds are managed by professional investment managers and are limited to a small number of "accredited investors." Hedge fund managers receive a percentage of the profits earned by the fund as an incentive to generate performance. Unlike most traditional investment managers, hedge fund managers usually have a significant amount of their own wealth invested in the fund. This minimizes conflicts of interest and gives a substantial amount of comfort to the investor, who knows that the manager's interests are aligned with the investor's interests in protecting and growing the investment.

Today, the term *hedge fund* generally is considered a misnomer. Many hedge funds do not hedge risk at all; many create additional risk. The term was introduced in the 1940s, when Alfred Winslow Jones established the first hedge fund by employing long and short strategies enhanced with leverage. Since those early days, hedge funds have grown in both number and complexity. Although the types of hedge funds and the tools of the trade have changed over the decades, the use of the catchy name has not.

Inside the Hedge Fund Trade

Hedge fund service companies track anywhere from 4,000 to 6,000 hedge funds, although many experts estimate that there are over 9,000 hedge funds in the world today. Many hedge funds are not tracked because of their lack of size and thus are not represented in those numbers.

The hedge fund business has grown by leaps and bounds over the last couple of decades. For instance, in 1990 hedge funds managed nearly $40 billion in assets; 15 years later, assets under management had grown to more than $975 billion. Much of this increase in assets is attributed to new money, or cash inflows, with the rest of the growth coming from appreciation of principal. Growth rates for net inflows of new assets into hedge funds have averaged in the high teens per year, with some years experiencing nearly 50 percent growth in assets. Today the growth rate of new assets is approximately 10 to 11 percent per year.

At the same time assets were flowing into hedge funds, new hedge funds were being established to capitalize on that growth. Since 1990, the number of hedge funds has increased dramatically to over 9,000 worldwide, with assets under management of between $1 and $1.5 trillion. Between 2001 and 2004, over 600 new hedge funds were established on average each year.

Hedge funds and mutual funds differ substantially in regard to the amounts of assets they manage. There are some hedge funds that are quite large and some that are quite small. Typically, however, hedge funds are much smaller than mutual funds. Much to the surprise of many investors, there are numerous hedge funds with assets under management of less than $10 million and few with assets under management of more than $5 billion. With hedge funds, smaller is considered better because it means that the fund managers can take investment action much faster and without artificially moving the market as some mutual funds often do. In addition, smaller hedge funds allow managers to take positions in smaller investments and generate opportunistic gains, whereas mutual funds cannot do that because even a small investment on their part would equate to a large investment, artificially moving the market and drying up opportunities. The performance incentive fee for hedge funds is used to support this kind of activity to capitalize on smaller investments. The Securities and Exchange Commission established a rule in 1998 that prohibits mutual funds from engaging in short-term trading and obtaining related returns. That presented an opportunity to hedge funds. Hedge funds are not required to follow the rule, the so-called short short rule.

ORIGINS OF HEDGE FUNDS

Most investment professionals would agree that the first recorded hedge fund was established in the late 1940s by Alfred Winslow Jones, a 1923 Harvard graduate, a 1941 doctoral graduate from Columbia University, and a journalist with *Fortune* magazine early in his career. During his days with *Fortune*, Jones became a student of the financial markets and immersed himself in their inner workings. While researching and writing an article in 1948 on the current investing landscape and on how hedging can enhance returns and reduce risk, Jones concluded that he could design a better way to manage money and achieve abnormally high returns over time. As a result, in 1949 he established what many consider the first recorded hedge fund to take advantage of market swings, both up and down, to generate the enhanced returns and reduced risk he had written about. To establish that hedge fund, Jones pooled $60,000 from investors with $40,000 of his own money. Soon afterward, he was employing the tools he hypothesized would deliver returns in both up and down markets. The two primary tools he employed in his hedge fund were selling short and leverage. These are the same tools that many hedge fund managers use today.

His investment general partnership, A.W. Jones & Co., attempted to take long positions in individual equity securities when the market was rising and short positions in individual securities when the market was falling. Betting correctly, regardless of the change in the market, of course would produce a positive return. In times when he had greater confidence about the direction in which the market would move, Jones employed leverage—borrowing from a prime broker to buy more of an investment—thus magnifying the returns of his long or short positions. Jones called the use of selling short and leveraging "speculative tools used for conservative purposes." In 1952, he changed the legal structure of his hedge fund from the established general partnership into the more advantageous and commonly used structure of today, the limited partnership. About the same time, he introduced a performance incentive fee that he set at 20 percent of the profits. Jones also was the first hedge fund manager to place a significant amount of his own money in the fund he managed. Most hedge fund managers today use the same two concepts—performance incentive fees and investing managers' money in the fund—introduced by Jones.

In light of Jones's stellar track record, in 1966 *Fortune* published an article on him and his hedge fund titled "The Jones That Nobody Can Keep Up With." The article praised Jones and his track record and revealed that his performance had bested even the top-performing mutual fund by 44 percent and the top five-year mutual fund of the day by 85 percent, returns net of fees. Jones's popularity skyrocketed. The *Fortune* article grabbed the attention and interest of numerous investors and investment professionals. The allure of earning 10 to 20 times what was being earned in traditional investments resulted in the creation of 140 new hedge funds between 1966 and 1968. The Jones hedge fund in one shape or another existed into the 1970s and maintained its solid track record.

The 10 Defining Characteristics of Hedge Funds

Here are the 10 defining characteristics of hedge funds, an executive summary of sorts:

- Hedge funds have minimal organizational structures and typically are operated by one or two key decision makers.
- Hedge funds receive minimal oversight and regulation by the Securities and Exchange Commission (SEC).
- Hedge funds are restricted by the SEC to fewer than 100 accredited investors, a term used by the SEC to describe investors with substantial wealth and income.
- Hedge funds offer their investors limited liquidity and impose restrictions on withdrawing invested capital.
- Hedge funds are limited in the types of marketing and promotions they can offer to potential clients, a restriction imposed by the SEC.
- Hedge funds have extensive strategies and tools available to them for the management of their funds.
- Hedge funds aim to generate attractive absolute returns, or returns that are positive in both bull and bear markets.
- Hedge funds offer investors low correlations with the total market but also with equity assets.
- Hedge funds have incentivized fee arrangements in which they charge an industry average 20 percent fees on the profits they generate for their investors.
- Hedge funds offer their investors performance safeguards to ensure that performance incentive fees are suitable and appropriate.

Sports Cars and Minivans

The investing marketplace uses many different traditional and alternative methods of investing, with the pooling of funds being one of the most popular. Two of the most popular vehicles for pooled funds are hedge funds and mutual funds. A good way to think about the differences between hedge funds and mutual funds is to consider the differences between a sports car and a minivan. If mutual funds resemble minivans, hedge funds resemble sports cars. Both minivans and sports cars are conceptually the same in that both transport one or more people from location A to location B. However, minivans and sports cars are classic examples of how two things with similar purposes can differ. This is the beginning of the great divide between mutual funds and hedge funds. Sports cars are faster off the line, have higher top speeds, are more nimble, are significantly more maneuverable, and can go where many other vehicles dare not venture. At the same time, sports cars are limited in the number of passengers they can carry, attract the attention of the police more frequently than do minivans, require a somewhat more polished driver, and have substantially fewer safety features in case of a crash. The same positives and negatives apply to hedge funds and mutual funds.

By far the greatest drawback of hedge funds is the potentially higher risk involved. This risk can be controlled by the driver, or the manager in the case of hedge funds. Moreover, it is not a foregone conclusion that investing in hedge funds is riskier to an investor than is investing in mutual funds. Going back to our analogy, the driver and the actions he or she takes dictate the risk. Driving fast, darting in and out of traffic, and going through red lights can be done by drivers of sports cars or minivans. That means that hedge fund risk is often the result of manager-specific actions. However, one can argue that different types of drivers select different types of vehicles. More conservative drivers typically will not drive, let alone buy, a sports car. Thus, hedge funds probably attract managers who prefer higher risk and are comfortable taking that risk. Furthermore, regardless of the type of driver behind the wheel of a sports car, at some point that driver is going to open things up to see what the vehicle can do. The same can be said for hedge fund managers. Regardless of their view of risk taking, hedge fund managers may feel motivated at some point to assume more risk than they ordinarily would assume.

The final part of this analogy is the way each vehicle protects passengers in an accident. There is no arguing with the fact that minivans provide substantially greater protection than do sports cars. The same thing holds for mutual funds and hedge funds. Mutual funds tend to safeguard investor assets more than hedge funds do. However, regardless of the vehicle, passengers are at greater risk traveling on expressways and major streets than they are traveling on side streets. For example, if small-cap stocks are expressways and blue-chip stocks are side streets, it is the type of street you are traveling on rather than your vehicle that determines the risk. Applying this logic to hedge funds, it is the investments or assets held in the mutual fund or hedge fund that dictate overall risk. Figure 15.1 summarizes the differences between hedge funds and mutual funds.

Figure 15-1. Comparing Mutual Funds and Hedge Funds

CATEGORY	MUTUAL FUND	HEDGE FUND
Liquidity	Daily Liquidity and Redemption	Liquidity Varies from Monthly to Annually
Performance Objective	Attractive Relative Return	Attractive Absolute Return
Regulation	SEC Regulated Investments	Non-Regulated Private Investments
Investors	Unlimited	Highly Limited
Minimum Initial Investment	Typically Very Small, > $1,000	Typically Very High, > $1 Million
Availability	Open to All Investors	Open ONLY to Investors where net worth exceeds $2.5 million or individual income must have been in excess of $200,000, or joint income must have been in excess of $300,000 in the past two years. Plus investor must expect the same level of income in the subsequent year
Selling Short	Maximum of 30 percent of profits from selling short	Unlimited Freedom to Sell Short
Performance Incentive Fee	Typically No Performance Incentive Fee	Performance Incentive Fee of 20 Percent is Common
Investment Management Fee	Common Usage of 1-2 Percent	Common Usage of 1-2 Percent
Leverage	Practically No Use	Freedom to Use Extensively
Primary Sources of Risk and Return	Market, Strategy, and Skill	Strategy and Skill
Structure	Typically a Large Company	Typically a Small Company
Marketing and Promotions	Unlimited with Disclosure Requirements	Restricted to Only Accredited Investors
Offerings	Prospectus	Private Placement Memorandum
Manager Participation	Little to No Manager Participation	Substantial Capital from Manager Invested
Derivatives	Restricted from Trading	Free to Trade

Types of Hedge Funds

In the realm of hedge funds, there are four broad categories, or styles, that can be subdivided into multiple hedge fund strategies. The strategies hedge fund managers employ at times deviate slightly from the following strategies; however, those strategies still resemble one of those in the broad category. Combining strategies in multiple categories is also common. Regardless of the strategy, each one has the aim of generating attractive absolute returns. The following are the strategies employed by hedge fund managers, grouped by style:

- **Style:** Tactical (also called directional)
    - *Macrocentric*: Strategy in which the hedge fund manager invests in securities that capitalize on the broad markets of both domestic and global opportunities.
    - *Managed futures*: Strategy in which the hedge fund manager invests in commodities with a momentum focus, hoping to ride the trend to attractive profits.
    - *Long/short equity*: This strategy is named for the practice of going long or going short equity securities.
    - *Sector specific*: Strategy by which the hedge fund manager invests in both a long holding of equities and a short sale of equities or equity market indexes.
    - *Emerging markets*: Strategy by which the hedge fund manager invests in international markets with a specific emphasis on emerging markets.
    - *Market timing*: Strategy by which the hedge fund manager either times mutual fund buys and sells or invests in asset classes that are forecast to perform well in the short term.
    - *Selling short*: Strategy by which the hedge fund manager sells short securities with the aim of buying them back in the future at lower prices.
- **Style:** Relative-value (also called arbitrage)
    - *Convertible arbitrage*: Strategy by which the hedge fund manager takes advantage of perceived price inequality that offers low-risk profit opportunities.
    - *Fixed-income arbitrage*: Strategy by which the hedge fund manager purchases a particular fixed-income product and immediately sells short another fixed-income security to minimize market risk.
    - *Equity market neutral*: Strategy by which the hedge fund manager buys an equity security and sells short a related index to offset the market risk.
- **Style:** Event-driven
    - *Distressed securities*: Strategy by which the hedge fund manager invests in the equity or debt of struggling companies, often at steep discounts to the manager's estimated values.
    - *Reasonable value*: Strategy by which the hedge fund manager invests in securities that are selling at discounts to their perceived value as a result of being out of favor or being relatively unknown in the investment community.

Figure 15-2. Spectrum of Hedge Fund Correlations

- ○ *Merger arbitrage*: Strategy by which the hedge fund manager invests in event-driven scenarios in which there are unique opportunities for profit.
- ○ *Opportunistic events*: Strategy by which the hedge fund manager invests in securities when there are short-term event-driven opportunities.
- **Style:** Hybrid
  - ○ *Multistrategy*: Strategy by which the hedge fund manager employs two or more strategies at one time.
  - ○ *Funds of funds*: Strategy by which the hedge fund manager invests in two or more hedge funds rather than directly investing in securities.
  - ○ *Values-based*: Strategy by which the hedge fund manager invests according to certain personal values.

Figure 15.2 shows the spectrum of hedge fund correlations.

Common Practices of Hedge Fund Managers

UTILIZE EQUITY FUTURES AND OPTIONS

Hedge fund managers can utilize options and futures to speculate or to hedge their positions. For instance, if an equity hedge fund manager believes that the equity market will decline, he or she can protect the value of the hedge fund by buying S&P 500 put options or selling short S&P 500 futures contracts. Thus, if the market declines, the hedge fund manager can exercise the S&P 500 put options to offset the loss with the long equity position or profit from the decline of the market with the short futures contract.

Both futures and options are considered derivative products. Many people have a bias against derivatives because of all the media hype surrounding a couple of high-profile scandals. Nevertheless, derivatives offer investors and hedge fund managers an opportunity to protect their positions in case of adverse price movements and to speculate on the direction of the market.

USE SHORT SELLING

Short selling consists of selling a security that is not owned by the hedge fund. Many nations around the world restrict this technique, but such restrictions are not present in the United States. With short selling, a hedge fund manager borrows shares of a security from a brokerage firm and sells those shares on the open market. The hedge fund receives the proceeds from the sale but owes the shares to the brokerage firm.

As long as the price of the security declines, the hedge fund will profit. This follows the tried and true investing wisdom of buy low and sell high. However, if the price rises, the hedge fund will lose as it essentially will have to replace the borrowed shares by purchasing them at a higher price. This translates into buying high and selling low, which is not what hedge fund managers should be doing.

Hedge fund managers use short selling in one of two primary ways. First, they use it as a way to hedge exposure to a single investment. For example, a certain hedge fund holds $25 million in equity securities, which accounts for 90 percent of the entire fund. Because of recent strong price increases, the manager believes that the risk and price of equities are too high. To offset some of the risk, the manager sells short $5 million, thus reducing open equity exposure to $20 million. Regardless of the price change, up or down, the remaining $5 million in equities is offset by $5 million in short equities. The second way hedge fund managers use short selling is to *profit* from securities that are perceived to be overvalued. Thus, if a hedge fund manager believes that a certain investment is priced too high, he or she can short sell shares in the hope that the price will fall, allowing the manager to buy back the borrowed shares and return them to the lender.

EMPLOY LEVERAGE

Leverage is best described as borrowing to buy more of an investment. Leverage also entails assuming more investment exposure than what an investor would be exposed to in light of the assets that investor holds. For example, a hedge fund manager expects that a certain investment will experience strong performance over the next year and will deliver a return that exceeds the cost of borrowing funds. As a result, the manager invests $2 million in the investment and borrows funds to place another $1 million in the same investment. Thus, the hedge fund will own an investment worth $3 million but used only $2 million of its own assets.

With leveraging, investors and hedge fund managers anticipate a higher return on the borrowed funds in excess of the cost to borrow the funds. Hedge funds borrow the funds from prime brokers that charge them a rate of interest tied to a standard rate, such as LIBOR. Leverage increases risk and therefore should be used cautiously. Leverage magnifies investment performance on the upside and the downside. When the market is performing well, leverage will generate greater returns. However, in falling markets or when there are declines in the price of an investment, leverage can be your worst enemy.

Because of the heightened risk with employing leverage, many hedge fund managers have found more low-risk ways of using it to their advantage. Two of the most common ways they use leverage are to purchase a new investment without being forced to sell another investment to free up capital to make the purchase and to increase the size of an existing investment in the hope of magnifying results. When used judiciously, leverage can work in your favor.

CONDUCT HEDGING

Hedging is used when a manager believes that a certain investment offers an opportunity for profit but does not want to be exposed to other risks, such as market risk. For instance, a hedge fund manager believes that a particular S&P 500 stock is significantly overpriced. As a result, the manager short sells the stock and simultaneously buys an S&P 500 index fund. Thus, the investment is protected from market influences and only price movement attributed to overvaluation is experienced. The same can be done for undervalued securities. In this case, a hedge fund manager can buy the security and sell short an S&P 500 index fund. Thus, if the stock declines because the market in general is weakening, the hedge fund manager will lose money on the long stock position held but offset that loss with the gain from the short S&P 500 index fund. This tool eliminates and isolates market risk and emphasizes investment-specific risk.

PURSUE ARBITRAGE

Arbitrage is defined in the academic world as a riskless investment. Unfortunately, that term has been overused and used out of context by those in the investment profession as a way to push their funds. Arbitrage is the simultaneous purchase and sale or two securities that are tied explicitly in some fashion. One of the most popular uses of arbitrage is to take profit from differences in the prices of stock and a bond that converts into shares of that stock. For example, Mega Stores stock is selling for $50 a share, and its convertible bond is selling for $1,030. If the convertible bond allows for conversion into 20 shares of stock, the value an investor will receive from doing that is $1,000 (20 shares multiplied by $50). However, with the bond selling for $1,030, the investor would be foolish to convert the bond for stock with less value. To profit on this price discrepancy, a hedge fund manager will short sell the convertible bond and buy the stock with the proceeds. The hedge fund will make $30 on each transaction ($1,030 – $1,000). The manager will continue to place this transaction until the prices of the convertible bond and the stock become closer and the spread narrows.

TARGET SPECIFIC MARKETS

Hedge funds often target specific markets, sectors, and asset classes. This is done to give a fund focus and take advantage of perceived opportunities specific to that market. Hedge funds often differentiate between geographic locations, such as European and Asian markets, and asset type, such as equities and fixed-income. By targeting specific markets, hedge funds can gain exposure to opportunities that are not necessarily available in the overall market. For instance, although many United States–based companies have operations in Europe and profit from gains made there, a hedge fund may get more exposure to European markets simply by buying European companies with more extensive European operations. This can be ideal for investors since modern portfolio theory says that investing in additional markets or asset classes can enhance returns and reduce risk.

INCORPORATE POSITION LIMITS

To safeguard against a loss on any single investment, hedge funds can institute position limits that restrict the size of an investment in any one company to a certain percentage. In addition, position limits can trigger hedge funds to liquidate certain holdings once losses become too large. For example, a hedge fund institutes a 20 percent limit on how much any one holding may constitute of its holdings. Regardless of how well the asset is performing, no new investments can be made in the asset above the 20 percent limit. This protects the hedge fund from large swings in value if the price of the asset begins to go in the other direction.

SET BUY/SELL TARGETS

In simple terms, a buy/sell target is the point at which a hedge fund manager will sell a held asset because it is fairly valued or buy an asset because it is perceived as being undervalued. Hedge fund managers frequently place target prices on securities; when the investment hits one of those price targets, it triggers a buy or sell transaction.

FOLLOW STOP-LOSS RESTRICTIONS

Regardless of the estimated value of an investment, hedge funds are very conscious of the losses they suffer. Investors do not appreciate losses. In consequence, hedge funds are motivated to sell once a particular investment reaches a predetermined level of losses. That predetermined point is the maximum loss the manager is willing to incur on any particular investment. Preferably, a hedge fund will not need to initiate a stop-loss provision, but those provisions can protect the fund from additional downside pressure.

Sourcing Hedge Funds

Years ago, obtaining information on hedge funds was very difficult. Investors had to rely on contacts and referrals. This has changed because the popularity of hedge funds has grown exponentially. The hedge fund industry is a well-connected network of professionals who gather and disseminate information much more easily than was the case in the past. Word of mouth continues to be the favorite source for investors seeking hedge fund investments. In light of the restrictions on hedge fund marketing, this approach seems to work for both investors and managers. With rating services becoming involved in ranking hedge funds, the sources of information will grow. Another solid source of information is brokerage firms. These firms often host seminars on hedge fund investing and invite hedge fund managers to give talks about their funds. Investors may find this venue a good source. Websites such as HedgeWorld.com provide research on hedge funds for a fee. Over time more sources of information will surface, providing additional help to small or new hedge fund investors.

Gathering information on hedge funds begins with obtaining their offering memorandums, disclosure documents, and legal partnership forms. Some of these documents provide information about each hedge fund, but many do not because of a lack of disclosure. Some of the questions that sometimes are answered in these documents are the following:

1. What is the minimum initial investment?
2. What are the annual management fee and the incentive performance fee?
3. What is the hurdle rate, if any?
4. Is there a watermark safeguard?
5. What are the provisions for making withdrawals?
6. When can additional contributions be made?
7. How and when are performance and holdings communicated?
8. What strategies are employed, and what is the stated goal?

Quiz for Chapter 15

1. Approximately how many hedge funds exist today?
   a. 1,000
   b. 5,000
   c. 9,000
   d. 15,000

2. Alfred Winslow Jones is credited with establishing the first hedge fund.
   a. True
   b. False

3. There are four types of hedge fund management styles. Which style emphasizes directional price bets?
   a. Tactical
   b. Arbitrage
   c. Relative-value
   d. Strategic

4. Which of the following hedge fund styles does not invest directly in securities but instead invests in stand-alone hedge funds?
   a. Event-driven
   b. Relative-value
   c. Fund of funds
   d. Multistrategy

5. The Securities and Exchange Commission mandates that only certain investors can invest in hedge funds. What are these investors called?
   a. Certified
   b. Accredited
   c. Permitted
   d. Approved

6. The first hedge funds typically employed which two strategies?
   a. Selling short and arbitrage
   b. Leverage and derivatives
   c. Selling short and leverage
   d. Arbitrage and emerging markets

7. Ownership of shares is required before one can sell short those shares.
   a. True
   b. False

8. What is the benefit of employing leverage?
   a. Increased risk
   b. Ability to profit in both rising and falling markets
   c. No cost
   d. Magnifying performance

9. Which of the following obligates the owner to exercise the contract?
   a. Options
   b. Futures
   c. Both
   d. Neither

10. Why are position limits used by hedge fund managers?
    a. To enable more efficient use of leverage
    b. To promote greater use of hedge fund resources
    c. To safeguard a hedge fund against losses from a single investment
    d. To offset lack of compliance

16 CHAPTER

Futures and Options:

About Managed Futures Funds and Self-Directed Participation

When you participate in the futures market, you can use the do-it-yourself approach or hire a professional to manage your money. The second approach involves the use of a managed futures fund, which is a collective portfolio, much like a hedge fund, in which multiple investors pool their money and a professional manages the money for them through the purchase and sale of commodity futures and options. The costs are high with managed futures funds, but most investors do not have the experience or skills to trade futures or options. Often it is beneficial to pay a professional to handle complex investment management. However, for investors who are comfortable with futures and options or are willing to learn about them, self-directed participation, in which the investor makes all the decisions about futures and options transactions, may be the better approach.

Clearinghouses

Buyers of futures contracts obligate themselves to take delivery, and sellers obligate themselves to make delivery. If your futures contract is generating gains, you are certain to perform on your obligation. But what about the counterparty who is losing money on the trade? Can he or she be counted on to perform as he or she promised when the trade was executed? There is an obvious risk here. To eliminate it, each exchange has a related clearinghouse that guarantees the performance of all participants and all futures contracts cleared on the exchange. This means that buyers and sellers do not have to track down counterparties to ensure contract performance but can look to the clearinghouse for that purpose. Clearinghouses have significant assets and can borrow if necessary to cover nonperformance by any participant. Initial margin and maintenance margin are used by clearinghouses to ensure participant performance.

Clearinghouses obtain their assets from the members of the exchange, who must post deposits and make sizable capital commitments. Thus, a clearinghouse is able to weather any issues arising from participant nonperformance. Clearinghouses serve the dual roles of ensuring performance and ensuring the financial integrity of the markets.

Volume and Open Interest

Aside from price, volume and open interest are the two variables that are important with futures contracts. Volume refers to the amount of futures contracts that trade during a specific day for a particular delivery month. Whether a trade takes a long or a short position, volume will increase. For instance, if you went long a December 2008 crude oil futures contract, the volume would rise by one to reflect your long trade. If you went short—essentially closing your position—the same futures contract later in the day, volume would rise by one to reflect your short trade. Going long and then going short does not have an offsetting effect; volume remains the same.

Open interest is similar to volume in that it attempts to capture the degree of trading in a specific commodity in a particular delivery month. However, open interest is composed of the number of futures contracts that remain outstanding. This means that open interest tracks the total number of outstanding futures contracts that have not been settled by delivery or offset with a trade on the opposite side of the market.

For example, if you went long five June 2009 natural gas futures contracts, open interest would rise by five to reflect the five purchased contracts. However, if you go short four of the same futures contracts on the next trading day, open interest will decline by four to reflect the four trades executed on the second day. Open interest provides traders with a look into what the market is thinking about a particular commodity. The more open interest there is, the more traders believe the commodity will change in price. If traders did not believe that the price would move, there would be more balanced long and short trades, thus offsetting trades and keeping open interest lower.

Volume and open interest are two excellent measures of liquidity for a futures contract. When volume is greater, this means higher interest from traders—and therefore greater liquidity—for a futures contract. In reviewing a futures contract for a possible trade, you should look at price, volume, and open interest together. For more on what moves commodities prices, see Chapter 6.

Margin

Most investors have heard of margin and understand how it works in stock trading. When an investor purchases stocks on margin, he or she must deposit a certain amount of money in the account; that amount initially is set at 50 percent by government regulations. Investors purchase on margin to enable them to leverage the investable capital they have to purchase more of a security. With margin, $1 of invested capital can become $2 of stock value. Margin does not work the same way with futures trading.

In futures trading, margin serves as a good-faith deposit to ensure the performance of the investor to the counterparty in case the investment generates losses and helps maintain investor confidence and efficient futures trading. Both sides—buyer and seller—of the futures trade are required to post margin to protect the other party. The margin is an estimate of the maximum loss the investment could generate during the next trading session.

If an investment generates losses on the second trading day after the initial investment was made, the margin is expected to cover those losses. If the margin is not large enough to cover the loss, a margin call will be issued that requires the investor to deposit additional funds or sell the investment to close the position outright. Margin calls are generated whenever the posted margin declines below a fixed level: the maintenance margin. The level that triggers a margin call is typically around 66 percent of the initial margin required. Thus, a futures contract with a $1,200 initial margin will have an $800 maintenance margin; that means that margin calls will not be issued until the margin falls below $800. In this example, an investor with $900 of margin, which is $300 below the initial margin, will not receive a margin call because margin is still higher than the maintenance margin of $800. The maintenance margin is best defined as the portion of the initial margin that the investor must satisfy in his or her account for the futures position before a margin call is triggered.

Let's look at one more example. Suppose you go long (purchase) one copper futures contract that has an $8,100 initial margin requirement, which you satisfy by depositing $8,100, and a $6,000 maintenance margin requirement. The next trading day, the price for copper declines and your contract experiences a loss of $1,000, leaving your margin at $7,100. Since your margin is above the $6,000 maintenance margin, no margin call is generated. However, on the third trading day copper falls even more, producing a loss of $1,600 and reducing your margin to $5,500. Since your margin is below the maintenance margin, a margin call is issued that requires you to post an initial margin of $2,600 ($8,100 – $5,500) or close your position by going short (selling) one copper futures contract.

Margin allows investors in commodity futures to purchase additional commodities through the use of substantial leverage. This adds extra risk and can enhance returns and magnify losses. Use caution when you purchase commodities on margin.

About Futures Contracts

With nonfutures investments, when you purchase an asset, you purchase it immediately for today's current market price. For instance, if you wanted to buy a share of stock with a market price of $50, you would pay $50 and take ownership. Again, you take ownership immediately and pay the current market price. With futures, the transaction is different: You pay an amount immediately for an asset that you will not take ownership of until a certain preestablished date in the future—thus the name *future*. For instance, if you want to buy crude oil with a market price of $90 but a futures price of $92 and want to take future delivery rather than immediate ownership, you will pay $92 rather than $90. Technically speaking, both prices are market prices, but only in futures trading do you call them the *spot price* ($90) and the *futures price* ($92). If you want to buy immediately, you buy at the spot price, and if you want to buy for a future delivery date, you buy at the futures price.

These examples provided only one futures price for the sake of simplicity. However, in reality there are many futures prices, depending on the date in the future when you want to take ownership of the asset. This date is referred to as the delivery month. Thus, if you buy a crude oil futures contract, you can buy the September, October, November, and so on, delivery months. Each month has its own unique price that is typically different from that of the previous month. Most futures prices increase month to month since commodities must be stored, financed, and insured. These extra costs add to the futures price. Inverted markets refer to futures prices

Figure 16-1. Forward Curve for Crude Oil, January 2008

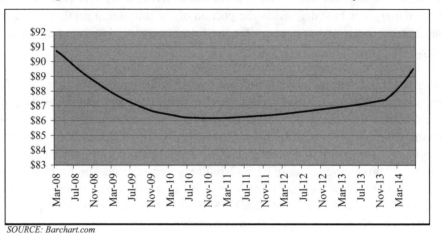

SOURCE: Barchart.com

that are lower than spot prices because investors demand the commodity now rather than wanting it in the future. The delivery month is only one of the unique contract specifications. Figure 16.1 shows the forward curve for crude oil in January 2008.

CONTRACT SPECIFICATIONS

Futures contracts are standardized products that allow for the future ownership of a commodity executed today. The specifications of any futures contract include the following:

- *Commodity*: denotes which underlying commodity you wish to transact. Each commodity is identified by a unique symbol that signifies the specific commodity and the delivery month.
- *Action*: denotes whether you wish to execute a purchase or a sale transaction.
- *Delivery month*: denotes which futures contract you wish to transact.
- *Quantity*: denotes how many contracts you wish to transact. Note that grains and soybeans are specified not in contracts but in thousands of bushels.
- *Order type*: denotes the execution contingencies you wish to be applied to your transaction.

TYPES OF ORDERS

Order type refers to how you want an order executed with regard to time, price, and fill. Although each exchange has its own unique set of rules regarding order types, the following are the most accepted types:

- *Market*: stipulates that you want the order executed immediately at the current price. Market orders are the most basic orders.
- *Limit*: stipulates that the order is not to be executed until the price hits a certain level. Thus, an order with a $40 limit when the contract is trading at $41 will not be executed until the price drops by $1.
- *Stop*: stipulates that the order does not go live until the current market price hits a certain level. Once the order is live, it is executed as a market order.
- *Stop-limit*: similar to the simple stop order but with one difference: Instead of the order becoming a market order, it becomes a limit order.
- *Day only*: this order type stipulates that the order is good for only the current trading day. Placing day orders is not relevant with market orders since they are executed immediately; however, limit orders may not be executed immediately, and thus an amount of time must be stipulated in the order. Most orders are assumed to be day orders unless otherwise stipulated.
- *Good till canceled*: essentially stipulates what the name implies. Your order will remain open until it is executed or until you cancel it.
- *Market if touched*: referred to as an MIT order, this order is executed as a market order if and when the commodity trades, or is offered, at a specified price or lower.
- *Market on close*: an order to execute at the end—usually within the last five minutes—of the trading session at a price near the closing price.

DELIVERIES

When you go long a futures contract, you essentially are stating your intention to take delivery of the physical product in a certain delivery month. For a commodities producer and a user of that commodity, that sounds good. However, as someone looking to speculate or provide efficiency in the market through futures contract trading, taking the physical product is not practical. Would you like to take possession of barrels of crude oil if you purchased a crude oil futures contract? Of course you would not. As a result, most futures contracts do not settle, or terminate, by having the owner take physical possession. Rather, most contracts are closed when the long is offset by a short of the exact same futures contract.

Each delivery month has a last trading day during which the contract settles and ceases to exist. The last trading day can vary with the commodity and the exchange. It is therefore important to identify which day your futures contracts settle so that you can plan accordingly. Figure 16.2 shows the abbreviations used for delivery months.

Figure 16-2. Abbreviations for Delivery Months

Month	Abbreviation	Month	Abbreviation
January	F	July	N
February	G	August	Q
March	H	September	U
April	J	October	V
May	K	November	X
June	M	December	Z

About Options

Options are one of the most complex financial instruments in the marketplace today. With traditional investing, such as stocks, options are somewhat less difficult to understand and employ. However, with futures contracts, option trading is not easy because options are derivatives and so are futures contracts. As a result, when you purchase an option, you purchase a derivative on a derivative.

With futures contracts both participants—buyer and seller—are obligated to perform on their trades. That is not true of options—hence the name. With options, buyers have the right to execute an option or let it expire. Therefore, the buyer has an option. Sellers of options are not afforded the same right and are obligated to perform, depending on what the buyer decides. If the buyer elects to execute his or her right, the seller must perform. However, if the buyer elects to have the option expire—which principally is done only when the option is worthless—the seller does not have to do anything more.

So what is an option exactly? An option is a financial instrument that gives the owner the right to purchase or sell an underlying instrument—a futures contract—at a specific price before a specified expiration date. For example, a trader can purchase an option on crude oil by which the trader has the right, but not the obligation, to purchase a January 2009 crude oil futures contract by a specific date. If the price of crude oil rises, you most likely will exercise your right to purchase the futures contract since you will gain on the difference between the new higher price and the set price established in the option. If the price of crude oil declines, you may let the option expire since you will not want to take a loss in exercising the option and therefore purchase a futures contract at a set price that is above current market prices. In this example, you will lose the money you paid to buy the option. The money you pay to buy an option or receive if you sell the option is called the premium and is one of the option specifications.

Like futures contracts, options can be exercised, in which case the buyer takes ownership—this applies to a call option only—of the underlying futures contract, or the buyer can sell an option to close or offset the long position. By closing the position, you will gain on the spread between the option purchase and the option sale. For example, suppose you purchase an option for $5 and the price of the underlying asset is $70. One month later the price of the underlying asset rises to $75, and the option price rises to $10 as a result. Seeing the gain of $5 in your option, you sell, or go short, the exact same option and receive the $10 premium from the option buyer. You thus have locked in $5 ($10 – $5). When the option settles, the clearinghouse considers you to have closed out your position without further action.

CALL OPTIONS

Call options are used to take advantage of expected rising prices for the underlying futures contract. Call options give the buyer the right, but not the obligation, to purchase the underlying futures contract at a preestablished price before a preestablished date: the expiration date. If you are bullish on a specific commodity, purchasing an option will allow you to profit if prices rise before the option expiration date. If prices rise, you exercise the option and purchase the futures contract below the market price for a gain. If prices fall, the options buyer is out the premium, or the price paid for the call option.

Market Sentiment and the Purchase Decision:

Buying a call option: bullish on the price of the underlying
Selling a call option: bearish on the price of the underlying

PUT OPTIONS

Put options are used to take advantage of expected falling prices for the underlying futures contract. Put options give the buyer the right, but not the obligation, to sell the underlying futures contract at a preestablished price before a preestablished date: the expiration date. If you are bearish on a specific commodity, purchasing a put option will allow you to profit if prices fall before the option expiration date. If prices fall, you exercise the option and sell your existing futures contract above the market price for a gain. If prices rise, the options buyer is out the premium, or the price paid for the put option.

Market Sentiment and the Purchase Decision:

Buying a put option: bearish on the price of the underlying
Selling a put option: bullish on the price of the underlying

OPTIONS SPECIFICATIONS

Aside from the premium, there are four specifications related to options that you should be aware of before purchasing or selling options. These options specifications are as follows:

- *Premium*: denotes the amount of money you pay to purchase the option or receive if you sell the option.
- *Expiration date*: denotes the last day the buyer of the option has to exercise the option and purchase the underlying futures contract.
- *Strike price*: denotes the price at which the call buyer must pay to purchase the underlying futures contract or the price that the put buyer will receive to sell the underlying futures contract.
- *Underlying asset*: the futures contract attached to the options contract by which the call option buyer purchases and the put buyer sells.

MAXIMUM GAINS AND LOSSES

Call Buyer:

Maximum gain: unlimited (the price of the underlying could skyrocket and keep going)
Maximum loss: premium paid

Call Seller:

Maximum gain: premium received
Maximum loss: unlimited (the price of the underlying could skyrocket and keep going)

Put Buyer:

Maximum gain: strike price (assuming an underlying price of $0)–premium paid
Maximum loss: premium paid

Put Seller:

Maximum gain: premium paid
Maximum loss: premium paid–strike price (assuming an underlying price of $0)

Managed Futures Funds

Managed futures funds are pools of money from multiple investors that are managed by professionals called commodity trading advisors (CTAs). The money put into these funds is invested in both futures contracts and options at the discretion of the commodity trading advisor. Managed futures funds have much in common with hedge funds in terms of pooling of funds, professional management, active management, correlation benefits, unique risks, and fee structure.

Managed futures funds have been around for over 30 years and today have nearly $175 billion under management. The money inflows to managed futures funds have increased steadily over the last several years as more investors have come to recognize the benefits. Commodity trading advisors must register with the Commodity Futures Trading Commission, a U.S. government entity, pass background checks by the FBI, and offer significant disclosures to potential and existing clients.

Commodity trading advisors employ their own proprietary trading systems for investing in futures contracts for commodities such as crude oil, natural gas, gold, coffee, sugar, and foreign currencies. Investing techniques such as going long and going short typically are used to take advantage of perceived opportunities on both sides of the market.

Managed futures funds are not for everyone in light of the higher risk, fees, wealth requirements, and initial investment requirements. Nevertheless, there are benefits to investing in managed futures funds that can offset the drawbacks, such as higher return potential, higher absolute returns, and favorable correlation benefits that can reduce portfolio volatility.

FEE STRUCTURE

Although fees vary from fund to fund, most managed futures funds charge a 2 percent annual investment management fee and a 20 percent performance incentive fee. The performance incentive fee is assessed only against the profits earned in the fund rather than the total market value of the portfolio. In contract, the annual investment management fee is assessed against the total market value of the portfolio in both good and bad years. Thus, even when the fund losses money, the portfolio will be assessed the typical 2 percent fee. Performance incentive fees are assessed only when performance is positive, and this motivates the CTAs to generate attractive positive performance year in and year out. You may think that a 20 percent fee is excessive—and perhaps it is—but it is the bottom line or net return that matters most. Thus, if CTAs can generate returns well in excess of the market or what you can earn with traditional stocks and bonds, they have earned their fees. To grow their fees, they must grow your portfolio; this means your interests are aligned with the interests of the CTA.

BENEFITS

As was mentioned above, the most important benefits of investing in a managed futures fund are the potential to earn strong returns, the potential to earn positive returns regardless of what the commodities markets are doing, and the ability to

reduce the volatility in your total portfolio because of investments that do not move in the same direction as traditional stocks and bonds.

Commodities futures contracts are typically highly volatile. This means there is greater opportunity to profit if the right decisions are made. Commodities trading advisors are highly skilled experts who have significant experience with and knowledge of the commodities futures markets; this enables them to take advantage of opportunities and generate attractive returns. This is not always the case, however, and the risk rises when one is trading futures contracts.

Since CTAs can go both long and short, they have the ability to profit in both rising and falling markets. As a result, you have the capacity to earn positive returns each year, an occurrence referred to as *absolute returns*. Traditional money managers do not typically employ both long and short strategies while most traditional money managers are not permitted to do so. Absolute strategies depend on the skills of the CTA and therefore increase the risk in an investment. As a general rule, the more influence a money manager has on your portfolio, the greater the risk is. However, greater risk also means greater return potential.

An important benefit to investing in managed futures funds is a reduction in portfolio volatility as a result of favorable correlations. According to the modern portfolio theory (MPT) developed by the Nobel Prize economist Harry Markowitz, investing in asset classes that have low to negative correlations with equity and bond asset classes is beneficial since it creates a more properly allocated portfolio that can weather market weakness. During times of stock market declines, an investment in commodities via managed futures funds typically provides gains that will offset losses in other asset classes. As a result, the total market value of your portfolio will not fluctuate as much as it would if no investment in commodities were made. Lower portfolio volatility leads to higher risk-adjusted returns or higher performance for the same level of risk assumed.

DRAWBACKS

The primary drawbacks to managed futures funds include elevated risk, high fees, high requirements to invest, and high initial investment requirements. As was mentioned above, typical fees with managed futures funds are a 2 percent annual investment management fee and a 20 percent performance incentive fee. Traditional investments, such as mutual funds and exchange-traded funds, do not charge these high fees. Only with alternative investing funds do you find performance incentive fees; this is the nature of the investment. Nevertheless, traditional investments have more favorable fee structures than do managed futures funds.

Risk is highly dependent on the CTAs since those advisors make all the investing decisions and employ both long and short strategies. Although its fund is not a managed futures fund, Amaranth Advisors, a hedge fund, invested in natural gas futures contracts and lost billions for its clients. Managed futures funds can do the same thing if they are not careful and do not use proper risk management.

Risk is double-edged since it increases the potential to generate strong returns but also increases the potential to generate large losses.

Private managed futures funds are targeted to wealthy individual investors and institutional investors that can verify their assets and income. To be able to invest in a managed futures fund, individual investors typically have to have $1 million in total assets and $200,000 in annual income. These high hurdles cause problems for some investors, but there are alternatives. Recently there has been a push to market managed futures funds to investors who do not have a high net worth. Thus, funds with lower minimums and index-related funds have been created to allow the mass of investors to invest in managed futures funds. Regardless, if you want to invest in managed futures funds, you may have to qualify before you consider making the initial investment. If you do not qualify for the private managed futures fund, a fund that markets itself to the mass investing public is a possible backup choice.

Finally, most managed futures funds require sizable initial investments, some around $1 million, although most are much lower. For wealthy individuals and large institutions this is not necessarily a problem, but for others it is. Sometimes it is nice to invest a small amount in a new investment until you feel comfortable enough to invest larger amounts. Larger initial investment requirements will not affect your performance, but this can make some investors uneasy and uncertain, which is a form of risk by definition.

Self-Directed Participation

For investors who are uncomfortable paying the high fees associated with managed futures funds but are comfortable trading futures and options, self-directed participation can be a good alternative. When you do all the work, you save the annual investment management fees and performance incentive fees associated with managed futures funds. In addition, you are in control of the way your account will be managed, from the commodity futures you purchase and sell to the timing decisions for executing those deals. There is a level of freedom in taking control of your own money that you cannot get from having a professional control your money. Unfortunately, there are bigger risks involved with self-directed participation: making mistakes because of inexperience, lack of information, poor technology platforms, and emotional behavior that impedes sound judgment.

For aspiring futures traders with little to no experience in the commodities markets, gaining real-life practice through the use of a trading simulator is the best first step. Lind-Waldock offers one of the best all-around trading simulation platforms, in which you obtain an account, use simulated money, and can place simulated futures trades. Once you know how futures trading is done, you can begin trading with actual money and the profits and losses will be real. If you go this route, you may want to consider a full-service broker-dealer who can provide recommendations and guidance during the learning phase. After you feel comfortable about your abilities, you can switch to a discount broker-dealer whose commission is low; that means more money in your pocket for each trade.

Figure 16.3 shows select margin requirements.

Figure 16-3. Select Margin Requirements

Commodity	Symbol	Initial Margin	Maintenance Margin
Brent Crude Oil	IB	$9,100	$7,280
Cocoa	CC	$2,660	$1,900
Coffee	KC	$5,390	$3,851
Copper Comex	HG	$8,927	$6,613
Corn	C	$1,485	$1,100
Cotton	CT	$4,900	$3,500
Crude Oil	CL	$13,602	$10,075
Ethanol	AC	$5,468	$4,050
Feeder Cattle	FC	$1,486	$1,100
Gold Comex	GC	$4,388	$3,250
Heating Oil	HO	$14,918	$11,050
KC Wheat	KW	$4,250	$3,400
Lean Hog	LH	$1,215	$900
Live Cattle	LC	$1,080	$800
Lumber	LB	$1,898	$1,265
MN Wheat	MW	$10,400	$8,000
Natural Gas	NG	$11,644	$8,625
Oats	O	$1,350	$1,000
Orange Juice	OJ	$1,890	$1,350
Palladium Comex	PA	$3,713	$2,750
Platinum Comex	PL	$8,100	$6,000
Pork Belly	PB	$3,726	$2,760
Rough Rice	RR	$3,416	$2,530
Silver Comex	SI	$6,750	$5,000
Soybean Meal	SM	$1,823	$1,350
Soybean Oil	BO	$1,620	$1,215
Soybeans	S	$5,198	$3,851
Sugar	SB	$1,540	$1,100
Wheat	W	$11,300	$8,370

Quiz for Chapter 16

1. What is the primary job of clearinghouses?
   a. Govern commodity markets
   b. Guarantee the performance of all participants and all futures contracts traded
   c. Ensure fair prices for all commodities participants
   d. Resolve problems with the supply of commodities

2. Exchange members are required to post deposits.
   a. True
   b. False

3. All but which of the following are excellent measures of liquidity for a futures contract?
   a. Volume
   b. Spread
   c. Price
   d. Open interest

4. Which of the following is not a specification of futures contracts?
   a. Underlying commodity
   b. Commodity source
   c. Delivery month
   d. Quantity

5. Which of the following types of orders is best described as an order that becomes a market order once a certain price threshold is achieved?
   a. Limit
   b. Stop
   c. Stop-limit
   d. Market-limit

6. Which of the following types of orders will remain open until executed or canceled by the trader?
   a. Open till canceled
   b. Wait till canceled
   c. Good till canceled
   d. Outstanding till canceled

7. Buying on margin refers to borrowing money to buy more of an investment.
   a. True
   b. False

8. Buying a call option is a bullish strategy. Which of the following strategies is also bullish?
   a. Buying a put

    b. Selling a call

    c. Selling a put

    d. None of the above

9. Commodity trading advisors manage the derivatives trading of which of the following types of investments?

    a. Mutual funds

    b. Index-based funds

    c. Closed-end funds

    d. Managed futures funds

10. Managed futures funds typically charge which of the following fees?

    a. 2 percent annual fee and 20 percent of profits

    b. 1 percent annual fee and no fee for profits

    c. No annual fee and 20 percent of profits

    d. 1 percent annual fee and 10 percent of profits

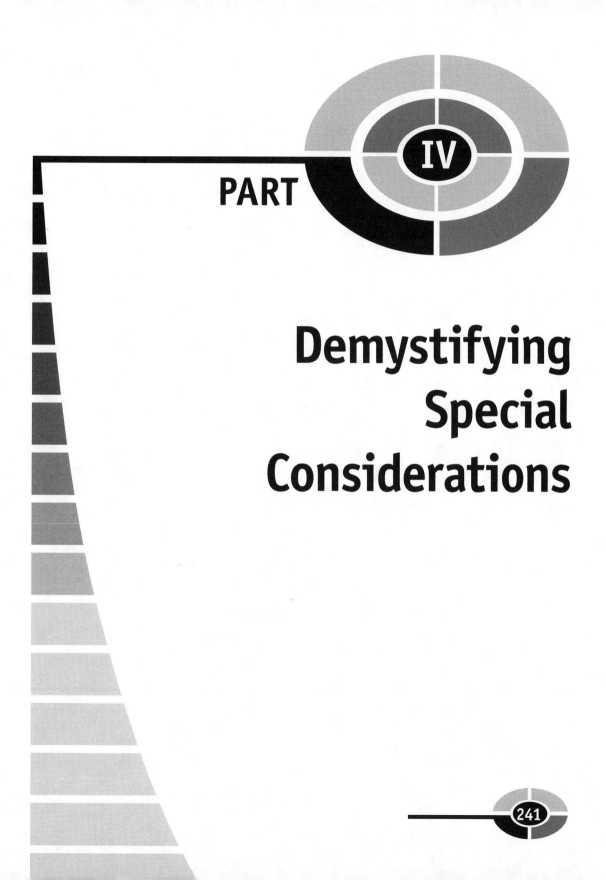

PART

IV

Demystifying Special Considerations

CHAPTER 17

Peak Performance Investing:

Inside Optimal Commodity Portfolios

This chapter presents 17 rules for building and maintaining peak performance portfolios. These rules touch on both concepts and actions. By following these rules for peak performance, you will build a portfolio that will position you to achieve and exceed your financial goals over the long term. Although the rules apply to all investors in all conditions, the content of this chapter will refer to commodities to help you understand and apply the rules to your pursuit of incorporating commodities in your portfolio.

17 Immutable Universal Strategies for Peak Performance Portfolios

1. MANAGE WITH A PRUDENT MIND-SET

The first rule of investing is to manage your portfolio as a rational and informed investor. If you are able to accomplish this task, everything else will fall into place.

To become a rational and informed investor, you will have to be proactive about learning what rational investors do and do not do. There are many pitfalls along the way. In addition, you will need to learn some of the immutable lessons of investing. By knowing these lessons, you will position yourself to manage your portfolio going forward.

What are rational investors? Rational investors do not fall victim to the most common behavioral blunders other investors often make. Those behavioral blunders involve things such as the illusion of control, blinders, overconfidence, denial, and the herd instinct. Rational investors are objective and do not let emotions cloud their judgment. Rational investors can evaluate investment opportunities and make wise decisions.

By definition, rational investors become informed investors over time. Being informed means knowing and fully understanding the immutable lessons of investing: Sector leadership does not continue forever, market timing is extremely difficult, no investment is guaranteed, and you should not invest more than you can afford to lose. The list of investment adages goes on and on, but you must make it a priority to become a rational and informed investor and manage your portfolio with a prudent mind-set.

2. ESTABLISH SMART FINANCIAL GOALS

Imagine that you are competing in an arrow-shooting contest in which you are blindfolded and are spun around many times. Now imagine trying to hit the target. Can you hit the target easily? Of course not. The same thing goes for investing: You cannot hit a target you are not aiming for. A majority of people begin investing before identifying their financial goals: why they are investing in the first place and what they are looking to accomplish by investing. Establishing financial goals allows you or your professional money manager to tailor the management of your portfolio.

However, establishing your financial goals is only half the battle. Ensuring that those goals are specific, measurable, achievable, and realistic and have a time constraint (SMART) is the other critical part. Establishing financial goals that do not adhere to this rule can cause some investors to assume more risk than is appropriate and others to assume less risk than is needed to generate the desired returns. This is the direct result of making ad hoc decisions with little or no guidance. Make it a personal priority to establish SMART financial goals to ensure that you hit your target with prudent investing.

3. UNDERSTAND YOUR RISK PROFILE

Your risk profile is critical for building your optimal portfolio. What is a risk profile? Your risk profile is a measurement of the amount of risk you can, should, and are willing to take in your portfolio to accomplish your SMART financial goals. Let's explore those three variables—can, should, and willing—in greater detail. First, your risk profile is based on your tolerance for risk, or your *willingness*. All people have a certain point where they are comfortable taking risk, but beyond that point they cannot stomach it. Your tolerance for risk is perhaps the easiest of the three risk profile components to assess. Second, your risk profile is dependent on your need to assume risk: the *should* factor. The term *need* is used here to communicate how much risk you are required to assume to attain your SMART financial goals.

Let's explore an example to help you understand your risk profile. Consider an investor who owns a portfolio worth $100,000 and needs an additional $20,000 over the next year to keep the portfolio on track to provide a certain amount of wealth at a future point in time; the portfolio will have to generate a return of 20 percent over the one-year period. Thus, the investor knows the amount of risk that needs to be assumed to accomplish the 20 percent return. Significant risk must be taken in this case.

The third variable of risk profile is capacity, or the *can* part. Capacity is best defined as the ability of the investor to assume risk so that any losses experienced will not affect the attainment of SMART financial goals. Capacity basically indicates how much risk an investor can take regardless of how much he or she wants or needs to take. Your portfolio asset allocation should be built with your risk profile in mind.

4. IDENTIFY YOUR OPTIMAL ASSET MIX

Numerous landmark studies have concluded that the way you allocate your assets rather than which individual investments you select or when you buy or sell them is the leading determinant of investment performance over time. Moreover, some studies show that asset allocation is responsible for approximately 10 times more of a portfolio's performance over time than security selection and market timing combined. As a result, it is essential that you allocate your portfolio properly. Asset allocation is defined as the strategy of dividing an investor's wealth among the different asset classes and subclasses to achieve the highest expected total rate of return for that investor's risk profile and SMART financial goals. The advantages of properly allocating your portfolio, even when investing in commodities, include greater certainty of returns over time, the most efficient use of portfolio assets, and a higher risk-adjusted portfolio return. The four primary asset classes that you need to consider when allocating your assets are equities, fixed-income, cash and equivalents, and alternative investments.

5. *MAXIMIZE ASSET LOCATION*

Most investors have heard of asset allocation, but few have heard of its cousin, asset location. Asset location can refer to one of two important things. First, it can refer to which type of investment account you own, either a taxable or a tax-exempt account. Second, it can refer to which individual investments you select for your type of account. With a tax-exempt account, you do not need to worry about capital gains taxes or ordinary income taxes on the dividends and interest payments you receive. That means you are free to select investments that deliver the highest return regardless of the tax consequences. In contrast, taxable accounts, the typical investment account, require you to consider the tax consequences of an investment before making a purchase or sale. For example, if you are in a high federal tax bracket, you need to consider municipal bonds since the tax-equivalent yield often will be greater than the fully taxable corporate bond yield. It is the net return that matters. Other considerations you want to explore are related to investing in asset classes that deliver higher returns for their inherent level of risk. In other words, they offer return premiums. This means that over the long term you can generate higher returns for little or no additional risk. High-yield bonds, small-cap stocks, value stocks, and of course commodities are four of those investments.

6. *DIVERSIFY, DIVERSIFY, DIVERSIFY*

One of the important rules of investing is to diversify a portfolio. Diversification is a strategy designed to reduce total portfolio risk by combining a large number of investments within a particular asset class that have similar risk and return trade-off profiles. By doing this, you will reduce the negative impact of any single investment on the portfolio. Diversification within equity securities is most beneficial since those securities have the greatest amount of investment-specific risk. Index investments provide a quick and easy method to diversify a portfolio since they represent all the securities within that investing space or market.

It is very important to understand that diversification is not the same as asset allocation. This is one of the leading misconceptions about asset allocation and is discussed in my book *Understanding Asset Allocation*. Asset allocation involves investing in asset classes that have certain risk and return trade-off profiles; asset diversification involves investing in a significant number of securities within each asset class to minimize investment-specific risk. Both are vitally important for peak performance investing.

7. *INDEX IT!*

It's no secret that most portfolio managers do not beat the return of the market each year. Furthermore, portfolio managers who do beat the market in any specific year have a lower probability of beating the market the next year. As a result, index funds not only offer a low-cost approach to building an optimal portfolio but do so in a quick, easy, and efficient manner.

Index funds are much like mutual funds in that they are pools of investments and are typically highly diversified with low company-specific risk. However, index funds do not employ security selection to guide their investment choices, as mutual funds do. Rather, index funds are considered passive investments that are managed in such a way that their return matches that of a specific underlying index, for example, the S&P 500. What does this mean to you? It translates into lower management fees, greater tax efficiency, more complete asset class diversification, maximum liquidity, and higher net investment performance over time than what the average professional money manager can provide. You can build an entire portfolio by using index funds exclusively.

Index funds are most beneficial for large-cap investing. The more specialized a money manager must be to evaluate certain asset classes, such as small-caps or high-yield bonds, the less benefit index funds provide. The reason for this is that the more challenging asset classes typically have fewer money managers evaluating them. The less an investment is followed by the street, the greater is the impact an investment manager can make. This means that more sophisticated investors may want to consider using money managers for these asset classes.

Figure 17.1 shows a scale of active-passive management styles.

8. *EMPLOY TIME, NOT TIMING*

Think in the long term and emphasize decisions that will affect your portfolio in the long term; do not play the market. This is another of the golden rules of investing. As you can see, this rule is simple and straightforward. In addition, do your best to abandon all gambling tendencies and behaviors. Remember to approach investing as a rational and informed investor.

Study after study has shown that market timing determines only a small portion of total investment performance over time. As a result, trying to time your purchases and sales is generally a waste of time and resources. Rather than attempting to time

Figure 17-1. Scale of Active-Passive Management Style

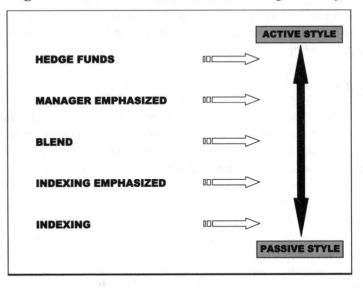

the market, concentrate your time and resources on employing a sound asset allocation strategy. A peripheral benefit of emphasizing asset allocation instead of market timing is lower turnover. Many people who use market timing have significant turnover, and that can trigger capital gains taxes.

It is difficult, if not impossible, to predict future returns in the short term. However, this task becomes significantly less difficult as the holding period increases. Having confidence in future returns allows for the selection of the optimal asset mix. Depending on your goals, investing for the short term can be a form of market timing. As a result, employing time rather than timing is by far the best solution.

9. THINK TOTAL PORTFOLIO, NOT COMPONENT INVESTMENTS

One of the most common errors investors make is to focus on certain individual investments within their portfolios rather than focusing on the portfolio as a whole. Portfolios behave in a much different way than do the individual investments that constitute them. Thus, a portfolio that consists only of fixed-income investments will be more risky, with a lower expected return, than a portfolio that includes both fixed-income and equity investments. Investors who want a more conservative portfolio therefore should allocate their investments to multiple asset classes.

By focusing on the individual investments in a portfolio, investors tend to lose sight of their overall SMART financial goals. In addition, many investors are tempted to make short-term ad hoc investment decisions that could be detrimental to overall portfolio performance.

The best way to avoid the problem of focusing on individual investments and instead focus on the overall portfolio is to allocate your portfolio properly, diversify your investments, and employ index funds when and where appropriate.

10. *MINIMIZE FEES AND COMMISSIONS*

Looking for a great way to gain performance without affecting future portfolio gains or adding an ounce of risk? You can accomplish this goal by minimizing management fees and commissions related to your portfolio. Depending on what financial instruments you employ to build your optimal asset mix, management fees and commissions can vary significantly. If you follow my suggestion and explore the idea of using index funds, your management fees should be relatively low. In contrast, if you invest in mutual funds or invest with select money managers, your management fees can be quite expensive, perhaps in the range of 1.5 to 2 percent. Regardless of the broker or investment professional, minimizing management fees and commissions leads to higher net returns. That of course is a very good thing.

11. *MINIMIZE TAXES AND EMPHASIZE AFTER-TAX RETURNS*

From time to time I hear financial advisors touting the returns they generated for some of their clients. They always quote what is known as gross returns rather than net returns. Although it is not always easy to identify net returns, in an ideal world that is what financial advisors and money managers should do. Here's something to think about. If an investor earns an 18 percent return but must pay 5 percent in taxes, did that person really earn 18 percent? If you cannot spend your earnings or reinvest them, did you earn them in the first place? It's the bottom line that ultimately counts.

Unacceptably high capital gain tax consequences can take a significant bite out of your performance. You have to earn those costs back or you are losing value. At the same time, for investors in the highest federal tax bracket, ordinary tax on interest and dividends can be severe and rob them of returns. Always think in terms of your after-tax return and minimize it where appropriate.

A final note: Although you need to beware of taxes and attempt to avoid them, never hold an investment that is not suitable. Tax consequences take a backseat to appropriateness and suitability.

12. *DRAFT A WRITTEN INVESTMENT PLAN*

Much like a blueprint for building a house, a written investment plan (investment policy statement) serves as a blueprint for building an optimal portfolio. First and foremost, a written plan helps you to learn more about what your needs and priorities are, how to address them, and the risks involved in investing. Second, a written investment plan allows you and your portfolio manager (if you elect to employ one) to gain a better understanding of your objectives and constraints and how to manage your portfolio to accomplish your SMART financial goals.

Other benefits of a written investment plan are that it (1) defines your optimal asset mix, asset allocation strategy, and construction method, (2) establishes what management style to follow, (3) provides a benchmark with which to evaluate the performance of your portfolio and manager, (4) safeguards the portfolio against ad hoc decisions that will impede your long-term strategy, and (5) allows misunderstandings and miscommunication to be resolved quickly and easily.

13. *REINVEST DIVIDENDS, INTEREST, AND CAPITAL GAINS*

Unless you need the income from your investments to supplement your normal income, reinvesting is a solid way to keep your money working for you. Over time the accumulation and compounding will become quite significant. This alone will result in strong portfolio growth.

. Choosing not to reinvest automatically in a taxable portfolio can be a good decision. Because you'll need to account for each and every reinvestment when you sell your investments, you may be faced with considerable hassles at tax time. No one wants to match up asset positions that were sold with those which were purchased to identify the gain or loss. One solution is to let your income accumulate in your money market and reinvest that money every three to six months. Doing that not only will help you avoid accounting hassles but also will allow you to reinvest in the areas that are underallocated in your portfolio. The key point is to reinvest regardless of the method.

Remember that all reinvested dividends, interest, and capital gains must be reported as income on tax returns. Uncle Sam always wants his cut.

14. *MONITOR, MEASURE, AND EVALUATE*

After you establish your portfolio, your work is not complete. Depending on how you look at it, it is essentially just beginning. What you do after you build your portfolio is arguably just as important as if not more important than what you do before that point.

With this strategy, you will take a proactive approach to monitoring not only your performance results but also the strategic fit. This means that you need to ensure that the commodities manager has not made any material changes since your initial investment and has delivered on any promises he or she made before investing. If you believe the strategic fit has weakened, you have every right to consider your alternatives and even explore the idea of terminating the relationship. Portfolio performance is only part of the reason you selected the commodities manager in the first place, and so any breach of fit with the other areas justifies taking action. Monitoring your portfolio also involves keeping an eye on how well it is performing. Poor performance is another strong reason for terminating the relationship.

When you measure your performance, you can measure it against similar commodities managers, the market as a whole, or stated goals if you have them. You also can employ mathematical measurements such as the Sharpe ratio, the Treynor ratio, and beta. These ratios measure portfolio risk in relation to portfolio return. Earning higher returns for a particular level of risk is ideal. Once you have a strong grasp of how well your portfolio is performing, you can determine that all is going well, decide to conduct more scrutiny, or terminate the relationship.

Regardless of the decision you make, this strategy is very important for keeping you on the right path with your commodity investing. Performing this strategy once each year is acceptable, but doing it semiannually or even quarterly is better.

15. *REOPTIMIZE YOUR PORTFOLIO*

Over time, a portfolio's asset mix, including the resulting risk and return trade-off profile, will change because of price fluctuations, with some fluctuations being quite large. Reoptimization may be an appropriate way to address this issue. Reoptimization consists of four different but somewhat similar tasks. The four R's of reoptimization are reevaluating, rebalancing, relocating, and reallocating.

Reevaluating is the process of examining recent changes in your life and evaluating them in the context of your portfolio. Many things may have changed in your life since you designed and built your portfolio, and those changes could affect your SMART financial goals and risk profile. As a result, you should take a long hard look at your original financial plan and portfolio and modify them if needed.

Rebalancing is the task of selling and buying investments to return a portfolio's current asset class mix to the previously established optimal asset mix. Rebalancing involves selling the asset classes that have become overweighted and buying the asset classes that have become underweighted.

Relocating is the task of exchanging certain assets for other assets without changing the overall asset mix or the risk and return trade-off profile. Relocating may involve exchanging a bond to obtain a higher or lower current rate of income, depending on how your need for income has changed.

Reallocating is the task of adjusting the investments your contributions are buying as well the amounts. In this context, reallocating does not change the mix of your assets, only how contributions will be made in the future.

16. *AMEND AS YOU CHANGE*

A sound investment plan is only as good as the quality of the way in which it is executed over the entire investment period. In the short term, investors find it easy to follow through and remain committed to their plans. Committing oneself over the long term is another story and is much easier said than done, but it is vital that investors do that.

Be driven, not motivated. Why be driven? Because being driven lasts a lifetime, whereas being motivated lasts only for the short term; motivation simply does not last. Avoid this very common pitfall and commit yourself to being driven.

In addition to committing yourself to being driven, you need to revisit your plan from time to time—at least annually—and modify it when and where appropriate. Pay careful attention to your current financial situation, your SMART financial goals, and the plan you have in place to bridge the gap. Changes should be made to your goals or plan if necessary. In addition, evaluate your portfolio within the context of any changes made and make changes to the portfolio and the written investment plan.

17. OBTAIN PROFESSIONAL HELP WHEN NEEDED

In an endeavor as critical as managing a portfolio, it is not wise to handle every situation without the help of a professional. Many individual investors do not have the time or the patience to manage their investments.

Obtaining professional counsel can be challenging and should not be approached lightly. As with investors and their objectives and constraints, professional advisors differ in their philosophy, processes, services, education, experience, and ability to add value. Professional advisors work in many fields and hold varied titles, such as investment advisor, financial planner, accountant, estate planner, insurance agent, and stockbroker. Figure 17.2 recaps the 17 points that were covered in this chapter.

Quiz for Chapter 17

1. Risk profile is composed of all but which of the following subsets of risk?
   a. Risk history
   b. Risk capacity
   c. Rick appetite
   d. Risk need

2. Commodities are considered alternative investments.
   a. True
   b. False

3. What is the golden rule of investing?
   a. Follow what the media say.
   b. Manage with a prudent mind-set.
   c. Compartmentalize your investments.
   d. Minimize tax consequences.

Figure 17-2. Immutable Universal Strategies of Peak Performance Investing

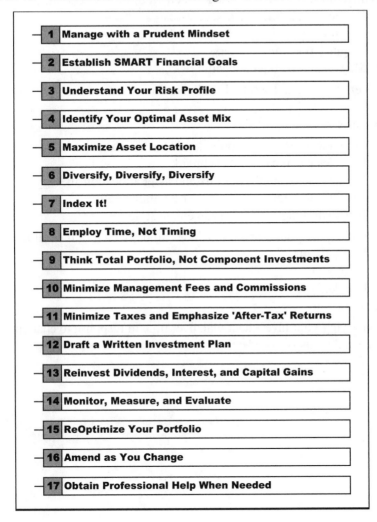

1. Manage with a Prudent Mindset
2. Establish SMART Financial Goals
3. Understand Your Risk Profile
4. Identify Your Optimal Asset Mix
5. Maximize Asset Location
6. Diversify, Diversify, Diversify
7. Index It!
8. Employ Time, Not Timing
9. Think Total Portfolio, Not Component Investments
10. Minimize Management Fees and Commissions
11. Minimize Taxes and Emphasize 'After-Tax' Returns
12. Draft a Written Investment Plan
13. Reinvest Dividends, Interest, and Capital Gains
14. Monitor, Measure, and Evaluate
15. ReOptimize Your Portfolio
16. Amend as You Change
17. Obtain Professional Help When Needed

4. Indexing all portfolio assets is a smart move and is highly encouraged.
   a. True
   b. False

5. For which of the following asset classes is indexing most effective?
   a. Large-cap stocks
   b. Small-cap stocks
   c. International stocks
   d. High-yield fixed-income investments

6. Which of the following is the key benefit of diversification?
   a. Isolate top-performing asset classes
   b. Minimize market risk
   c. Magnify portfolio returns
   d. Minimize investment-specific risk

7. Diversification and asset allocation are the same.
   a. True
   b. False

8. A written investment plan provides all but which of the following benefits?
   a. Provides a comparison benchmark
   b. Defines the optimal asset mix and asset allocation strategy
   c. Provides for significant manager flexibility
   d. Establishes the optimal management style

9. Reoptimizing your portfolio includes all but which of the following?
   a. Reevaluating
   b. Redividing
   c. Rebalancing
   d. Relocating

10. Modifying your investment plan over time in response to changing financial goals is a prudent move.
    a. True
    b. False

CHAPTER 18

Key Attributes of Commodities:

Highlighting the Top 10 Defining Characteristics

As is the case with nearly everything else, there are specific characteristics that define commodities. Commodities can be defined by a number of different characteristics that present them in a unique light. We have discussed each of these characteristics to some degree in this book, but this chapter zeroes in on what I consider the most important of these characteristics—the top 10 defining characteristics of commodities. We bring them all together in one chapter to reinforce their importance.

If there is anything or any lesson that you take away from this book, it should be an understanding and conceptualizing of these 10 defining characteristics. They are presented in no particular order because no single characteristic is more important than the others. After reading all the defining characteristics, you may want to review the material in this book relevant to those topics to gain a solid grasp. Note that the first seven characteristics are related to commodities, whereas the final three are related to adding commodities to a portfolio. Figure 18.1 provides a convenient list of these characteristics.

Figure 18-1. Top 10 Defining Characteristics of Commodities

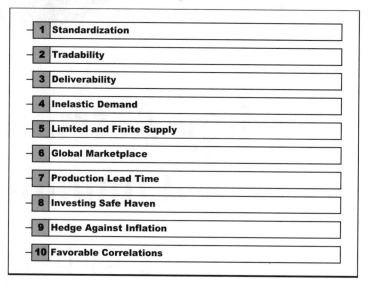

1. Standardization

The primary characteristic of a commodity is its standardization. This means that you can take one unit of a commodity and replace it with another unit of the same commodity without any difficulty. Thus, commodities are interchangeable. For example, if you are an orange juice producer, it does not matter to you if you obtain oranges from Florida, California, or Brazil as each location produces oranges that will produce the same final product. Moreover, it does not matter if the natural gas you use to heat your house or stove is sourced from the United States or Canada or is imported from the Middle East. Natural gas sourced from a far-off location and gas sourced from close to home will achieve the same result: the production of heat.

Some commodities, such as crude oil and coal, come in different grades. Each grade achieves the same end result and is priced according to the demand for it. In addition, through the interaction of people, commodities are not entirely pure. For instance, depending on the amount of other precious metals added, you can purchase pure gold—referred to as 24-karat gold—or gold that is only 37.5 percent gold and 62.5 percent other metals—referred to as 9-karat gold.

Standardization with commodities is essential since commodities are the raw materials needed to sustain any economic activity or society.

2. Tradability

Tradability refers to the market for buying and selling a particular commodity. Most commodities have very robust markets, but the markets for a few of the newest commodities, such as carbon emissions credits, are not as robust. With increasing interest, these newer markets are expected to gain in liquidity and become robust.

Tradability also refers to the way commodities are traded. Unlike trading in traditional stocks and bonds, commodity trading is unique because of the futures markets. With futures trading, a trader can purchase a commodity for future delivery but lock in that purchase at current market prices. This futures market is what distinguishes commodity trading from nearly all other investments. There are some commodities that do not have underlying futures contracts, but exposure can be gained through exchange-traded instruments such as funds and notes or through stock in companies involved in the commodities market.

3. Deliverability

Aside from financials, commodities can be delivered physically to the buyer by the seller. For instance, crude oil can be delivered in barrels and coal can be delivered in railway cars. Commodity traders have the option of receiving the physical commodity or closing the position with an offsetting transaction and thus not taking physical delivery.

Taking physical possession of a commodity is dependent on the delivery month stipulated in the futures contract. Physical delivery varies from commodity to commodity in regard to the delivery month and how far out in the future the futures contract extends. Delivery months are important since timing in making delivery by the seller and taking delivery by the buyer is essential. For example, farmers will provide delivery soon after they harvest their crops, whereas buyers want to take delivery at certain points that correspond with their production schedule. Without deliverability in terms of delivery months, commodities would all trade spot, meaning that they would be exchanged at the very moment a transaction between buyer and seller was executed. The efficiency and liquidity of the commodities markets would decline sharply as a result, and many consumers would experience times of excess commodities and times of no commodities.

4. Inelastic Demand

Elasticity is an economic concept that is used to measure how much supply of and demand for a particular product will change per unit of price change. This measurement captures the way in which price and the quantity demanded by consumers are related to each other. Products can be categorized as elastic or inelastic, although there are many gradations between the two. When quantity demanded changes in proportion to changes in price, a product is considered elastic. If the quantity demanded does not change in proportion, the product is inelastic. When prices rise, quantity demanded falls when the product is elastic. In other words, there is a high inverse correlation between price and quantity demanded for elastic products.

For example, suppose the price of baseball tickets rose by 30 percent. The result would be a sharp decline in the sale of baseball tickets since watching a movie at the theater is not a necessity. We thus can say that movie tickets are an elastic product and that any change in price will cause an inverse change in quantity demanded. However, if the price of natural gas increases by 30 percent, are you going to lower your thermostat temperature 30 percent on a freezing winter day? The answer is no. Natural gas is a necessity and therefore is considered an inelastic product. As a result, when the price for natural gas rises, the quantity demanded remains relatively stable.

No products are 100 percent inelastic so that there is no change in quantity demanded after a change in price. Even with natural gas, there is a price point at which you would start to make the temperature slightly lower, investigate alternative sources of heating, or save heat by placing plastic over the windows.

For the most part, commodities are considered inelastic products, and consumers thus have few options for reducing the quantity demanded when prices rise and costs increase. Without natural gas, many people would be unable to heat their homes. Without gasoline, many people would be unable to get to work and school. Without grain and corn, many people would be hard put to find food alternatives. The fact is that commodities are the raw materials of civilization and people cannot do without them. Unfortunately, that means that people pay more when prices rise, and there is little they can do about it.

5. Limited and Finite Supply

Unlike other goods, there is a limited and finite supply of commodities. There is more crude oil in the world today than there will be a month from now or a year from now. The same goes for the other energy fuels and for both precious metals and industrial metals. Once a commodity is exhausted, there is no way of producing more. Crude oil production has been in decline in many countries for the last couple of decades. Even Saudi Arabia is close to declines in production as more crude is extracted, leaving only the crude that is most challenging to extract. The same goes for coal and natural gas. Commodities that are the easiest to extract are sourced first. Metals and energy fuels have a finite supply that one day will be extinguished without the possibility of being replenished.

As for agricultural products, there is a limited supply of cropland, and much of the highest-quality cropland is being shifted to residential use. In the past, people gravitated to the best agricultural lands since producing food for local consumption was the key to survival. Over time, as towns transform into cities and the population grows, the best agricultural land is used for new homes rather than for cropland. At the same time, land that was less than ideal is used as cropland.

For investors, this characteristic is positive. Because of increasing demand, declining production, and finite supplies, prices can go in only one direction in the long term: higher.

6. Global Marketplace

When you invest in commodities, you generally invest globally rather than locally. This is the case because commodities are situated and produced in many different parts of the world and transported to many other parts. Thus, when you invest in palladium, you are investing in a metal that is produced principally in Russia and South Africa. Much of the copper in the world is produced in Chile, and much of the crude oil comes from the Middle East. Although many commodities—especially key commodities—are quoted in U.S. dollars, there are global factors that affect their quality and price. For example, when OPEC placed an embargo on oil, consumers in other parts of the world were affected as supplies dwindled and prices skyrocketed. When droughts occur in Australia and other grain-producing nations, consumers turn to the United States for wheat. Commodities exchanges work within a global marketplace in which purchasers and sellers from around the world can come together to execute transactions.

When a certain brand of car is in demand in Europe, that will not necessarily affect prices in the United States. Likewise, when a certain type of wine has high demand in New Zealand, that does not mean that Italians will demand the same type. Commodities are different in that global geopolitical factors and global demand and supply dynamics affect price. There is a great demand for stainless steel in China because of the economic transformation occurring in that country. As a result, the price for stainless steel in the United States has risen, with some consumers choosing alternatives. Commodities are defined by their global reach.

7. Long Production Lead Time

Unlike other goods in the marketplace, commodities can take years to produce and bring to market. This means that when demand for a particular commodity increases, the supply of that commodity will not increase quickly to match the new demand. When supply does not keep pace with demand, prices rise, and that equates to profits for commodities investors.

When an electronics company experiences greater demand for its high-tech televisions, it increases production to match the new demand. This increase in production can be achieved within a few months. The same thing cannot be said for commodities. If a commodity company experiences greater demand, it will take years rather than months to meet the new demand because many commodities must be explored, discovered, extracted, refined, and transported to the marketplace, and that process can take several years. For example, if the demand for uranium ore increases, mining companies will need to increase production at current mines and find new mining sites. It's a big world, and finding uranium ore is not an easy task. The mining company could spend years searching for new deposits that are worth mining and then begin the process of extracting uranium ore. Once the ore is mined, it must be transported to buyers, which will add extra time. If problems occur with mining operations, the time before buyers take delivery will be even longer. One of the largest uranium mines in the world is in Canada. In the mid–2000s the company that owns the mine reported that the mine was flooded with water and would be unable to provide uranium ore for an extended period. The price of uranium ore shot up literally overnight.

For investors, longer production lead times are a positive factor since less supply is available to meet higher demand, resulting in higher prices and greater profits. Many investments do not exhibit this characteristic.

8. Investing Safe Haven

Some commodities, such as gold and silver and to some extent U.S. dollars, provide safety during times of global unrest and instability. Investors view precious metals as an asset that provides strong value during uncertain times when investments such as stocks are falling sharply. As was mentioned above, one of the reasons for this is the perception of the value precious metals provide; another reason is the perception that large cash inflows occur during troubling times, and this thus becomes a self-fulfilling prophecy. If you look at any price chart for silver and gold over the last 20 years, you can see price increases that were caused by specific global events.

Aside from precious metals, other commodities, such as crude oil, provide some degree of safety from world troubles. When political tensions escalate in the Middle East, the price of crude oil typically rises. Most other types of investments do not offer the same degree of safety from turmoil that otherwise would decrease their value.

9. Hedge against Inflation

In addition to providing safety, commodities provide investors with a natural hedge against inflation. Inflation causes purchasing power to decline since a dollar earned today will not buy the same amount of goods tomorrow. When inflation increases, the market value for nearly all assets declines in response to the lower future earnings that result from higher costs. Thus, there is an inverse relationship between inflation and the value of most assets. When inflation is tame, the prices for assets typically rise. However, when inflation is high, prices fall. Commodities are the raw materials required to sustain any society and the underlying materials for business and industry. When inflation is rising, commodity prices are rising. Actually, inflation is based on commodity prices rather than commodity prices being based on inflation. Thus, when crude oil is rising, inflation typically increases.

For investors looking to hedge the assets in their portfolios, investing in commodities is a good move. For instance, suppose you invest in a crude oil exchange-traded note (ETN) and crude oil prices rise over the next year. This increase in prices will mean a higher value for your ETN, which will help offset losses in any stock positions in your portfolio. Stocks typically will fall since higher energy costs attributed to the rise in crude oil prices leave consumers with less money to spend on products, and that translates into lower revenues and earnings.

By investing in commodities, you turn what is typically a destroyer of value into a driver of value. Another popular asset class that provides a hedge against inflation is a real estate investment trust (REIT). When inflation is rising, real estate prices rise, and that means profits for investors.

10. Favorable Correlations

Correlation is a measurement of how closely the market prices of two assets move together over time. Thus, high correlation means that the prices of two assets are changing and moving in very similar ways and patterns. Low correlations mean that the prices of the two assets are moving differently. The lower the correlation is, the less the prices move together. Low correlation could mean that they still move in roughly the same direction—positive correlation—or in totally opposite directions—negative correlation. Holding a portfolio of assets with low correlations to other assets is ideal since when one asset is moving down in price, another will not fall as much or even rise in value.

Most commodities have low correlations with other investments and thus provide a safety net during times of stock market turmoil. This means that the value of your portfolio will not decline during stock market crashes. Low correlation means that the value of your portfolio will be more stable since while some investments are falling, other investments are remaining stable or rising. The end result is a portfolio that has a higher risk-adjusted return than do portfolios with only traditional stock and bond investments.

Quiz for Chapter 18

1. Which of the following is not a top 10 defining characteristic of commodities?
   a. Inelastic demand
   b. Limited and finite supply
   c. Standardization
   d. Adaptability

2. The commodities market is considered a global marketplace.
   a. True
   b. False

3. Which defining characteristic is described as being interchangeable, or replacing one unit with another unit without difficulty?
   a. Tradability
   b. Standardization
   c. Deliverability
   d. Commonality

4. Tradability is defined by robust trading and which other unique attribute?
   a. Exercisable
   b. Stable prices
   c. Volatile prices
   d. Futures market

5. Demand for commodities is generally independent of commodity prices. This describes which defining characteristic of commodities?
   a. Independent demand
   b. Inelastic demand
   c. Demand neutrality
   d. Elastic demand

6. Commodities have favorable correlations compared with other asset classes. What type of correlation does the term *favorable* attempt to convey?
   a. Positive correlations
   b. Negative correlations
   c. No correlations
   d. None of the above

7. The production of most commodities has very long lead times.
   a. True
   b. False

8. Which of the following commodities is considered an investing safe haven during uncertain times?
   a. Copper
   b. Crude oil
   c. Wheat
   d. Lumber

9. Taking physical possession of a commodity describes which defining characteristic of commodities?
   a. Tradability
   b. Deliverability
   c. Standardization
   d. Inelastic demand

10. Commodities are defined by their relatively unlimited supply.
    a. True
    b. False

9-P Performance Plan:

Selecting the Right Commodities Money Manager

The discovery and pursuit of the right commodities money manager is the ideal first step in investing in commodities. Regardless of your experience with investing, you need to ensure that some very basic and important tasks are done before you select a commodities money manager. The following are some of the critical considerations you should investigate about each manager before making the initial commodities investment. This chapter deals mostly with professionally managed commodities funds rather than commodity brokers or financial advisors.

The process of investing in commodities can be illustrated in a nine-step process-oriented plan I call the 9-P Performance Plan. This plan covers everything from formulating your initial ideas and goals to monitoring your portfolio for performance and continued strategic fit. Each of the nine steps involves just one task, with the exception of the fifth step, which covers probing or investigating a professional money manager for suitability, appropriateness, and performance. Although the plan is presented in the context of commodities, it can be employed with all types of investments when one is investigating a professional money manager. Some of the steps may differ from investment type to investment type, but the overall intent and theme will be beneficial. For instance, although you may employ the plan in searching for a commodities money manager you also may employ it if you decide to seek the help of a financial planner or a traditional investment manager. The steps of the 9-P Performance Plan follow.

1. Prioritize

In the first step investors need to identify exactly what they are hoping to accomplish by investing in commodities. Perhaps an investor is looking to build a better portfolio or wants to profit from the anticipated rise in energy prices during the summer months. In either case, identifying what one is hoping to achieve is the first step. In addition, investors need to determine that allocating portfolio assets to commodities is suitable and appropriate for their goals and risk profile. Once your goals and objectives are established and prioritized, you can decide which approach to commodity investing to take. Perhaps you will invest in a commodities mutual fund or in commodities-related exchange-traded notes. Maybe you are willing and able to assume greater risk and can afford the time required to trade futures contracts and participate in commodities directly without the help of a professional money manager. This step is all about laying the foundation for successful commodity investing.

Having investment goals and striving to attain those goals will give your investing purpose and direction. In formulating your investment goals, make sure that they adhere to the SMART strategy:

- *Specific*: Your goals should be unambiguous, clear, and well defined.
- *Measurable*: Your goals should be quantifiable and calculable.
- *Accepted*: Your goals should be acknowledged and motivational.
- *Realistic*: Your goals should be achievable and attainable, not lofty.
- *Time-centric*: Your goals should be for a set period, not indefinite.

2. Plan

In this step investors establish and formalize their thoughts on investment goals and objectives in a written plan that often is called an investment policy statement (IPS). Some of the important items that need to be addressed in the plan are the desired investing approach (commodities mutual funds, commodities trading advisors, exchange-traded commodities, or investing in the stock of companies involved in the commodities market), the number of commodities funds (if you elect to use this investing approach), the degree of portfolio allocation to commodities, and the breadth of commodities included (all classes or only select classes).

A properly drafted IPS outlines the asset classes selected for investment and their respective weightings within the portfolio. In addition, many policies mention security selection and timing strategies. A properly drafted IPS clearly articulates your objectives and constraints as well as ways to address and incorporate them within the portfolio management process. A written plan will not guarantee success in protecting and growing your portfolio. Rather, it will shelter your portfolio from ad hoc revisions made by you or your portfolio manager.

3. Pinpoint

In this step investors take a proactive approach to finding and investigating ways to invest in commodities. Perhaps the investor has decided to invest in commodities through a mutual fund. As a result, the investor will seek out mutual funds that target commodities and information on each of those funds. In this example, the investor will want to collect data on key characteristics such as performance, manager tenure, investment turnover, management fees, minimum investment amounts, and investment objectives and philosophies. Once this information is collected, the investor can evaluate all the material before screening out certain mutual funds and selecting others for additional research.

4. Pursue

Once an investor has performed the initial research on different investing alternatives, that investor will select the investment alternatives that appear attractive and screen out those which do not overcome the essential hurdles. Investors should evaluate performance numbers for each alternative against the performance of its peers. For example, an investor should identify and evaluate the 1-, 5-, and 10-year performance history of a certain commodity mutual fund not only against its peer commodity group but also against the S&P 500 as a whole. Why the S&P 500? The S&P 500 is the benchmark return investors can earn from simple and straightforward investing. If the performance of a certain investment does not beat the performance of the S&P 500, the investor needs to reevaluate that investment. Performance comparison is only one factor in evaluating investment alternatives. Other factors include correlation, capital gains consequences, volatility, and expenses such as management fees. For more astute investors, comparing an investment's risk-adjusted return is by far the most important task in conducting research. Although an investment may offer a stronger performance history, that investment may have a much higher volatility risk history, which means greater overall risk. Investments that offer the highest return per unit of volatility risk are the ideal investments, all else being equal, such as correlation to the market. This is the essence of modern portfolio theory. Once all the initial evaluations have been made and a group of investments has been selected, the investor will pursue more information on each one.

5. Probe

In this step investors need to be diligent in evaluating commodities and key people. To remain consistent, I have included nine areas, each beginning with the letter P, that investors should investigate. Make sure you understand the level of risk, the initial investment minimum, any withdrawal provisions, and other important considerations. Evaluate this information within the context of your goals and objectives and ensure that they are suitable to your investing goals, time horizon, and risk profile (tolerance, capacity, and need). As with any investment, the higher the potential returns for a commodity, the higher the potential risk you must assume. Risk and return are linked.

PRODUCTS

The first step is to identify the various commodity offerings available to you. Do they offer high-risk and high-potential-return investments, low-risk and low-potential-return investments, or a combination of the two? Can the commodities money manager integrate the offerings with your current portfolio or will this be a stand-alone investment? Does the commodity advisor offer multiple funds to provide investors with a choice of strategies? Once the question of offerings is answered, you can make an informed decision on whether to go any further in your probing task.

PERFORMANCE

Investors should conduct a quantitative investigation of a commodities money manager by targeting areas such as the level of historical returns, the volatility of historical returns, and the dispersion of historical returns. Risk measurements should be conducted.

Most commodities money managers will provide some type of performance composite for review. When reviewing performance, be sure to learn which benchmark or benchmarks are employed, how well the manager performed against his or her peer group, how consistent performance has been over long periods, what type of volatility is typical in those commodities, what the growth of assets under management has been, and how and when the performance composite was created. A statement claiming that the performance composite conforms to CFA Institute standards is your best assurance that the results are accurate. Some commodities funds go a step further and have an external party review their performance composites and give them their stamp of approval. If any of these items are not provided, ask the manager for them.

PEDIGREE

Investors should conduct a qualitative investigation of the commodities manager by targeting things such as the educational background, investment experience, and possible disciplinary history of key people.

Conducting a background check on the commodities manager is one of the golden rules of commodity investing. Know with whom you are investing your money. Make sure the commodities manager and other key decision makers are qualified to manage your money. Investigate what type of education the manager has: a bachelor's or perhaps a master's degree. Investigate whether the manager has earned a professional designation such as a CFA (Chartered Financial Analyst), CPA (Certified Public Accountant), CFP (Certified Financial Planner), or ChFC (Chartered Financial Consultant). Having a designation illustrates commitment and specialized knowledge, both of which separate the top managers from the rest of the pack. Investigate how long the manager has been managing commodities and how much experience he or she has with investments and portfolio management. Also inquire how long the manager has been in his or her current role.

PROCESS

Investors should conduct investigations into the investment process employed by a commodities manager. This includes items such as investment strategy, use of derivatives and leverage, and buying and selling methodology. Some commodities managers employ top-down investment styles, and others use bottom-up investment styles. Top-down refers to evaluating the macro investing marketplace first and then narrowing the focus in subsequent steps until individual commodities or companies are investigated. Bottom-up is the opposite approach. With this strategy the manager emphasizes individual commodity or company research first, widens the analysis in subsequent steps, and concludes the process once the macro investing marketplace has been researched.

Many commodities managers exercise significant discretion in the method and timing of valuing securities. Make every effort to identify the timing of the valuation (e.g., monthly, quarterly) and how the assets are valued. It is always wise to understand the valuation process and learn whether the assets are valued by an independent external source.

PROVISIONS

Investors should conduct due diligence of the operational aspects of commodities managers. Some of the key areas to investigate are liquidity and lock-up provisions, performance safeguards, and the quality of the technology systems.

The vast majority of commodities-related funds typically restrict investors from redeeming their interest. These restrictions include the first-year period of withholding the right to withdraw from the fund and the periods when withdrawals can be made. Most funds include the first-year provision, in which your investment is locked up for one year or more. Thereafter, funds are typically available only on a quarterly or annual basis. These provisions are instituted to give commodities managers the opportunity to employ their strategies and the time needed to liquidate investments to cover withdrawals from clients.

PAYMENTS

Fees have a big impact on your net return. Most commodities funds typically charge an investment management fee of 1 to 2 percent of assets under management, plus an incentive performance fee, which is typically 20 percent of the profits. This fee is used to motivate commodities managers to generate positive returns. If the manager does not perform, the investor will not have to pay this fee; this is a win-win situation for both. At the same time, this fee could motivate a commodities manager to take greater risks than warranted in pursuit of even greater returns and thus more fees. Most commodities funds charge both the annual investment management fee and the performance incentive fee. Remember to get all this information on the table from the outset.

Some managers underemphasize tax management, whereas others overemphasize it. Specifically, ask about the general degree of turnover, how they incorporate tax management into the management process, and how they approach the issue of tax loss-harvesting and exchange strategies. Many commodities managers strive to maximize the top line, or gross return, but the top managers focus on maximizing the bottom line, or net return. Remember, if you cannot walk away with the money, did you really earn it in the first place? It does not matter if you earned a substantial return if you must turn around and give Uncle Sam a big chunk of that return.

PERSONAL

Ask about the commodities manager's personal investments in the commodities funds. Hedge fund commodities managers should have a substantial amount of their investable assets in the commodities hedge funds they are managing. Moreover, the commodities manager should not have any investments of a similar type outside his or her commodities fund. Ask the commodities manager about both of these issues. Exercise caution with commodities managers who invest actively in similar investments outside the commodities fund they manage. Owning nonsimilar assets such as Treasuries and real estate is not a concern as it does not cause conflicts of interest or signal that better investments can be found outside the fund. Commodities managers who invest a substantial amount of their personal assets in the fund have an extra incentive to generate attractive returns. This is a win-win situation for everyone involved and tells the investor that the interests of the manager and those of the client are aligned. If commodities managers are investing outside their funds, perhaps investors should do the same thing.

PERSONALITY

Investors need to consider the personality fit before deciding to invest with a manager. Usually, after the first meeting you will know if there is a fit. Is the manager serious or humorous? Is the manager intense or low-key? Is the manager professional or down to earth? Does he or she play golf? Did a friend refer you? Are your interests similar? Personality fit is not a high-priority item, but not having a good relationship with your commodities manager will make things more challenging over time.

PRINCIPLES

Nothing can cause a commodities fund to collapse quite like unethical behavior. The top commodities managers want to remain in the business over the life of their careers and therefore value ethical behavior. Building a top commodities fund can take a significant amount of work, time, and money, but a single unethical action can make it come crashing down. The top commodities managers are at the pinnacle of the industry and therefore do not want to risk this.

This is obviously very subjective and not always easy to determine when you first meet a commodities manager. A good way to approach it is to investigate whether either a regulatory organization or a private association he or she might be a member of has disciplined the manager publicly. You can obtain this type of information by reviewing the manager's Form ADV-II if it is available. Depending on whether this form is available, it may be possible to review the firm's Form ADV-II by using the SEC's Investment Adviser Public Disclosure (IAPD) website. For managers with less than $25 million in assets under management, the state securities regulator where the manager's principal place of business is located can provide this type of information. Also check with the National Futures Association (NFA) for background information on commodities fund managers. This step can prevent problems that arise from unethical behavior down the road.

6. Ponder

In this step investors conduct a serious review and evaluate all the information obtained during the probing step. This step is best thought of as the final assessment and filtering before the selection of one or more commodities funds in which to invest. Remember to consider all the factors presented in the probing stage as each one plays an important role in the decision process. You probably will not identify any one manager who will be the best in all categories, so be prepared to make a difficult decision.

7. Pick

In this step investors make the formal selection of one or more commodities funds that meet their criteria and provide them with the greatest amount of confidence that the investment will go well. Preferably, the investor will have selected a commodities fund that has demonstrated good performance over the long term, offers suitable and appropriate products and offerings that meet the investor's needs, has demonstrated excellence in ethical behavior, has managers with strong experience in commodities and money management, and does not charge excessive fees and hit investors with high capital gains consequences. As with traditional investing, there are money managers who are solid fits for investors and some who are not. The same holds true for commodity investing and the use of commodities money managers.

8. Position

In this step investors make the initial commodities investment, or purchase, and position that investment within the context of their overall portfolios. Investment decisions involving the total portfolio should include the commodities allocation regardless of whether the invested capital is combined under one money manager or reported on the same monthly account statement. From this point forward, all decisions involving the portfolio should include the commodities allocation. For instance, over time the asset class allocations within a portfolio will change with changing market conditions. This means that your allocations to equities, fixed-income investments, and alternative investments will change. Some asset classes will advance in price and therefore increase their allocation within the portfolio, and others will decline in price and decrease their allocation. Reoptimizing is thus very important to keep the portfolio allocations as close to the optimal allocations as possible. This may involve purchasing more commodities investments or selling some commodities investments. Positioning of asset classes within a portfolio is critical for achieving an investor's long-term goals and objectives.

9. Police

In this step investors monitor, measure, and evaluate the commodities investment for continued strategic fit and satisfactory performance. If the investment is doing well, no action needs to be taken. However, if strategic fit or performance has weakened since the initial investment, perhaps a discussion with the commodities manager is appropriate or a termination of the engagement is needed.

PERFORMANCE MONITORING

Most money managers evaluate the portfolio performance on a quarterly basis to appease investors. However, evaluating portfolio performance is not as easy as it might appear. First, there is the issue of evaluating a portfolio's short-term results when you have designed and implemented a long-term strategy. Any comparisons made using short-term periods are measuring security selection and market timing, nothing more. Second, there is difficulty in comparing a multiple-asset-class portfolio to a benchmark. Which benchmark or benchmarks do you select? Simply selecting the S&P 500 for a multiple-asset-class portfolio will not suffice. The S&P 500 is composed of equity securities only. Thus, a portfolio that includes fixed-income securities or alternative assets would not be appropriate. The solution is to segment each asset class and compare it with an appropriate benchmark, such as the S&P 500 for U.S. equity securities and the EAFE for international equity securities.

It is very important to ensure that the performance data supplied by your money manager, if you elect to use one, are created using geometric returns rather than arithmetic returns because otherwise the results can be misleading. For instance, you invest $1,000,000 with a certain money manager. During the year your portfolio suffers a huge loss and is worth $500,000 at the end of the year. That's a negative 50 percent return. The following year your portfolio gains the $500,000 lost in the previous year, giving it a total market value of $1,000,000 at the end of the second year. This equates to a return of 100 percent for year 2. Using arithmetic returns, your money manager may claim to have earned you +25 percent (−50 percent +100 percent divided by 2) during the two-year period. As you can see, your portfolio has not appreciated whatsoever, and +25 percent is not accurate. Geometric returns compensate for this issue whereby your two year portfolio performance would be 0 percent. The CFA Institute requires all members to measure their portfolio performance using geometric returns.

REBALANCING TO REOPTIMIZE

Over time, a portfolio's asset mix, including the resulting risk and return trade-off profile, will change as a result of price fluctuations, with some fluctuations being quite large. To address this issue, reoptimization may be needed. Reoptimization consists of four different but somewhat similar tasks. The Four R's of reoptimization are reevaluating, rebalancing, relocating, and reallocating. Each is described below.

Reevaluating

Reevaluating is the task of examining recent changes in your life in relation to your current portfolio. Many things may have changed in your life since you last designed and built your portfolio and could affect your SMART financial goals and risk profile. You may have changed jobs, married, divorced, had more children, or experienced an upheaval in your life. As a result, you should take a long and hard look at your original financial plan and portfolio and modify them if needed.

Rebalancing

Rebalancing is the task of selling and buying investments to return a portfolio's current asset class mix to the previously established optimal asset mix. Rebalancing involves selling a portion of asset classes that have become overweighted and buying a portion of asset classes that have become underweighted. Rebalancing is the key to maximizing a portfolio's risk and return trade-off profile over time.

Relocating

Relocating is the task of exchanging certain assets for other assets without changing the overall asset mix or risk and return trade-off profile. Relocating may involve exchanging a certain bond to obtain a higher or lower current rate of income, depending on a changed need for income. It also may involve switching to tax-exempt U.S. Treasury securities from taxable corporate bonds if there has been a change in tax status resulting from greater taxable income.

Reallocating

Reallocating is the task of adjusting which asset classes you make investment contributions to and in what proportion you make those investments. In this context, reallocating does not change the mix of your assets, only how contributions will be made in the future.

Quiz for Chapter 19

1. Which of the following is the first step in selecting the right commodities manager/advisor?
   a. Pinpoint
   b. Prioritize
   c. Police
   d. Ponder

2. An investment policy statement is vitally important for all investors?
   a. True
   b. False

3. SMART financial goals are all but which of the following?
   a. Specific
   b. Measurable
   c. Accountable
   d. Realistic

4. With SMART financial goals, which strategy stipulates that goals should be acknowledged and motivational?
   a. Specific
   b. Accepted
   c. Realistic
   d. Time-centric

5. Which of the following steps is defined as a proactive approach to investigating and sourcing ways to invest in commodities?
   a. Plan
   b. Prioritize
   c. Pursue
   d. Pinpoint

6. Which step includes nine substeps to ensure a proper fit with a commodity manager/advisor?
   a. Probe
   b. Pinpoint

    c. Ponder

    d. Police

7. Once all the relevant data are collected, investors move to the ponder step.
    a. True
    b. False

8. All but which of the following substeps are included in the probe step?
    a. Performance review
    b. Pedigree review
    c. Process review
    d. Premium review

9. Which of the following is the golden rule of investigating potential managers/advisors?
    a. Ask about tenure.
    b. Conduct background checks.
    c. Ask for client references.
    d. Investigate holdings.

10. In which step do investors execute rebalancing?
    a. Probing
    b. Pinpointing
    c. Policing
    d. Pursuing

CHAPTER 20

Electronic Commodity Trading:

An Introduction to Online Opportunities

In the past, investing in commodities was the turf of big players who had large portfolios, access to placing trades, and money to pay commissions and fees. Today, electronic trading is commonplace, and that has opened commodity trading to the mass of investors. You do not have to be a big player anymore to gain access to trading platforms and commodities exchanges. Discount futures brokers such as Lind-Waldock make trading much more quick and simple than it was in years past. At the same time, investors have more choices and have the option of working with a full-service broker, discount broker, or introducing broker.

Full-Service Broker

Full-service brokers provide an array of services that inexperienced investors may find of value and be willing to pay for. Those services include research, recommendations, and service from a dedicated account representative. Account representatives can provide advice about which commodity to trade and perhaps what trading strategy to employ. Some of the top brokerage firms offer this type of service, and that means added comfort for investors who wish to begin a program of commodities trading.

Discount Broker

For do-it-yourself investors, discount brokers are ideal since they assess lower fees and commissions than do full-service brokers. As long as you are comfortable conducting all your research and making all your investing decisions, a discount broker is probably your best bet. These brokers do not provide all the bells and whistles that full-service brokers do, but they do not charge extra for services you do not need. The typical discount broker allows you to place trades online or with a representative by telephone at a slightly higher commission rate.

Introducing Broker

Introducing brokers are companies that offer services very much like those of full-service brokers but defer the execution of futures trading orders to another type of firm called clearing firms, which must be members of a commodities exchange. Introducing brokers are ideal for an investor who is investing in commodities for the first time, wants the extra services not provided by discount brokers, or both. The fees are higher than those of discount brokers and more comparable to those of full-service brokers.

Pros and Cons of Trading Online

Trading commodities online has unique challenges and opportunities not seen with trading and investing through a representative such as a financial advisor or through approaches such as commodity exchange-traded funds and mutual funds. As a result, keeping these challenges in mind before and during trading will help you avoid pitfalls that could lead to sizable losses. Let's begin with a discussion of the pros of online trading.

PROS

Low Commissions and Fees

The most important reason for trading online and with a discount broker is lower commissions and fees. Always remember that it is the bottom line that matters most; anything that reduces that number should be minimized wherever and whenever possible. Commissions and fees can have a material impact on your overall performance.

Desired Access

Online trading provides significant access to trade commodities, and that means more choices. As a general rule, the more choices an investor has, the more opportunity he or she has to maximize gains, minimize losses, and control risk.

More Control

When you trade online, you often trade on your own. That can be good or bad, depending on your experience level. For experienced commodities investors, online trading affords the opportunity to retain control over trading without the influence of someone else.

CONS

No Mentor

By far the most important drawback to online trading is the lack of a qualified and experienced mentor: an account representative. Some investors do not need mentors, whereas others, such as novice investors, find their help invaluable. Without a mentor some investors may feel that they are flying blind, and doing that in the high-risk and high-return field of commodities futures can be extremely risky.

Potential for Excessive Trading

When you trade online, you typically do not have contact with an account executive, or at least with one who provides input for your purchase and sale decisions. As a result, some investors may trade their portfolios excessively, and that can cost them in losses and higher fees and commissions. A dedicated full-service account executive is a good sounding board and can help you avoid excessive trading.

Potential for Identity Theft

Online trading, whether commodities trading or equity trading, comes with the potential for identity theft. Nearly one in six people will fall victim to identity theft sometime in their lives, and those who transact online have a higher chance. The end of this chapter lists eight things investors can do to avoid falling victim to identity theft.

Extra Time and Effort

Do-it-yourself investors spend significantly more effort managing their portfolios than do more passive investors who seek the advice of professionals. As long as you have the time and are willing to invest the effort in researching investing opportunities, there should be no issues. For investors with less time and motivation, online trading may not be the best approach to commodities investing. Investors who want to use a passive approach should consider going with a professional money manager.

Contracts Traded

For investors looking to trade commodities online, the following section will provide some insight into the top U.S. commodities exchanges and which key commodities can be purchased and sold on those exchanges. Take note that both physical and financial instruments of the same commodity can be listed for trading on each exchange.

NEW YORK MERCANTILE EXCHANGE (NYMEX)

The NYMEX is one of the leading commodities exchanges in the world. Many key commodities trade on the NYMEX, with the most popular being energy fuels and metals. Since 2006, the NYMEX has placed a significant degree of emphasis on electronic trading through the CME Globex. The traditional trading pits are still in operation, but now trading in the pits and electronic trading are conducted side by side. The aim is to give all investors, large and small, equal access to the markets. Some of the most important physical and financial NYMEX commodities that trade on the CME Globex are the following:

- Henry Hub natural gas futures (NG)—physical
- Light sweet crude oil futures (CL)—physical
- Heating oil futures (HO)—physical
- Platinum futures (PL)—physical
- Palladium futures (PA)—physical
- Crude oil financial futures (WS)—financial
- Natural gas (last-day) financial futures (HH)—financial
- Brent crude oil financial futures (BB)—financial

CHICAGO BOARD OF TRADE (CBOT)

Electronic trading at the Chicago Board of Trade occurs on its e-CBOT platform, which allows for the simultaneous trading of commodities and futures contracts. Electronic trading on the CBOT began in 1998 after the CBOT partnered with the Chicago Mercantile Exchange to provide commodity trade clearing and electronic services. The primary commodities available for purchase and sale on the e-CBOT are agricultural products such as corn and wheat. Some of the most important commodities (including financials) that trade electronically on the e-CBOT are the following:

- Corn (ZC)
- Soybeans (ZS)
- Wheat (ZW)
- Oats (ZO)
- Rough rice (ZR)
- CBOT mini-sized Dow

CHICAGO MERCANTILE EXCHANGE AND GLOBEX

As the pioneer of electronic trading, the Chicago Mercantile Exchange (CME) provides access for both traders and investors to the realm of trading commodity futures contracts. Established in 1992, Globex is the electronic platform that enables the trading of futures contracts via a computer order-matching system in a significant number of commodities, including many nonhard assets such as foreign currencies and stock index futures. All trades executed with Globex are matched with an anonymous counterparty, and the CME ensures performance. To access Globex, you need an authorized system to trade and an account with a futures commission merchant or an introducing broker. Some of the most important commodity futures contracts that trade electronically on Globex are the following:

- 3-Month eurodollar
- S&P 500 Index
- E-mini S&P 500
- E-mini NASDAQ–100
- E-mini Russell 2000
- Euro FX

Trading Costs

In trading commodities futures contracts, investors incur commissions and sometimes fees. Fees are charged on nontrading activities such as statement requests and annual account summaries. Commissions are charged when you purchase or sell a futures contract, whether online or with an account representative. Trading online without the help of a live person will cost the least, and placing orders with account representatives will increase the commission slightly. Commission rates vary from firm to firm but are relatively comparable for the same trade. Each firm lists its commission rates on what is called a commission schedule, a document that can be obtained directly from the broker. Most commission rates are based on the number of futures contracts you purchase or sell during a particular month. The more trades, the better the pricing. An infrequent trader should expect commissions to be about $4 to $7 per trade/side of the contract, whereas high-frequency traders can have commission rates as low as $3.50 round turn, which means both the purchase and the sale transactions on one specific futures contract. To obtain the best commission rates, you must trade dozens of contracts per day, which is not feasible for most people. Nevertheless, discount brokers provide a low-cost means for investors to purchase and sell commodities futures contracts. Full-service brokers cost much more.

Online Trading Simulations

For those who are looking to gain experience with futures trading but do not want to risk their own money when learning how the system works, using an online trading simulation can be beneficial. One of the most popular trading simulations is offered by the discount futures broker Lind-Waldock of Chicago. Lind-Waldock offers free access for 15 days and gives you $50,000 in virtual money to start your online trading. Furthermore, you receive online execution of your trades, can trade most types of futures contracts, and even have your virtual account marked-to-market just as actual trading accounts are. Marked-to-market means that your account is valued at the end of the trading session and gains and losses are calculated. In real trading, if your losses drop below your maintenance margin, additional margin is required. Online trading simulations let you make mistakes and try different strategies without incurring real money losses. Even more advanced traders can use a trading simulation to experiment with new strategies without placing their money at risk. Other discount futures brokers provide online trading simulations, as do nonbrokers. One website that allows trading simulation is www.tippingmonkey.com. This is a new website, and the owner has grand plans for it. Regardless of which trading simulation you choose, the experience will help you hit the ground running when you trade futures online for real gains and losses.

Protecting Your Online Brokerage Account

Safeguarding sensitive personal information should always be on your mind when you open an online brokerage account and place trades. Identity theft is a major problem in today's Internet-savvy world. There are some things you can do to ensure that you do not fall victim to identity theft and the consequent loss of money in your online brokerage account.

EIGHT WAYS TO PROTECT YOUR ONLINE ACCOUNT

Use Security Software

One of the best moves you can make to protect sensitive account information is to use security software. The software must include personal firewalls, antivirus, antispam, spyware detection, and browser patches. Always remember to download the latest updates and patches for your programs to keep one step ahead of the hackers.

Employ a Security Token

Security tokens are number-generated passwords that provide you with a second layer of protection against someone learning your password. Token passwords typically change every 60 seconds, making your password extremely difficult to obtain.

Be Password-Smart

To ensure that your password is difficult to guess, use as many different variables as possible. This means including uppercase and lowercase letters, numbers, and special characters such as # and *. Changing your password frequently is a good practice, as is having a unique password for each online account.

Use Caution When Downloading

Downloading programs may seem harmless but can put you at risk of downloading malicious files. Extra caution is always a smart idea.

Access Your Account from Your Own Computer

Accessing your online accounts and typing in sensitive personal information is much safer on your own computer. For one thing, you do not know if another computer has all the necessary antivirus and firewall protections.

Exercise Caution with Wireless Connections

Wired connections almost always provide more security than wireless connections, which are much easier to compromise.

Do Not Respond to E-Mails Asking for Personal Information

As a general rule, you should never provide sensitive information in response to an e-mail request. Legitimate companies do not send e-mails asking for personal information. Report any suspicious e-mails to the company from which they are supposed to be coming.

Log Out Completely

Always remember to terminate an online session because closing or minimizing your browser is not enough to protect your security. Also, do not store your user name and password in the browser.

List of Online Brokers

Lind-Waldock
141 W. Jackson Boulevard
Chicago, IL 60604
(800) 445–2000
www.Lind-Waldock.com

Man Financial-Retail Division
440 South LaSalle Street
Chicago, IL 60605
(800) 621–3424
www.ManFutures.com

Interactive Brokers Group
Two Pickwick Plaza
Greenwich, CT 06830
(877) 442–2757
www.InteractiveBrokers.com

Terra Nova Trading
100 South Wacker Drive, Suite 1550
Chicago, IL 60606
(800) 228–4216
www.TerraNovaFutures.com

PTI Securities & Futures
411 South Wells Street, Suite 900
Chicago, IL 60607
(800) 821–4968
www.PTISecurities.com

Infinity Futures
111 West Jackson Boulevard, Suite 2010
Chicago, IL 60604
(800) 322–8559
www.InfinityFutures.com

RJO Futures
222 South Riverside Plaza
Chicago, IL 60606
(312) 373–5000
www.RJOFutures.com

Quiz for Chapter 20

1. All but which of the following are types of brokers?
   a. Full-service brokers
   b. Discount brokers
   c. Joint listing brokers
   d. Introducing brokers

2. The typical discount broker offers the same services and advice as a full-service broker and charges a lower commission.
   a. True
   b. False

3. Which type of broker is similar to a full-service broker but defers trading execution to clearing firms?
   a. Full-service broker
   b. Discount broker
   c. Introducing broker
   d. Executive broker

4. All but which of the following are advantages of trading online?
   a. Low commissions
   b. Trading access
   c. Little time and effort required
   d. Greater control

5. All but which of the following are disadvantages of trading online?
   a. Mentorship
   b. Potential for excessive trading
   c. More time and effort
   d. Potential for identity theft

6. Which of the following brokers typically charges the lowest commissions?
   a. Full-service broker
   b. Discount broker
   c. Introducing broker
   d. Pit broker

7. Typically, only discount brokers provide mentors and offer advice.
   a. True
   b. False

8. Which of the following commodity exchanges offers the most trade listings for energy fuels?
   a. Chicago Mercantile Exchange
   b. Chicago Board of Trade
   c. London Metals Exchange
   d. New York Mercantile Exchange

9. Globex is affiliated with which commodity exchange?
   a. Chicago Mercantile Exchange
   b. New York Mercantile Exchange
   c. New York Board of Trade
   d. London Metals Exchange

10. All but which of the following are ways to protect an online account?
    a. Use security software.
    b. Be password-smart.
    c. Emphasize wireless communications.
    d. Log out completely.

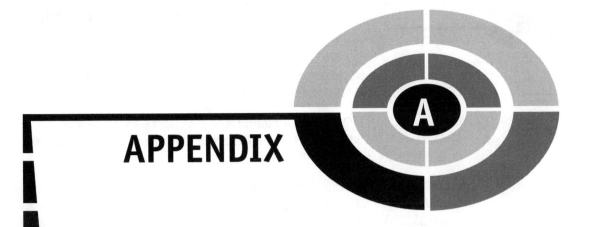

APPENDIX

Commodity Resources

Books

The Commodity Trader's Almanac 2008, edited by Scott W. Barrie and Jeffrey A. Hirsch; 192 pages, John Wiley; November 2, 2007; ISBN: 0470109866

Hot Commodities: How Anyone Can Invest Profitably in the World's Best Market, by Jim Rogers; 272 pages; Random House Trade Paperbacks; March 27, 2007; ISBN: 0812973712

Commodities for Every Portfolio: How You Can Profit from the Long-Term Commodity Boom, by Emanuel Balarie; 240 pages; John Wiley; September 10, 2007; ISBN: 0470112506

Commodities for Dummies, by Amine Bouchentouf; 384 pages; For Dummies; December 6, 2006; ISBN: 0470049286

Hedge Funds Demystified, by Scott Paul Frush; 300 pages; McGraw-Hill; September 20, 2007; ISBN: 0071496001

Understanding Asset Allocation, by Scott Paul Frush; 208 pages; McGraw-Hill; September 25, 2006; ISBN: 007147594X

Trading Commodities and Financial Future: A Step by Step Guide to Mastering the Markets, third edition, by George Kleinman; 288 pages; FT Press; October 18, 2004; ISBN: 0131476548

Commodities and Commodity Derivatives: Modeling and Pricing for Agriculturals, Metals and Energ, by Helyette Geman; 416 pages; John Wiley; March 25, 2005; ISBN: 0470012188

Getting Started in Commodities, by George A. Fontanills; 507 pages; John Wiley; July 9, 2007; ISBN: 0470089490

Handbook of Alternative Assets, second edition (Frank J. Fabozzi Series), by Mark J. P. Anson; 720 pages; John Wiley; September 1, 2006; ISBN: 047198020X

The Handbook of Managed Futures and Hedge Funds: Performance, Evaluation, and Analysis, second edition, by Carl Peters; 500 pages; McGraw-Hill; December 1, 1996; ISBN: 1557389179

Commodity Trading Advisors: Risk, Performance Analysis, and Selection (Wiley Finance), edited by Greg N. Gregoriou, Vassilios Karavas, Fran#alcois-Serge Lhabitant, and Fabrice Douglas Rouah; 424 pages; John Wiley; September 24, 2004; ISBN: 0471681946

Associations:

Alternative Investment Management Association (AIMA)
Meadows House

20-22 Queen Street

London W1J5PR

United Kingdom

44-20-7659-9920

www.aima.org

Chartered Alternative Investment Analyst Association
29 South Pleasant Street

Amherst, MA 01002
413-253-7373
www.cais.org

Financial Industry Regulatory Authority (formally NASD)
9513 Key West Avenue
Rockville, MD 20850-3351
301-590-6500
www.finra.org

Managed Funds Association
2025 M Street N.W., Suite 800
Washington, DC 20036
202-367-1140
www.mfainfo.org

National Futures Association
200 W. Madison St., #1600
Chicago, IL 60606-3447
312-781-1300
www.nfa.futures.org

CFA Institute
560 Ray C. Hunt Drive
Charlottesville, VA 22903-2981
800-247-8132
www.CFAInstitute.org

Commodity-Specific Organizations:

GENERAL

National Grain and Feed Association: www.ngfa.org
U.S. Department of Agriculture: www.usda.org

ALUMINUM

International Aluminium Institute: www.world-aluminium.org
The Aluminum Association: www.aluminum.org
aluNET International: www.alunet.net

COPPER

Copper Development Association: www.copper.org

COFFEE

International Coffee Organization: www.ico.org
National Coffee Association of the USA: www.ncausa.org

COCOA

World Cocoa Foundation: www.worldcocoafoundation.org

International Cocoa Foundation: www.icco.org
Cocoa Producer's Alliance: www.copal-cpa.org

CORN

National Corn Growers Association: www.ncga.com
Corn Refiners Association: www.corn.org

WHEAT:

Wheat Foods Council: www.wheatfoods.org
National Association of Wheat Growers: www.wheatworld.org
U.S. Wheat Associates: www.uswheat.org

SOYBEANS:

American Soybean Association: www.soygrowers.org
Soy Protein Council: www.spcouncil.org

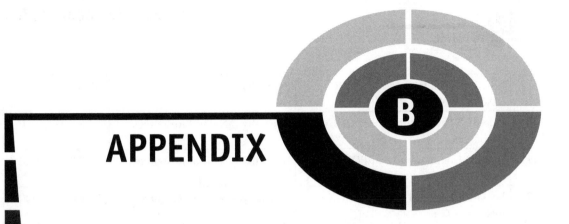

APPENDIX

B

Top 25 Commodity Mutual Funds

	Fund Name	Symbol	Category	Net Assets
1	Vanguard Energy	VGENX	Specialty—Natural Resources	8,360,000,000*
2	T. Rowe Price New Era	PRNEX	Specialty—Natural Resources	6,390,000,000
3	PIMCO CommodityReal-Ret Strat Instl	PCRIX	Specialty—Natural Resources	5,780,000,000
4	Vanguard Energy Adm	VGELX	Specialty—Natural Resources	5,160,000,000
5	Ivy Global Natural Resources A	IGNAX	Specialty—Natural Resources	4,900,000,000
6	Vanguard Precious Metals and Mining	VGPMX	Specialty—Precious Metals	4,360,000,000
7	Fidelity Select Energy	FSENX	Specialty—Natural Resources	2,900,000,000
8	Fidelity Select Energy Service	FSESX	Specialty—Natural Resources	2,450,000,000

9	RS Global Natural Resources A	RSNRX	Specialty—Natural Resources	2,000,000,000
10	Fidelity Select Natural Resources	FNARX	Specialty—Natural Resources	1,870,000,000
11	PIMCO CommodityRe-alRet Strat A	PCRAX	Specialty—Natural Resources	1,840,000,000
12	Ivy Global Natural Resources C	IGNCX	Specialty—Natural Resources	1,640,000,000
13	Fidelity Select Gold	FSAGX	Specialty—Precious Metals	1,560,000,000
14	Jennison Natural Resources A	PGNAX	Specialty—Natural Resources	1,350,000,000
15	U.S. Global Investors Global Res	PSPFX	Specialty—Natural Resources	1,310,000,000
16	Oppenheimer Gold & Special Minerals A	OPGSX	Specialty—Precious Metals	1,310,000,000
17	Fidelity Select Natural Gas	FSNGX	Specialty—Natural Resources	1,280,000,000
18	Franklin Gold and Pre-cious Metals A	FKRCX	Specialty—Precious Metals	1,170,000,000
19	Tocqueville Gold	TGLDX	Specialty—Precious Metals	1,130,000,000
20	American Century Global Gold Inv	BGEIX	Specialty—Precious Metals	1,090,000,000
21	PIMCO CommodityRe-alRet Strat Admin	PCRRX	Specialty—Natural Resources	929,780,000
22	USAA Precious Metals and Minerals	USAGX	Specialty—Precious Metals	918,460,000
23	ING Global Resources S	IGRSX	Specialty—Natural Resources	916,320,000
24	PIMCO CommodityRe-alRet Strat D	PCRDX	Specialty—Natural Resources	891,380,000
25	PIMCO CommodityRe-alRet Strat C	PCRCX	Specialty—Natural Resources	886,130,000

*In U.S,. dollars.

Note: Separate share classes with unique symbols are considered single mutual funds.

Source: Morningstar.com, October 15, 2007.

APPENDIX C

Top 25 Largest Commodity Exchange-Traded Commodities

	Name	Symbol	Type	Asset Class	Exp Ratio	Net Assets
1	streetTRACKS Gold Shares	GLD	ETF	Commodities - Precious Metals	0.40%	$13,804,000,000
2	Energy SPDR	XLE	ETF	Sector - Energy	0.26%	$5,048,000,000
3	Oil Services HOLDRs	OIH	ETF	Sector - Energy	0.00%	$3,646,000,000
4	iPath DJ-AIG Commodity	DJP	ETF	Commodities - General	0.75%	$2,193,000,000

5	iShares GS Nat Res	IGE	ETF	Sector - Natural Resources	0.50%	$2,145,000,000
6	PowerShares Water Resources	PHO	ETF	Sector - Natural Resources	0.67%	$1,992,000,000
7	iShares Silver Trust	SLV	ETF	Commodities - Precious Metals	0.50%	$1,959,000,000
8	Materials Sel SPDR	XLB	ETF	Sector - Basic Materials	0.26%	$1,759,000,000
9	iShares DJ US Energy	IYE	ETF	Sector - Energy	0.60%	$1,234,000,000
10	DB Commodity Index	DBC	ETF	Commodities - General	0.83%	$1,205,000,000
11	iShares COMEX Gold Trust	IAU	ETF	Commodities - Precious Metals	0.40%	$1,194,000,000
12	PShares WilderHill Clean Energy	PBW	ETF	Sector - Natural Resources	0.71%	$1,128,000,000
13	Market Vectors Gold Miners	GDX	ETF	Sector - Natural Resources	0.55%	$894,000,000
14	Vanguard Energy	VDE	ETF	Sector - Energy	0.25%	$719,000,000
15	iShares DJ Basic Mat	IYM	ETF	Sector - Basic Materials	0.60%	$690,000,000
16	PowerShares DB Agriculture Fund	DBA	ETF	Commodities - General	0.91%	$620,000,000
17	United States Natural Gas	UNG	ETF	Sector - Energy	0.60%	$478,000,000
18	PowerShares Dyn Oil & Gas	PXJ	ETF	Sector - Energy	0.64%	$448,000,000
19	United States Oil	USO	ETF	Commodities - General	0.65%	$395,000,000
20	iShares GSCI Commodity Id	GSG	ETF	Commodities - General	0.75%	$367,000,000
21	Vanguard Materials	VAW	ETF	Sector - Basic Materials	0.26%	$335,000,000
22	iShares DJ US Oil Equip	IEZ	ETF	Sector - Energy	0.48%	$294,000,000
23	SPDR Metals & Mining	XME	ETF	Sector - Natural Resources	0.36%	$265,000,000
24	iPath GSCI TotRet Idx ETN	GSP	ETF	Commodities - General	0.75%	$215,000,000
25	SPDR Oil&Gas Equip & Serv	XES	ETF	Sector - Energy	0.36%	$195,000,000

Source: IndexPublications, LLC; As of September 30, 2007.

Glossary of Commodities Terms

- **Arbitrage:** The simultaneous purchase and sale of like-kind commodities in different markets to take advantage of a price discrepancy between the markets.

- **Basis:** The difference in price between the current cash price and the futures price for the same commodity.

- **Bear spread:** Selling the nearby contract month and buying the deferred contract for a single financial instrument to capture profits from any change in the price relationship.

- **Bid:** A formal offer to buy a commodity at a predetermined price.

- **Broker:** A person or company that accepts and executes transactions on behalf of financial and commercial institutions and/or the general public.

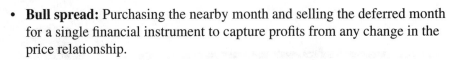

- **Bull spread:** Purchasing the nearby month and selling the deferred month for a single financial instrument to capture profits from any change in the price relationship.

- **Call option:** A financial instrument that provides the buyer the right, but not the obligation, to purchase the underlying asset at the strike price on or before the expiration date of the contract.

- **Carrying charge:** Also referred to as carry or cost of carry; the cost to warehouse a commodity: storage space, insurance, and finance charges incurred by holding a physical commodity. Typically seen with grains, metals, and other commodities.

- **Cash commodity:** An actual physical commodity a person or company is purchasing or selling at the present time. Examples include maize, orange juice, gold, and Treasury bonds.

- **Cash contract:** A sales agreement for the immediate or future delivery of an actual product, such as maize or cocoa.

- **Cash exchange:** Involves two back-to back transactions in which one party purchases futures and sells a correlated cash product and the counterparty sells futures and buys the correlated cash product.

- **Cash market:** The marketplace where buyers and sellers transact for commodity goods in real time.

- **Cash settlement:** In contrast to physical delivery settlements, cash settlements typically involve index-based futures contracts that are settled in cash—based on the real-time value of the index—on the last trading day.

- **Clear:** The process by which a clearinghouse updates and maintains records of all trades and settles margin flows daily for its clearing members by using a mark-to-market approach.

- **Clearinghouse:** A corporation affiliated with a futures exchange that is responsible for settling trading accounts, clearing trades, collecting and maintaining margin capital, regulating delivery of physical products, and reporting trading data. Each clearinghouse acts as a third party to all futures and options contracts; it acts as a buyer to every clearing member seller and as a seller to every clearing member buyer.

- **Clearing corporation:** The independent legal corporation that settles all trades executed on a specific commodities exchange. The primary roles include guaranteeing all trades executed, establishing and adjusting clearing member firm margins for mark-to-market, and ensuring that all gains and losses are posted to member firm accounts.

Glossary of Commodities Terms

- **Clearing member:** A member of an exchange clearinghouse, typically a company. Clearing members are responsible for the financial commitments of the customers that clear through their firm.

- **Closing price:** Also referred to as settle price; the final price paid for a commodity on a particular trading day. On trading days on which a range of closing prices exist, the closing price is determined by averaging all prices.

- **Commission fee:** Fee charged by brokers for executing buy and sell transactions. Also referred to as brokerage fee.

- **Commodity:** An article of commerce or a product that can be used for commerce. Commodities are basic products traded on an authorized commodity exchange.

- **Commodity Credit Corporation (CCC):** A branch of the U.S. Department of Agriculture that supervises the government's farm loan and subsidy programs.

- **Commodity Futures Trading Commission (CFTC):** A federal regulatory agency established under the Commodity Futures Trading Commission Act that is charged with overseeing futures trading in the United States.

- **Commodity pool:** An investment fund in which capital contributed by a number of persons is combined for the purpose of trading futures contracts or commodity options.

- **Commodity pool operator (CPO):** An individual or organization that operates and solicits investable capital for a commodity pool.

- **Commodity trading adviser (CTA):** A duly registered person who, for compensation, profit, or both, advises others, directly or indirectly, about the value or advisability of buying or selling futures contracts or commodity options.

- **Consumer price index (CPI):** A major inflation indicator computed by the U.S. Department of Commerce that measures the change in prices of a fixed market basket of some 385 goods and services.

- **Contract month:** The specific month in which delivery occurs under the terms of a futures contract.

- **Crop reports:** Reports compiled by the U.S. Department of Agriculture on various agricultural commodities. Information includes estimates on planted acreage, yield, and expected production.

- **Current yield:** The ratio of the coupon interest payment to the current market price of a fixed-income investment.

- **Delivery:** The transfer of a cash commodity from a futures contract seller to a futures contract buyer. Each futures exchange has specific procedures for commodity delivery.

- **Delivery month:** A future month in which futures and forward trading takes place. This is in contrast to the nearby (delivery) month.

- **Delta:** A statistical measure of how much an option premium changes for every unit change in the underlying futures price. Often interpreted as the probability that an option will be in-the-money by the expiration date.

- **Discretionary account:** A legal arrangement by which an investment account owner gives written power of attorney to a person—typically a broker or financial advisor—to make and execute investment decisions.

- **Equilibrium price:** The market price at which commodity quantity supplied equals commodity quantity demanded.

- **Exchange for physicals (EFP):** A transaction commonly executed between two hedgers who want to exchange futures for cash positions rather than take physical possession of a commodity.

- **Exercise:** The action executed by the owner of a call or put option when he or she wants to purchase or sell an underlying futures contract.

- **Exercise price:** Also referred to as strike price; the price at which an underlying position (a call or a put) for a futures contract can be purchased or sold.

- **Expiration date:** The specific date on which options on futures generally expire, typically during the month preceding the futures contract delivery month.

- **Floor broker (FB):** An individual who executes orders on behalf of others for the purchase or sale of any commodity futures or options contract.

- **Floor trader (FT):** An individual who executes trades on his or her own behalf for the purchase or sale of any commodity futures or options contract.

- **Foreign exchange market:** Also called the forex market; an over-the-counter marketplace where buyers and sellers execute foreign exchange transactions electronically, by telephone, or by other means.

- **Forex market:** An over-the-counter market where buyers and sellers conduct and execute foreign exchange business and transactions. Also referred to as foreign exchange market.

- **Forward (cash) contract:** A cash contract in which a seller agrees to deliver a predetermined and specific cash commodity to a buyer some time in the future. In contrast to futures contracts, forward contracts are privately negotiated between the buyer and the seller and are not standardized.

- **Futures commission merchant (FCM):** An individual or organization that solicits or accepts orders to buy or sell futures contracts or options on futures and accepts money or other assets from customers to support those activities. Also referred to as a wire house or commission house.

- **Futures contract:** A legally binding agreement, executed on the trading floor of a futures exchange, to buy or sell a commodity or financial instrument at a predetermined date some time in the future. In contrast to forward contracts, futures contracts are standardized by quality, quantity, and delivery time and location for each commodity. The only variable is price, which is set on an exchange trading floor.

- **Futures exchange:** A central marketplace with established rules and regulations where buyers and sellers meet to transact futures and options on futures contracts.

- **Globex:** A global after-hours electronic trading system.

- **Hedging:** The act of offsetting the price risk or related volume risk inherent in any cash market position by taking an equal but opposite position in the futures market.

- **Hog/corn ratio:** A statistical measure of the relationship of feeding costs to the dollar value of hogs; calculated by dividing the price of hogs ($/hundredweight) by the price of corn ($/bushel).

- **Initial margin:** The amount of money required for deposit by a futures market participant at the time of order execution to buy or sell a futures contract.

- **In-the-money option:** A call or put option that has intrinsic value. A call option is in-the-money if the strike price is below the current price of the underlying asset; a put option is in-the-money if the strike price is above the current price of the underlying asset.

- **Intrinsic value:** The dollar amount by which an option is in-the-money.

- **Last trading day:** The final day for trading in a specific futures or option contract month. Any contract outstanding at the end of the last trading day must be settled by physical delivery, securities delivery, or agreement for monetary settlement.

- **Leverage:** The practice of buying additional positions with borrowed capital. The end result is the ability to control large dollar amounts of a commodity with a comparatively smaller amount of capital.

- **Liquidate:** The act of transacting futures contracts of the same delivery month to offset either an existing long position with a short position or an existing short position with a long position; also refers to making (or taking) delivery of the cash commodity represented by the futures contract.

- **Long:** A position representing an asset that is purchased rather than sold.

- **Maintenance margin:** The established minimum margin, or invested capital, a customer must maintain in his or her account to cover borrowed capital. Similar in concept to a down payment with a house purchase.

- **Managed futures:** An investment pool in which invested capital from multiple investors is pooled and managed by professionals known as commodity trading advisors. These accounts are managed on a discretionary basis.

- **Margin call:** An alert communication call from a clearinghouse to a clearing member or from a brokerage firm to a customer that requires the deposit of additional capital or the sale of positions to bring margin to the required minimum level.

- **Marking-to-market:** An accounting method by which debits and credits are posted to investors' accounts on a daily basis, based on the change in asset prices occurring on each trading day.

- **National Futures Association (NFA):** A self-regulatory organization that supports and monitors the futures and options markets. The primary responsibilities of the NFA are (1) enforcement of ethical standards and customer protection rules, (2) screening of futures professionals for membership, (3) auditing and monitoring of professionals for financial and general compliance rules, and (4) providing for arbitration of futures-related disputes.

- **Offer:** The term given to the act of placing an asset for sale in the marketplace at an established minimum price.

- **OPEC:** Acronym for the Organization of Petroleum Exporting Countries, an international organization established by the major petroleum-producing nations in 1973 to control the price of crude oil sold on global commodities exchanges.

- **Open interest:** The total number of futures or options contracts—either buy or sell—of a specific commodity that have not been offset by an opposite futures or option transaction or fulfilled by delivery of the commodity or option exercise.

- **Open outcry:** A method of trading by which verbal bids and offers are conducted in trading pits or rings in a public auction platform of an exchange.

- **Option:** A contract that gives the owner the right, but not the obligation, to buy or sell a specific asset at a predetermined price for a limited time.

- **Option premium:** The price of a call or put option; paid by the option buyer and received by the option seller.

- **Option spread:** The simultaneous purchase and sale of one or more options contracts, futures, and/or cash positions to take advantage of pricing discrepancies.

- **Out-of-the-money option:** A call or put option that has no intrinsic value. A call option is out-of-the-money if the strike price is above the current price of the underlying asset; a put option is out-of-the-money if the strike price is below the current price of the underlying asset.

- **Over-the-counter (OTC) market:** A virtual market with no tangible trading floor—in contrast to commodity exchanges—where physical and financial products are transacted by purchasers and sellers.

- **P&S (purchase and sale) statement**: A financial statement sent by a commission house to a customer reporting the account details, such as the number of contracts bought or sold, the prices at which the contracts were bought or sold, the gross profit or loss, the commission charges, and the net profit or loss on the transactions held by the account owner.

- **Position:** A market commitment: the holding of a long or short asset.

- **Position limit:** The maximum number of assets an investor can hold. Determined by the Commodity Futures Trading Commission and/or the exchange on which the contract is traded. Also called a trading limit.

- **Price discovery:** The practice of estimating future cash market prices when given current forward market prices.

- **Price limit:** Established by each exchange, the maximum advance or decline permitted for a futures or options contract in one specific trading session over the previous day's settlement.

- **Reserve requirements:** Established by the Federal Reserve; the minimum amounts of cash and liquid assets—as a percentage of demand deposits and time deposits—that member banks must maintain.

- **Settlement price:** The price at which the final trade of each trading day is executed for any commodity. Also called the closing price.

- **Short:** A position representing an asset that is sold rather than purchased.

- **Speculator:** A market participant who attempts to make a profit from buying and selling futures and options contracts on the basis of forecast future price movements. Speculators assume market price risk and add liquidity and capital to the futures marketplace.

- **Spot:** The cash market price for a physical commodity that is available for immediate delivery.

- **Spot month:** The futures contract month that is nearest to expiration.

- **Spread:** The price difference between two related commodities or markets.

- **Strike price:** The price at which an options or futures contract can be purchased or sold. Also referred to as the exercise price.

- **Technical analysis:** The practice of forecasting future asset price movements by using historical prices, trading volume, open interest, and other trading data.

- **Tick:** The smallest incremental price movement permitted for a futures or options contract.

- **Time value:** The amount of the option premium buyers of call or put options are willing to pay in the anticipation that a change in the underlying futures price will cause the option to increase in value before the expiration date. Also referred to as extrinsic value.

- **Underlying futures contract:** A futures contract that is bought or sold by exercising an option on a specific futures contract.

- **Volatility:** A statistical measurement representing the change in price for an asset over a specific period; typically expressed as a percentage and computed as the annualized standard deviation of the percentage change in the daily price changes.

- **Volume:** The quantity represented by a single purchase or sale or total position held at any specific time for any specific period desired.

- **Yield curve:** A chart in which yield is plotted on the vertical axis and the term to maturity is plotted on the horizontal axis. The yield curve illustrates the relationship between yield and time and is typically upward-sloping—a positive yield curve. Downward-sloping yield curves are referred to as negative or inverted.

Conclusion

Commodities Demystified was written for investors who want to learn more about one of the most important asset classes in the investing marketplace today. The information provided is intended to help investors optimize their portfolios and generate attractive portfolio performance over the long term. Commodities, as well as the other alternative investments, may be the missing component for many investors who are looking for an edge.

I hope you have enjoyed reading *Commodities Demystified* and have learned how to invest in commodities. If you are interested in learning more about how my firm can help protect and grow your wealth through the use of commodities, please contact us for a brochure and more information.

Scott Paul Frush, CFA, CFP, MBA
Frush Financial Group
6001 North Adams Road, Suite 250
Bloomfield Hills, MI 48304
Voice: (248) 642–6800
E-mail: Contact@Frush.com
Website: www.Frush.com

I encourage you to visit my official author website, which provides information on all my books, including the latest news and information on upcoming books, at www.ScottFrush.com.

Other books by Scott Frush include the following:

Optimal Investing, Marshall Rand Publishing, 2004

Understanding Asset Allocation, McGraw-Hill, 2006

Understanding Hedge Funds, McGraw-Hill, 2006

Hedge Funds Demystified, McGraw-Hill, 2007

Final Exam

1. What is the official name for a commodity exchange?
   a. Commodity trading market (CTM)
   b. Designated contract market (DCM)
   c. Obligated futures bourse (OFB)
   d. Single clearing center (SCC)

2. Which of the following market indicators is not a technical indicator?
   a. Volume
   b. Price
   c. Relative strength
   d. EIA inventory reports

3. Industrial metals have a higher resistance to corrosion and oxidation than do precious metals.
   a. True
   b. False

4. To-arrive was the original name for what financial instrument?
   a. Futures contract
   b. Delivery asset

    c. Exchange-traded note

    d. Closed-ended fund

5. Which of the following organizations regulates futures contracts?

    a. Organization of Petroleum Exporting Countries (OPEC)

    b. Energy Industry Association (EIA)

    c. Commodity Futures Trading Commission (CFTC)

    d. National Commodities Regulatory Association (NCRA)

6. A managed futures fund most closely resembles which of the following?

    a. Closed-end fund

    b. Exchange-traded fund

    c. Hedge fund

    d. Exchange-traded note

7. Which of the following is an example of geopolitical risk?

    a. Damaging the environment

    b. Highly volatile commodity prices

    c. Knowledge and expertise risk

    d. Nationalizing natural gas projects

8. What is the most common percentage managed futures and hedge funds charge as a performance management fee?

    a. 20 percent

    b. 15 percent

    c. 10 percent

    d. 5 percent

9. Morningstar is an example of which type of commodity participant?

    a. Rating agency and data source

    b. Commodity fund risk manager

    c. Prime broker

    d. Futures commission merchant

10. An American company that purchases cocoa in western Africa and brings that product into the United States is considered what type of participant?

    a. Exporter

    b. Importer

    c. Producer

    d. Storage

11. What is the objective of most producers when participating in the futures market?

    a. To hedge price risk

    b. To ensure steady demand

    c. To gain favorable tax treatment

    d. To profit from price speculation

12. What information do EIA inventory reports provide?

    a. Inventory storage for all commodities in the United States

    b. Regulatory oversight of storage companies

    c. Open interest on U.S. commodity exchanges

    d. Supply and demand for energy products in the United States

13. Which market indicator is a measurement of the market of individuals with paid wages employed exclusively by businesses throughout the country?

    a. Nonfarm payrolls

    b. Consumer price index

    c. LIBOR

    d. Purchasing Managers Index

14. Which market index is considered the benchmark for spot gold prices worldwide and serves as a measure of inflationary pressure?

    a. NYMEX gold index

    b. Kruger bond exchange

    c. Amsterdam gold index

    d. London Gold Fix

15. Which of the following was the first commodity index established?

    a. Goldman Sachs Commodity Index

    b. Dow Jones-AIG Commodity Index

    c. Deutsche Bank Liquid Commodity Index

    d. Reuters/Jefferies CRB Index

16. Which commodity class typically has the highest weighting on average on commodity indexes?

    a. Energy fuels

    b. Metals

c. Livestock and agriculture

d. Exotics and financials

17. Financial commodities are excluded from commodity indexes.

a. True

b. False

18. Which of the following metals is necessary to produce stainless steel?

a. Bronze

b. Tin

c. Nickel

d. Platinum

19. About what percentage of total annual lead production is attributed to recycled scrap?

a. 5 percent

b. 15 percent

c. 25 percent

d. 50 percent

20. Which of the following industries accounts for the greatest demand for palladium?

a. Automotive

b. Jewelry

c. Electronics

d. Photography

21. Which of the following refers to crude oil with low levels of sulfur?

a. Sweet

b. Diesel

c. Sour

d. Ethanol

22. Approximately what percentage of global consumption of natural gas is attributed to the United States?

a. 10 percent

b. 20 percent

c. 30 percent

d. 40 percent

23. All but which of the following are types of coal?

    a. Lignite

    b. Subbituminous

    c. Arabitunimous

    d. Anthracite

24. Which of the following countries is the world's largest producer of soybeans, accounting for nearly 36 percent of the total supply?

    a. China

    b. Indonesia

    c. United States

    d. Brazil

25. Barley and which other commodity were the first two cereals to be domesticated?

    a. Wheat

    b. Corn

    c. Soybeans

    d. Rice

26. Which category of agricultural commodities is defined by seasonal growing patterns and described as either tropical or fiber?

    a. Grains and oil seeds

    b. Softs

    c. Tropics

    d. Caribbean ags

27. Which of the following commodity exchanges was the first to list foreign currencies for trading?

    a. NYBOT

    b. NYMEX

    c. CBOT

    d. CME

28. Which exotic energy fuel is produced chiefly from sugar and corn?

    a. Heating oil

    b. Ethanol

    c. Methane

    d. Biomass

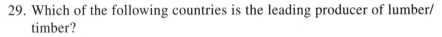

29. Which of the following countries is the leading producer of lumber/timber?

    a. United States

    b. Canada

    c. Russia

    d. Sweden

30. All but which of the following are considered benefits of commodity mutual funds?

    a. Low cost

    b. Instant exposure to commodity classes

    c. Diversification

    d. Professional management

31. Shareholders of commodity mutual funds can incur capital gains consequences even when no transaction to sell is made.

    a. True

    b. False

32. All but which of the following are considered drawbacks to commodity mutual funds?

    a. Year-end capital gains distributions

    b. High fees

    c. Market underperformance potential

    d. Only for high-net-worth investors

33. All but which of the following are advantageous characteristics of exchange-traded instruments?

    a. Low costs

    b. Favorable diversification

    c. Stocklike tradability

    d. Ability to outperform the underlying index

34. What is the primary advantage of exchange-traded notes over exchange-traded funds?

    a. Favorable tax treatment

    b. Lower expense ratios

    c. Higher distribution of dividends

    d. No market risk

35. As an asset class, commodity exchange-traded funds and notes typically have the highest expense ratio of all ETFs and ETNs.

    a. True

    b. False

36. Which of the following approaches allows investors to take an ownership stake in companies involved in the commodities trade?

    a. Purchasing shares of stock of a publicly traded corporation

    b. Purchasing units of a master limited partnership

    c. Purchasing American Depositary Receipts

    d. All of the above

37. Which of the following documents do unit holders of partnerships receive for tax reporting purposes?

    a. W-2

    b. 1099

    c. W-4

    d. K-1

38. All but which of the following are excellent measures of liquidity for a futures contract?

    a. Volume

    b. Spread

    c. Price

    d. Open interest

39. Commodity trading advisors manage the derivatives trading of which type of investment?

    a. Mutual fund

    b. Index-based fund

    c. Closed-end fund

    d. Managed futures fund

40. Which common commodity characteristic is described as being interchangeable, or replacing one unit with another unit without difficulty?

    a. Tradability

    b. Standardization

    c. Deliverability

    d. Commonality

41. Taking physical possession of a commodity describes which defining characteristic of commodities?

    a. Tradability

    b. Deliverability

    c. Standardization

    d. Inelastic demand

42. Which of the following hedge fund styles does not involve investing directly in commodity futures but investing in stand-alone commodity hedge funds?

    a. Event-driven

    b. Relative-value

    c. Fund of funds

    d. Multistrategy

43. The Securities and Exchange Commission mandates that only certain investors can invest in hedge funds. What are those investors called?

    a. Certified

    b. Accredited

    c. Permitted

    d. Approved

44. What is the benefit of employing leverage?

    a. Increased risk

    b. Ability to profit in both rising and falling markets

    c. No cost

    d. Magnification of performance

45. Which of the following obligates the owner to exercise a contract?

    a. Options

    b. Futures

    c. Both

    d. Neither

46. Which of the following hedge fund styles emphasizes directional price bets?

    a. Tactical

    b. Arbitrage

    c. Relative-value

    d. Strategic

47. Risk profile consists of all but which of the following subsets of risk?

    a. Risk history
    b. Risk capacity
    c. Rick appetite
    d. Risk need

48. A written investment plan provides all but which of the following benefits?

    a. Provides a comparison benchmark
    b. Defines the optimal asset mix and asset allocation strategy
    c. Provides for significant money manager flexibility
    d. Establishes the optimal management style

49. Which of the following is the key benefit of diversification?

    a. Isolates top-performing asset classes
    b. Minimizes market risk
    c. Magnifies portfolio returns
    d. Minimizes investment-specific risk

50. For which of the following asset classes is indexing most effective?

    a. Large-cap stocks
    b. Small-cap stocks
    c. International stocks
    d. High-yield fixed-income

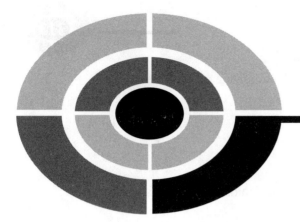

Answer Key

Chapter 1	Chapter 2	Chapter 3
1. C	1. A	1. D
2. B	2. B	2. A
3. D	3. C	3. B
4. B	4. C	4. B
5. A	5. A	5. D
6. C	6. B	6. A
7. A	7. A	7. A
8. C	8. B	8. C
9. A	9. D	9. B
10. D	10. A	10. D

Answer Key

Chapter 4	Chapter 5	Chapter 6
1. D	1. B	1. B
2. B	2. C	2. B
3. B	3. B	3. B
4. D	4. D	4. D
5. A	5. D	5. C
6. B	6. B	6. C
7. A	7. A	7. B
8. A	8. B	8. B
9. C	9. A	9. D
10. D	10. A	10. C

Chapter 7	Chapter 8	Chapter 9
1. D	1. C	1. D
2. B	2. A	2. A
3. B	3. C	3. C
4. C	4. B	4. A
5. D	5. D	5. B
6. C	6. C	6. A
7. B	7. A	7. A
8. D	8. B	8. D
9. B	9. A	9. C
10. B	10. D	10. C

Chapter 10	Chapter 11	Chapter 12
1. D	1. C	1. D
2. A	2. A	2. A
3. B	3. D	3. A
4. C	4. C	4. D
5. B	5. B	5. C
6. B	6. B	6. B
7. B	7. B	7. B
8. A	8. C	8. B
9. C	9. C	9. D
10. D	10. D	10. B

Chapter 13	Chapter 14	Chapter 15
1. C	1. D	1. C
2. A	2. A	2. A
3. D	3. C	3. A
4. B	4. A	4. C
5. A	5. D	5. B
6. B	6. B	6. C
7. B	7. B	7. B
8. D	8. D	8. D
9. A	9. C	9. B
10. A	10. A	10. C

Answer Key

Chapter 16

1. B
2. A
3. C
4. B
5. B
6. C
7. B
8. C
9. D
10. A

Chapter 17

1. A
2. A
3. A
4. B
5. A
6. D
7. B
8. C
9. B
10. A

Chapter 18

1. D
2. A
3. B
4. D
5. B
6. B
7. A
8. B
9. B
10. B

Chapter 19

1. B
2. A
3. C
4. B
5. D
6. A
7. A
8. D
9. B
10. C

Chapter 20

1. C
2. B
3. C
4. C
5. A
6. B
7. B
8. D
9. A
10. C

Final Exam

1. B	17. A	34. A
2. D	18. C	35. A
3. B	19. D	36. D
4. A	20. A	37. D
5. C	21. A	38. C
6. C	22. D	39. D
7. D	23. C	40. B
8. A	24. C	41. B
9. A	25. A	42. C
10. B	26. B	43. B
11. A	27. D	44. D
12. D	28. B	45. B
13. A	29. A	46. A
14. D	30. A	47. A
15. D	31. A	48. C
16. A	32. D	49. D
	33. D	50. A

Index

Index

Index

D

E

Index

M

N

Index

About the Author

Scott Frush, CFA, CFP, is a leading authority on asset allocation policy and portfolio optimization using alternative investments. He is president and senior portfolio manager of Frush Financial Group, a registered investment advisor in Bloomfield Hills, Michigan. Frush is the 2007 recipient of *CFA Magazine*'s prestigious "Most Investor Oriented" award, which recognizes a CFA Institute member who has made outstanding contributions to investor education.

Frush has helped investors protect, grow, and insure their wealth for more than a decade. In 2002, he founded Frush Financial Group to manage portfolios for individuals, affluent families, and institutions by using customized asset allocation solutions and an emphasis on alternative investments. His previous experience includes commodity risk management with DTE Energy in Ann Arbor, MI and mutual fund accounting with Stein Roe Mutual Funds in Chicago, IL.

Frush earned a master of business administration degree in finance from the University of Notre Dame and a bachelor of business administration degree in finance from Eastern Michigan University. He holds the Chartered Financial Analyst (CFA) and Certified Financial Planner (CFP) designations; is insurance licensed for life, health, property, and casualty; and is Series 7 and Series 66 licensed. Frush is a member of the CFA Institute, CFA Society of Detroit, National Association of Tax Professionals, and Detroit Economic Club.

Frush is the author of *Hedge Funds Demystified* (McGraw-Hill, 2007), *Understanding Hedge Funds* (McGraw-Hill, 2006), *Understanding Asset Allocation* (McGraw-Hill, 2006), and *Optimal Investing* (Marshall Rand Publishing, 2004). He has received two Book of the Year honors for business and investments.

The Frush Financial Group website is www.Frush.com.